rediscovering Vardis Fisher

centennial essays

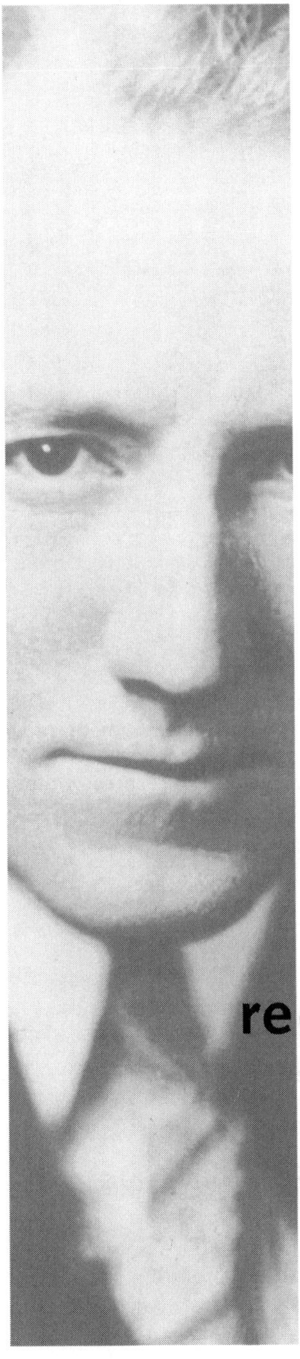

rediscovering Vardis Fisher

centennial essays

edited by
Joseph M. Flora

University of Idaho Press | Moscow, Idaho

04 03 02 01 00 5 4 3 2 1

The University of Idaho Press
Moscow, Idaho 83844-1107
Printed in the United States of America

Library of Congress Cataloging-in-Publication Data
Rediscovering Vardis Fisher : centennial essays / edited by Joseph M. Flora
p. cm.
Includes bibliographical references and index.
ISBN 0-89301-223-8 (alk. paper)
1. Fisher, Vardis, 1895–1968—Criticism and interpretation. 2. West (U.S.)—In literature. I. Flora, Joseph M.
PS3511.I744 Z84 2000
813'.52 21—dc21 99-043641

Design by A.E. Grey

This book is dedicated
to the memory of
Margaret Morgan Pace (1943–1999)
for her service to
Western American literature

Contents

Acknowledgments

The idea of this book was born in Ketchum, Idaho, in July 1996, during the meeting of the Hemingway Society. I hasten to acknowledge the encouragement and support of Peggy Pace, former director of the University of Idaho Press. Although illness would prevent her from seeing the book to completion, her spirit is abundantly evident in this book.

Tamara Shidlauski became acting director at the press and immediately added her support and enthusiasm to the project. I am much in her debt. Marie Prys worked with me on the editing and numerous details involved in making a book out of a manuscript. Jennifer Backer skillfully copyedited. I have valued the opportunity to work with them.

Following Peggy's death, Ivar Nelson as interim director proceeded enthusiastically, making the transition at the press as smooth as possible. Similarly, in a time of flux, Elizabeth Kliger, as the new editor, capably and energetically guided the production of this book honoring Idaho's most important author. Amy Grey, the new UI Press book designer, strengthened the team. Cooperation between West and East was exemplary.

For the Fisher estate, Grant Fisher has graciously granted permission for the writers of these essays to quote from the works of Vardis Fisher. For the pictorial essay on Vardis Fisher, Grant Fisher has given permission to reproduce the Fisher photographs. Grateful acknowledgment for photograph reproduction extends to T. Roberts Fisher; Boise State University Library, Special Collections Department; Idaho State Historical Society; Archives, Ricks College; the Library of Congress; and Syracuse University Library, Department of Special Collections.

William Mulder of the University of Utah and Louie W. Attebery of Albertson College of Idaho recognized the timeliness of this book and made helpful suggestions that have made it better.

Closer to home, I would be remiss if I did not acknowledge the support, good advice, and encouragement from several persons. My wife, Christine, and Susan Marston have lent me their good critical judgment, and Susan has also increased tremendously my comfort zone as I adjusted to IBM and Windows after happy years depending on Mac. My chairman, William Andrews, has been constant in his support of my work. And Senior Associate Dean Darryl Gless of the College of Arts and Sciences has given good counsel.

The University of North Carolina at Chapel Hill has provided financial assistance to help make this book a reality. I am grateful to the University Research Council and to the College of Arts and Sciences for subvention support.

Chronology

1895	Vardis Fisher born in Annis, Idaho, March 31.
1905	Moved to isolated river basin home.
1915	Graduated from Rigby High School, Rigby, Idaho. Entered University of Utah in Salt Lake City.
1917	Married Leona McMurtrey, September 10.
1918	Birth of son Grant; drafted into U.S. Army, corporal.
1920	Received Bachelor of Arts in English, University of Utah.
1921	Birth of son Wayne.
1922	Received Master of Arts in English, University of Chicago.
1924	Death of Leona McMurtrey Fisher, September 8.
1925	Received Ph.D. (magna cum laude), University of Chicago.
1925–28	Assistant professor of English, University of Utah; taught Wallace Stegner, freshman English, 1926.
1927	*Sonnets to an Imaginary Madonna.*

1928	Married Margaret Trusler, October 2; *Toilers of the Hills.*
1928–31	Assistant professor of English, Washington Square College, New York University. Became friend of Thomas Wolfe.
1930	Summer in Europe.
1931	Returned to Idaho ranch; *Dark Bridwell.*
1932	*In Tragic Life;* taught summer at University of Montana.
1933	Taught summer at University of Montana.
1934	*Passions Spin the Plot.*
1935	*We Are Betrayed.*
1935–39	Director, Idaho Writers' Project and Historical Records Project of Works Progress Administration; *The Neurotic Nightingale.*
1936	*No Villain Need Be.*
1937	*April: A Fable of Love;* birth of son Thornton Roberts. *Idaho: A Guide in Word and Picture,* first of WPA guides to appear.
1938	*Forgive Us Our Virtues: A Comedy of Evasions; The Idaho Encyclopedia.*
1939	*Children of God; Idaho Lore;* won Harper Prize for Fiction; divorced from Margaret.
1940	Married Opal Laurel Holmes, April 16; moved to mountainside acreage near Hagerman, Idaho.
1941	*City of Illusion.*
1943	*The Mothers; Darkness and the Deep,* first volume of the series *Testament of Man.*
1944	*The Golden Rooms.*
1946	*Intimations of Eve.*
1947	*Adam and the Serpent.*

1948 *The Divine Passion.*

1951 *The Valley of Vision.*

1952 *The Island of the Innocent.*

1953 *God or Caesar? The Writing of Fiction for Beginners;* trip to Europe, autumn and early winter, 1953–54.

1956 Alan Swallow assumed publication of *Testament of Man; Jesus Came Again; A Goat for Azazel; Pemmican.* Trip to Europe and Middle East, autumn and early winter, 1956–57.

1957 *Peace Like a River.*

1958 *My Holy Satan; Tale of Valor;* trip to Europe, autumn and early winter, 1958–59.

1959 *Love and Death.*

1960 *Orphans in Gethsemane,* last volume of the *Testament of Man* series.

1962 *Suicide or Murder? The Strange Death of Governor Meriwether Lewis*

1963 *Thomas Wolfe As I Knew Him, and Other Essays.*

1965 *Mountain Man;* won Distinguished Achievement Award of Western Literature Association.

1968 *Gold Rushes and Mining Camps of the Early American West,* with Opal Laurel Holmes; writer-in-residence, College of Idaho, January–February; died following bout of heavy drinking and overdose of sleeping pills, July 9.

Introduction

Although many view Vardis Fisher, widely acknowledged as Idaho's most important writer, as a curmudgeon increasingly out of touch with the realities of the twentieth century, he was not devoid of a sense of humor. He thought that he had a rather well-developed sense of the comic.[1] (It is true that his bent was for the sardonic, and probably few readers would consider humor one of his strengths.) In some moments, he could see himself as a ridiculous fellow. Born on March 31, 1895, he later expressed bemusement that he had escaped being born on April Fools' Day by a matter of hours; it would have been a fitting birthday, he sensed.

Were he able to notice, the centennial of his birth would have tested his sense of irony, even confirmed his vow to his longtime literary agent Elizabeth Nowell—and others—that if he could live his life over he would not be a novelist: the testing was too severe, the rewards too few. In truth, little attention was paid to the centennial, in Idaho or elsewhere. To its credit, the Pocatello Public Library sponsored an exhibit titled "Vardis Fisher: A Centennial View—1895–1995." The exhibit was funded by the Idaho Humanities Council, the Community Hospital Corporation of Idaho Falls, and the Idaho Commission on the Arts; it circulated in libraries throughout Idaho. Lectures on Fisher's work supplemented those exhibits. But there was no conference on his life and work. At the dedication of Albertsons Library at Boise State University, Professor Dorys Grover celebrated Fisher's legacy; Boise State has continued to build the Clore Collection of Vardis Fisher Materials in its Special Collections. Clearly, Fisher, once hailed as the first major writer from the Rocky Mountain West, is not forgotten.[2] (He rankled some Idahoans, pleased others, with the column "Vardis Fisher Says," which appeared in several Idaho newspapers in the 1950s and 1960s.) At the centennial of his birth—twenty-seven years after his death—few of his works were in print.

The anniversary was not noticed at the annual meeting of the Western Literature Association (WLA), though Fisher was counted "dean" of Western writers when the association was founded in 1965; he was the first recipient of the association's Distinguished Achievement Award and was the keynote speaker at the inaugural meeting. Opal Fisher, Fisher's widow, was deceased by the year of the centennial. But until declining health intervened, she had frequently attended WLA meetings, a visual reminder of her husband's legacy, and at many meetings (whether she attended or not) she presented all participants with a Fisher publication. At the Coeur d'Alene meeting in October 1989, the gift was a hardback copy of *Children of God* (1939), then under the imprint of Opal Laurel Holmes. It is not difficult to imagine her outrage had she witnessed the centennial neglect. But she might have been prepared for the slight by checking the annual bibliographies on Western writing that appeared in the association's journal, *Western American Literature*. She had surely observed that by the 1980s little attention was being paid Fisher in WLA sessions—and that given was typically by old hands. More often than not, there would be not a single Fisher paper. By the 1990s, in a growing association infused by young blood, Vardis Fisher was scarcely more than a name to many members. Yet regular attention was being paid at WLA to writers of his generation, writers he found shallow and sentimental and whom he considered writers for the market—most notably John Steinbeck and Willa Cather. Indeed, WLA Cather sessions became typically multiple. Opal Fisher doubtless noticed, too, that papers on Ernest Hemingway were also appearing with regularity. As Fisher's stock fell, Hemingway's stature as a "Western" writer was growing. The Fishers had long thought the nation hopelessly confused—the insanity had infected the Western Literature Association as well.

The neglect at the occasion of the centennial of Fisher's birth seems obvious when one considers the attention given at the birth centennials of writers who were Fisher's contemporaries and against whom he knew he must eventually be judged. Willa Cather's centennial in 1973 was the first of these. Years earlier, recognition of Cather as a major twentieth-century novelist and as the most successful female writer in America to that date was all but universal.[3] Her centennial was duly marked with ceremonies and conferences in Lincoln and Red Cloud. Indeed, special Cather conferences have been so numerous since the centennial that the commemoration, aided by an active Willa Cather Pioneer Memorial and Educational Foundation, may be said to be ongoing. A United States postage stamp was also issued to mark her centennial. F. Scott Fitzgerald, born in 1896 and almost Fisher's exact contemporary, was also remembered on a postage stamp, and the centennial markings were numerous. Nor was less done for William Faulkner, born in 1897.[4] Indeed, Faulkner's centennial was marked by a conference in France as well as in the United States. The commemorations of Fitzgerald and Faulkner were noted in the national press. Two modern writers whom Fisher greatly admired—Ellen Glasgow and James Branch Cabell—do not have the national visibility that Cather, Steinbeck, Fitzgerald, and Faulkner have maintained, but their centennials (1974 and 1979, respectively) were duly marked with conferences and resulting books of centennial essays, though neither has appeared on a postage stamp.

Centennial festivities took place for two writers whose careers had long engaged Fisher's attention. He felt a special kinship with Thomas Wolfe, with whom he had taught at New York University. For his centennial in 2000, Wolfe was honored with a commemorative stamp and with celebrations and meetings in Asheville and Chapel Hill. Those commemorations were preceded by numerous centennial markings in 1999 for Fisher's bête noire, Hemingway—an affront all the keener since Hemingway is now held as an Idaho author and is a permanent and highly visible part of its literary heritage.

Fisher might well scorn these celebrations as hero worship—but that would not be consistent with his protest of America's treatment of Meriwether Lewis. Fisher dedicated his *Suicide or Murder? The Strange Death of Governor Meriwether Lewis* (1962) "To the memory of/ MERIWETHER LEWIS/ the greatest American of his breed/ and the most neglected." The book includes a photograph of Lewis's monument, taken by Fisher himself, and a photograph of the Sgt. Floyd Monument near Sioux City, Iowa. In appendix C, "A Neglected American," Fisher writes, "Even Sergeant Charles Floyd, who did not reach the Mandan villages, but died August 20, 1804, on the first leg of the journey up the Missouri, has a shaft in his honor that towers far above anything that honors Lewis." Fisher's identification with Lewis was apparent; in fact, in Fisher's autobiographical novel *Orphans in Gethsemane* (1960), the protagonist makes the comparison precise. He tells his wife, "On that frontier of the mind I intend to be one of the first novelists—to be, if only I have the talent for it, its Meriwether Lewis."[5]

Fisher was a writer who kept his eye on the future, writing not so much for his own time, he liked to think, but for posterity. His career had several swings. In the early 1930s he commanded significant national attention with his Vridar Hunter tetralogy, but before the fourth volume appeared in 1936, many questioned his talent: the quality of the tetralogy seemed to have lessened with each succeeding volume. Fisher rallied with

Children of God in 1939, a novel that won him the Harper Prize for Fiction and again affirmed to many that he was a major writer. For several years, Fisher was able to maintain national visibility with other historical novels about the American West, *City of Illusion* (1941) and *The Mothers* (1943). The year that *The Mothers* appeared also saw publication of *Darkness and the Deep*, the first of twelve volumes that would be known as the *Testament of Man*. Fisher considered these historical novels that aim at tracing human development from its primitive beginnings to the present day the most important work of his career. Because of his national reputation, the series opened with respectable notice in important places, but enthusiasm soon waned, and his publisher concluded that publishing the series was not a sound financial investment. Midway through the series, Fisher was struggling frantically to find a publisher who would see the project to conclusion—arguing that the novels had moved into eras and arenas with good market potential. But for a long time the battle seemed a losing one. Even Caxton Printers of Idaho, the firm that had in 1932 published *In Tragic Life* (the first novel of the tetralogy) after it had met refusal in the East, would decline to continue the *Testament*.[6] The mid-1950s severely tested more than Fisher's sense of humor: he lived in despair and occasionally self-doubt. Eventually, Alan Swallow of Denver, with a modest publishing firm, came to Fisher's rescue; Swallow published volumes 7–12 and began reprinting the earlier *Testament* novels.

Using several forums to promote Fisher, Swallow may be credited with reopening the Vardis Fisher case. Although sales of the *Testament* volumes were modest, Doubleday and Company published new Fisher titles of Western Americana as well as his collected short stories. Swallow brought out his collected essays and the nonfictional study of the death of Meriwether Lewis. Although Fisher had not quite reached the end of troubles with publishers (Swallow's death in 1966 took away his safety net), he had regained much lost ground. Before Fisher died in 1968, he had become a subject for doctoral dissertations and had seen his work credited by a volume in Twayne's United States Author Series. Best of all, perhaps, his novel *Mountain Man* (1965) had sold well and had received gratifying praise. Honored guest of the Western Literature Association, he was also invited to other academic platforms in the West. Scholars were writing essays on his work. Though modest by some standards, a Fisher revival was clearly under way.

The reasons for the vicissitudes of Fisher's fortunes during his lifetime are numerous—some were not of his making, some were. The Great Depression qualified many financial endeavors—and publishing is always that. Although a New Deal project designed to help writers provided

Fisher with needed income and enhanced his reputation (he directed Idaho's federal writing projects and saw to it that Idaho's guide was the first in the nation), he scorned President Roosevelt and liberal politics. Indeed, he thought that he did not fare well with reviewers and critics because he had not joined the communist brigade. A turn to the left for literary success was not essential, of course. Willa Cather never turned that way and still prospered. During the 1930s Hemingway was often under attack for not developing a social conscience. Both Cather and Hemingway maintained that the artist's chief responsibility is to the art. They had, of course, the vision of the literary modernists, one Hemingway learned in part from Idaho-born Ezra Pound. Sometimes the experiments of the modernists failed, and those experiments exasperated Fisher. He favored the direct—the matter more than the manner concerned him. Probably the concern with matter over form was a result of his fierce efforts as a young man to deal with the various demons that tormented him. At the end of James Joyce's *A Portrait of the Artist as a Young Man* (1916), Stephen Dedalus is determined to fly above the nets that have previously ensnared him, vowing to "forge in the smithy of [his] soul the uncreated conscience of [his] race."[7] At the end of Fisher's *In Tragic Life,* Vridar Hunter—having endured similar conflicts with family, religion, and sexuality—makes a somewhat different vow: "'Some day,' he said, 'I'll laugh and be glad. I'll be happy as flowers some day.... I will, so help me God'" (ellipsis Fisher's).[8] By the time Fisher had concluded his tetralogy, reviewers warned that matter was dominating manner. Thereafter, charges of didacticism would become insistent in the response to Fisher. He paid them little heed. By the late 1930s, Fisher was reading very little fiction. His attention was given more to historical research, either for Western projects or for the *Testament of Man.* Like Pound's Hugh Selwyn Mauberly—but for very different reasons—he was an artist out of touch with his times.

When Fisher struggled to get a publisher to see the *Testament of Man* to completion, the adversary was no longer the communist brigade of the 1930s, but the eastern publishing establishment. Jewish presence in the publishing world was a large one, and Fisher increasingly feared that his material would turn Jewish support from him. The crucial novel was the sixth, *The Valley of Vision* (1951), which recreated the life and times of Solomon, one of Israel's most acclaimed kings. After the novel had met several rejections (Vanguard had retreated after publishing the first five volumes), Fisher revised it extensively to heighten its novelistic value: reports made clear that readers had not found fact and fiction sufficiently integrated. His own feeling was that he had made Solomon into a greater king than he probably was. Fisher argued to Elizabeth Nowell, his literary agent and continuing friend, that well marketed, the book could get good sales from the New York City Jewish community alone. He also argued that Jewish interest in *The Island of the Innocent* (1952), the seventh volume, would be even greater. With Hemingway in mind, he had emphasized a love story and made the stage of the novel the Maccabean wars. Because those wars are important to Jewish pride, he thought the sales potential all the greater. Although a Jewish publisher published those two novels, they did not achieve the result Fisher anticipated; Abelard also withdrew from the series. Surely it could have been better marketed, Fisher thought. The *Testament* had been at a disadvantage from the start, he repeated, because it did not have a publisher who knew how to promote it. The notion that he had been victim of a Jewish "conspiracy" would not die. Fisher did not, however, think of himself as anti-Semitic and thought the *Testament* proved the point. But he is probably at least as open to the charge as is Thomas Wolfe, the novelist with whom he is most often compared. In any case, and probably for reasons of his own mental health, he could not give much room to the thought that the series was artistically not viable to a commercial publisher. Ironically, Fisher argued that the series would become increasingly salable as it got closer to modern times.

In his mind, publishers' fears of the Catholic Church accounted for the difficult time he had in landing a publisher for *Jesus Came Again* (1956). Elizabeth Nowell and others tried to make him see that any number of works that would not square with Catholic theology were being published; Kinsey's report on male sexuality was the dramatic example. It is true that when James Gipson of Caxton declined to publish the novel, he gave as his reason that he could not publish works that undermined Christianity because that would give aid and support to the communist cause. In the cold-war climate, he wanted no part of that. Although the New York publishers had long before concluded that the *Testament* was not a marketable commodity, Fisher believed that fear of the Catholic Church was behind their decision. In *Orphans in Gethsemane* he provides the fictional account of his woes with publishers; it is fascinating, but it should be viewed with some skepticism.[9] Readers who persevere to the end of that long saga will take vicarious pleasure in the protagonist's triumph over compounded adversity, but they will also be aware that Vridar's personality often undermines his own best interests. With good reason, Martin Kich observed about Fisher, "Of all the obstacles that Fisher had to overcome in his determination to make his mark as a novelist, the most unyielding may have been his own personality."[10]

It is a truism that immediately after their deaths most writers' reputations decline. Certainly such was the case with Fisher. Fisher's decline was hastened by a well-meaning ally. A woman with a large motherly instinct but who had had no children, Opal Fisher had lived Fisher's agonies. Assaults on him, real or imagined, were assaults on her. She determined to be his protector even after his death, a death she could not at first even admit. Unfortunately, her good intentions worked against the very goals she had articulated. Her ally was to be Boise State University, which was setting aside a room in its library to be known as the Vardis Fisher Room. Fisher's library and other papers at his Hagerman home were to go there. Boise State set aside and named the room, but Opal was unable to part with the materials. They were never delivered, and eventually the designated room was rechristened the Frank Church Room. It houses the papers of the late senator—a nice piece of irony since Fisher (maintaining the right-wing bent of his politics) had attacked Church frequently in his newspaper columns.[11] Following Fisher's death, Opal had envisioned turning the Hagerman ranch into a retreat where scholars of Western literature could sojourn for research and think-tank sessions on such topics as the *Testament of Man*. But she took no action. The buildings there were repeatedly vandalized, Opal having moved to Boise.

Opal concluded, however, that she should keep Fisher's books before the public. Swallow Press had once taken this lead, but after it became a subsidiary of the Ohio University Press, expansion there was unlikely. Although *Mountain Man* was having a good life in a paper edition with Pocket Books, most Fisher titles were to be found only in rare book catalogs. Possibilities for teaching Fisher in college courses were limited. Opal decided that she would print the books herself and had several titles printed (using original plates) under her imprint. But she had little experience in marketing. She even turned to paperback editions. Eventually, her efforts were counterproductive to her goals.

"Truth" was Vardis Fisher's avowed goal, and in his company social occasions could turn into sessions of "truth or consequence" that could overwhelm the unwary or insecure ego. He wrote to Elizabeth Nowell that people could say about him whatever they liked. It is doubtful that he was quite as thick-skinned as he pretended, but he firmly believed in free speech. It is especially ironic, therefore, that Opal Fisher became so defensive about what could be said about her husband or his work. She was horrified when the historian of the Church of Jesus Christ of Latter-day Saints wrote an article opining that Fisher was closer to his Mormon roots than was commonly held.[12] Fisher would have laughed at the article, scorned it, but probably would have recognized that the attention counted for something. Few people familiar with him or his work would sincerely believe that Fisher was a closet Mormon. But Opal went on the offensive. Her paper edition of Fisher's *Dark Bridwell* (1931) contained an appended protest denying that Fisher had retained any Mormon belief, rendering the edition inappropriate for classroom use. She joined, on Fisher's behalf as it were, the American Atheists Association, Inc., and was active in the Utah chapter. Doubtless she felt better for the effort, but it did little to reverse the decline in Fisher's stock.[13]

Apparently sensing attack or slight everywhere, she kept watch over scholars who had been most sympathetic to Fisher. Any negative criticism would not be welcomed. Those scholars wished to cause her no anguish and responded by turning their energies elsewhere. The field of literature, even the field of Western American literature, is large. There were other pastures they could cultivate.

Opal Fisher is not, of course, the only reason that Fisher's stock was so low at the time of his centennial. The academy had altered profoundly. A great deal of Western and a great deal of American literature had come on the scene in the period—writers of stature addressing serious issues. The notions of canon and culture had been seriously challenged. Apparently, Fisher was not speaking to this new generation—probably because few in it had read him.

A remnant continued to lament the neglect. In 1989, Idaho newspaper journalist Tim Woodward called attention to it in a biography *Tiger on the Road: The Life of Vardis Fisher*, published by Caxton, the firm most crucial to the Fisher story—early and late. Biographies seldom restore writers to prominence, nor could Woodward's. But it did remind the academy that there is that core of readers to whom Fisher still matters. If Woodward's approach was more popular than scholarly, Martin Kich's *Western American Novelists, Volume 1: Walter Van Tilburg Clark, Dan Cushman, H. L. Davis, Vardis Fisher, A. B. Guthrie, Jr., William Humphrey, and Dorothy M. Johnson* (1995) reminded the academy of Fisher's claim and importance. Kich's introduction also provides a compelling image to accompany his protest of the "deepening silence" about Fisher: "Like an eroded cliff face, Fisher's cantankerous visage seems to glare at us out of the deep mists of remote Idaho, keeping us off with the pointedly unliterary threat of a bloodletting."[14]

In addition to these recent calls for reassessment, there are other encouraging signs. Following Opal Fisher's death in July 1994, the University of Idaho Press took over the handling of Fisher titles she had stored, and advertised them regularly in its catalogs. When Opal Fisher's estate was finally settled, those works then reverted to Boise State University and to Albertson College of Idaho, where Fisher had briefly taught as a writer-in-residence. The college is using the profits from the books to support the Vardis Fisher Scholarship Fund. The library at Boise State has heightened awareness of its Fisher collections. In spring 1998, *The Idaho Writers Archive Newsletter* announced that four new research collections about Fisher are now open for research at BSU. They include correspondence of Fisher to his oldest son, Grant; the papers of Opal Fisher; photocopies of letters Fisher and his siblings wrote to their mother in the 1910s, 1920s, and 1930s; and correspondence with his physician and friend Dr. George E. Brown, Jr., and with his friend Judge James P. Gossett.[15] What is most needed, of course, is that Fisher titles be available to introduce a new generation of students to his work. Prospects for that happening are now more propitious.

This collection of essays aims to give a more permanent marking of the centennial of the birth of Vardis Fisher. It honors the courage and tenacity of his pilgrimage—though its purpose is not to make exaggerated claims for his status. The collection does stem from the conviction that his work continues to merit serious study. It pays tribute to Fisher's legacy by making unhampered inquiry its base. It brings together persons of various backgrounds—with a sizable contingent of critics who have not previously turned their scholarly attention to Fisher. Accordingly, it accents approaches and views previously neglected. It does not, of course, intend to give the final word, but to invite reflection and even debate.

The essays gathered here concentrate on the work that mattered most to Fisher—his novels, the genre where he makes his greatest claims on posterity. Fisher certainly did interesting work in other genres—in short fiction, poetry, and criticism. His work for the Federal Writers' Project is itself a dramatic story. Although that work frustrated him, he made a large contribution to the project, and it served him well in many ways other than financial. His successes with the Idaho projects brought him national attention, and his research guided him to subjects for other fiction. His many newspaper commentaries also invite study and evaluation. There is easily room for a companion volume of essays of rediscovery and assessment. Here, however, the emphasis is on the novels.

Before turning to that task, the book takes a look at Fisher the man. Fisher scholars have long felt the need for a scholarly biography. The first two essays remind us of this need and the rich possibilities. Alan Virta's pictorial essay evokes the shape to an extraordinary life. Frederick Oyer's essay provides a more intimate view of a small part of the life, a look at a single friendship in Fisher's life. An Oregon physician, Dr. Oyer is representative of a steady body of Fisher readers through the years. Not of the academy, they have nevertheless found Fisher's a compelling voice. Their number has always been sizable among Fisher readers, and their contributions will be important to any revivals of interest, in the new century.

The next two essays consider early Fisher novels, those set in his native Idaho. James Maguire studies *Toilers of the Hills* (1928), *Dark Bridwell,* and *In Tragic Life* in the context of literary naturalism, the school in which many critics and readers first placed Fisher, to see if that designation continues to be a valid approach. Maguire, a student of naturalism steeped in the discourse of Western American literature, concludes that the novels are not "merely" naturalistic novels "that make the world seem a trap or even a torture chamber"; they convey as well "the sacrality of the earth." When Peter Blakemore approaches *Dark Bridwell,* he emphasizes the perspective of recent environmental studies, indicating that Fisher's novel merits the careful attention of the eco-critics, as Maguire implies. Blakemore's essay provides a new and compelling reassessment of Fisher's use of landscape.

A large part of Fisher's success as a novelist came from his novels that recreated stories of the American West. *The Mothers,* which recreates the history of the tragic Donner Party, has been among the most enduring of those novels. Doris Betts revisits that novel here. She brings to her task the insights of a highly acclaimed novelist whose most recent novel, *The Sharp Teeth of Love* (1997), came about in response to her own reaction to the Donner story, especially that of Tamsen Donner. Betts places *The Mothers* in the context of its time and studies it as a reflector of Fisher's approach to the concerns of women. The most famous of the novels that deal with Western American history—and the one that brought Fisher his greatest acclaim—is *Children of God.* In it Fisher recounts the founding of the Church of Jesus Christ of Latter-day Saints—from the vision of Joseph Smith in Palmyra, New York, through his martyrdom in Carthage, Illinois, to the march across the West to Utah under Brigham Young, and the triumph of the Mormon Church over continuing opposition. Mormons, inevitably, appear in numerous Fisher fictions. Fisher's readers included numerous Mormons; it is safe to say that throughout his career, Mormons kept a watchful eye on him. Six decades after the publication of *Children of God,* Stephen Tanner, professor of English at Brigham Young University, reexamines Fisher's use of Mormon material. It is a topic that will continue to be debated—especially in the Mormon West—but there is no gainsaying that Fisher presented one of the most influential accounts of the Mormon story.

In almost every novel Fisher set in the West, Native Americans appear. In *Pemmican* (1956), *Tale of Valor* (1958), and *Mountain Man,* they are central to the action and meaning. Fisher's first critics and reviewers did not look very critically at Fisher's use of Native Americans. In *Mountain Man* the issue demanded attention. No one has looked more carefully at Fisher's record on this matter than Mick McAllister. In his essay "Father to the Man: An Apology for Fisher's Indians," he brings a perspective that is much needed, one grounded in a knowledge of all of Fisher's work and in the traditions of the peoples Fisher came in time to see with more compassion and understanding. McAllister's essay is the only one in this collection that has been previously published, having appeared in *The Vardis Fisher Newsletter,* which was published by Dancing Badger Press as a "WLA Special First Printing." Its circulation was very small, and the *Newsletter* did not continue publishing. Inclusion of the essay here enables it to reach the larger audience it deserves.

Whatever the merit of Fisher's faulting of Hemingway for what he saw as fascination with violence, many readers have found Fisher's emphasis on violence excessive and problematic. In "Music, Violence, and Nature in Vardis Fisher's *Mountain Man,*" Barbara Meldrum focuses on the tension between the abundant depictions of torture and killing and the equally insistent references to the great music of the Western world. She identifies a protagonist who is repelled by the advance of civilization onto the Western landscape but who finds the artistic achievement of that civilization necessary to his definition of himself and the world he discovers. By extension, Vardis Fisher remains an enigma, our problematic mountain man.

In 1958 Fisher did not make the impact on the reading public with his novel about Lewis and Clark—*Tale of Valor*—that in the 1990s Stephen Ambrose made with the nonfictional *Undaunted Courage,* but, as has been noted, the story of Meriwether Lewis was major for Fisher. For this collection, an historian visits both *Tale of Valor* and Fisher's nonfiction study of Lewis's death. John D.W. Guice affirms the power of the novel, but as an historian he understandably is more engaged with Fisher's work as historian in *Suicide or Murder? The Strange Death of Governor Meriwether Lewis;* he expects that Fisher's thesis about Lewis's death may soon prove more influential.

Anyone reviewing the record of Fisher's scholarship would be struck by the paucity of attention paid to the work Fisher felt central to his career, the *Testament of Man* novels. The critics seem to affirm the judgment of the various publishers who turned from the *Testament* as well as the response of several reviewers. It was needful, therefore, that at least one essay of the commemoration deal with the totality of that achievement. The author of that essay, Marilyn Grunkemeyer, is an anthropologist, representative of an audience that Fisher targeted, but one that has not paid his *Testament* much attention. Although Grunkemeyer cannot speak for all anthropologists, she brings to her study a background versed in that discipline's literature, as well as a woman's perspective. Of all the essays in the collection, her assignment was, certainly, the most daunting. For her, the most problematic of the volumes is the last, *Orphans in Gethsemane*. She found the reading of it a "toxic" experience; she is among a small contingent that has read the novel more than once. She finds in it an importance for anthropologists of the future, but not the one Fisher envisioned.

Anne Zahlan, who lived in the Middle East for several years and knows its problems and politics well, read the *Testament* to see to what extent it might speak to current issues there. Primarily a literary scholar, she is a specialist in the literature of colonialism and the tensions across cultures. She looks at a discrete part of the *Testament*—the novels set in the Middle East, those that Fisher found most difficult to get published. Zahlan concludes that Fisher "foregrounds tensions similar to those that today plague the Middle East" and finds the novels compassionate and valuable, indeed exemplifying a religious sensibility.

If the essays gathered here point to some new directions for Fisher scholarship, the final essay will assist such explorers. Mark Canada surveys the entire territory (vaster than many had supposed); his essay will surely be useful to the next generation of explorers.

Notes

1. See his "How's Your Sense of Humor," in Vardis Fisher, *The Neurotic Nightingale* (Milwaukee: Casanova Press, 1935), 21–38.
2. See Ray B. West, *Writing in the Rocky Mountain West* (Lincoln: University of Nebraska Press, 1947).
3. Cather's position was signaled in Jackson R. Bryer's *Fifteen Modern American Writers* (Durham: Duke University Press, 1969). Cather is the only woman in this survey of research and criticism on the century's giants. Her company: Sherwood Anderson, Hart Crane, Theodore Dreiser, T.S. Eliot, William Faulkner, F. Scott Fitzgerald, Robert Frost, Ernest Hemingway, Eugene O'Neill, Ezra Pound, E.A. Robinson, John Steinbeck, Wallace Stevens, and Thomas Wolfe.
4. Fisher took a somewhat cautious stance in regard to Faulkner. He recognized the complexity of the writing, but apparently read little Faulkner.
5. Vardis Fisher, *Orphans in Gethsemane* (Denver: Alan Swallow, 1960), 790.
6. After *In Tragic Life* received a lead rave review in the *New York Times*, the tetralogy was jointly published by Caxton and Doubleday.
7. James Joyce, *A Portrait of the Artist as a Young Man* (New York: Viking, 1968), 252–53. The novel was first published in 1916.
8. Vardis Fisher, *In Tragic Life* (Caldwell, ID: Caxton Printers; Garden City, NY: Doubleday, 1932), 464.
9. Throughout Fisher's struggle to find a publisher for the *Testament*, Elizabeth Nowell advised and consoled him. Their correspondence is in the North Carolina Collection at

the University of North Carolina at Chapel Hill and at the Beinecke Library at Yale University. In addition to encouraging Fisher, Nowell tried to temper his judgments.

10. Martin Kich, *Western American Novelists, Volume 1: Walter Van Tilburg Clark, Dan Cushman, H. L. Davis, Vardis Fisher, A. B. Guthrie, Jr., William Humphrey, and Dorothy M. Johnson* (New York: Garland, 1995), 292.
11. Senator Church, of course, had been aware of Fisher's views of him, but he had a sense of humor about his critic. When my *Vardis Fisher* was published in 1965, Senator Church had notice of it entered into the *Congressional Record.*
12. Leonard J. Arrington and Jon Haupt, "The Mormon Heritage of Vardis Fisher," *Brigham Young University Studies* 18 (Fall 1977): 27–47.
13. Richard M. Andrews, "Vardis Fisher: An American Atheist Author," *American Atheist: A Journal of Atheist News and Thought* 35 (Summer 1997): 9–15.
14. Kich, *Western American Novelists*, 292.
15. "New Vardis Fisher Collections Open for Research," *Idaho Writers Archive Newsletter* 6 (Spring 1998): 1–4.

Bibliography

Andrews, Richard M. "Vardis Fisher: An American Atheist Author." *American Atheist: A Journal of Atheist News and Thought* 35 (Summer 1997): 9–15.

Arrington, Leonard J., and Jon Haupt, "The Mormon Heritage of Vardis Fisher." *Brigham Young University Studies* 18 (Fall 1997): 27–47.

Bryer, Jackson R., ed. *Fifteen Modern American Writers*. Durham: Duke University Press, 1969.

Fisher, Vardis. *In Tragic Life*. Caldwell, ID: Caxton Printers; Garden City, NY: Doubleday, 1932.

———. *The Neurotic Nightingale*. Milwaukee: Casanova Press, 1935.

———. *Orphans in Gethsemane*. Denver: Alan Swallow, 1960.

Joyce, James. *A Portrait of the Artist as a Young Man*. New York: Viking, 1968.

Kich, Martin. *Western American Novelists, Volume 1: Walter Van Tilburg Clark, Dan Cushman, H. L. Davis, Vardis Fisher, A. B. Guthrie, Jr., William Humphrey, and Dorothy M. Johnson*. New York: Garland, 1995.

West, Ray B. *Writing in the Rocky Mountain West*. Lincoln: University of Nebraska Press, 1947.

Courtesy of Grant Fisher.

1 Vardis Fisher: A Photographic Essay

Alan Virta

Vardis Fisher as a Young Novelist

Vardis Fisher was born on March 31, 1895, in Annis, Idaho, a small farming community along the upper reaches of the Snake River in the hills of eastern Idaho. He grew up in the shadow of the Rocky Mountains among hardworking Mormon families like his own, who, for reasons practical and spiritual, threw themselves with religious zeal into the task of transforming wilderness into civilization. Although Fisher discarded the Mormon faith into which he was born and baptized, the habit of hard work—both physical and intellectual—never left him. And though college and teaching took him far from home, he was always a westerner, an Idahoan, and, eventually, one of the creators of a new regional literature. Photograph ca. 1934.

Courtesy of Boise State University Library, Special Collections Department.

Courtesy of Idaho State Historical Society (73-221.77).

The Last Frontier

The Idaho that was Vardis Fisher's home is a land of wild and fearsome topography, a vast sagebrush desert cut by deep river gorges and surrounded by jagged mountain ranges. "For those who know it and have stood within its strength," wrote Fisher in 1937, "it is a splendid and timeless area upon which a thousand centuries will leave no mark of change; and they love its caves and craters and the weird terracing of its scene....This is the last frontier, delivered to rock and desolation and set apart of its own."[1] Fisher's friend Thomas Wolfe passed through Idaho a year later and was struck by the "abject loneliness underneath the huge light and scale and weather and the astounding brightness and dimension of everything—all given a kind of tremendousness and terror and majesty." Of Fisher, he added, "What I've seen today explains a lot about him."[2] This photograph of the Snake River in Idaho was taken by Robert Limbert in the early twentieth century.

The Snake River Country

The Snake River is the lifeblood of southern and eastern Idaho. Though the volcanic soil is rich, rainfall on this western side of the Rocky Mountains is insufficient to support agriculture without irrigation from the river and its tributaries. Before canals were built to water the valleys, early settlers, like the parents of Vardis Fisher, clung to the riverbanks and bottoms. It was in one such river bottom that Vardis Fisher spent his formative childhood years. This scene, captured in the early twentieth century by the photographer Clarence Bisbee, is near Twin Falls.

Donated in 1978 to Idaho State Historical Society by Idaho Association of Commerce and Industry. Courtesy of Idaho State Historical Society (78-37.20/A).

Courtesy of Grant Fisher.

The Mountains

Vardis Fisher grew up in the Antelope Hills, on the western flanks of the Rocky Mountains. "This toothed steppe, furrowed and gouged and spilled into pyramids, is not for persons whose homes are in tropical growth under cloudy skies," he wrote of his native region.[3] Fisher portrayed the harsh mountain environment vividly in his novel *Mountain Man* and the struggle of the pioneers to tame it in *Toilers of the Hills*. He dedicated both books to his parents. This is a view of the Teton range seen from eastern Idaho.

Vardis Fisher's Parents

Vardis Fisher's parents, Joseph and Temperance Fisher, were children of pioneers in the upper Snake River valley of eastern Idaho. Joseph Fisher's mother was reputedly the first white woman to winter in the valley in which her grandson Vardis was later born. Joseph and Temperance Fisher received little formal education and lived most of their lives in a log cabin with a dirt floor. Joseph farmed and hunted and avoided civilization; Temperance, a devout Mormon, was driven by an unrelenting passion to see her three children well educated. Neither parent was openly affectionate. In his autobiographical novel *In Tragic Life* (1932), Fisher wrote of the parents: "It was in this one matter, shame for their ignorance and a desire to lift their sons and daughters to a lofty estate, that they found the deepest intimacy. It was this desire that cemented their lives, that drove them forth into an epic of labor and self-sacrifice."[4] Three children were born to them: sons Vardis (the eldest) and Vivian, and a daughter, Irene. Photograph 1932.

Courtesy of Archives, Ricks College.

Courtesy of Archives, Ricks College.

Fisher's Childhood Home

Vardis Fisher spent much of his childhood in this cabin along the Snake River. The Fishers moved here from Annis when he was six. Far from any neighbors, Fisher found the river bottom a "well of loneliness."[5] With its marshes and bogs, dense undergrowth, and wild beasts, it was an "awful land of roaring sounds and hidden terrors.... My early years there were nightmare."[6] But that changed. In *In Tragic Life,* Fisher's teenage alter ego, Vridar Hunter, considered that river-bottom ranch the "center of the universe...and in later years, after he had traveled far, he felt himself always as one on a circumference, so many miles from his life's root and core."[7] Fisher returned to the ranch many times in his life, often for months at a time. Photograph by Rod Boam, 1990.

Vardis Fisher and His Brother, Vivian

There were no schools near their isolated ranch, so the Fisher children were first taught at home. Vardis and his brother, Vivian, were sent away to school in the village of Annis when Vardis was twelve and Vivian nine. The brothers were exceptionally close; their early social isolation created a strong bond that lasted through young adulthood. Later they attended high school together in the town of Rigby. This is a school portrait of Vardis (right) and Vivian from about 1914. Vardis graduated and went away to the University of Utah in 1915; Vivian followed a year later and roomed with him. Vivian eventually earned a doctorate in psychology from Johns Hopkins University.

Courtesy of Idaho State Historical Society (63-211.28).

Courtesy of Grant Fisher.

Rigby, Idaho

This is an early twentieth-century view of the main street in Rigby, Idaho. Rigby was the county seat and a town of several hundred residents when Vardis and Vivian Fisher went to high school there. The boys lived alone in a one-room hut built by their father. The town had "only a main street, with alleys running back to narrow lanes," Fisher wrote in *In Tragic Life,* "but it housed two banks, two drugstores, two poolhalls, a small dark theater, a dancing pavilion, and a dozen shops," and Fisher "found wonder in all these."[8]

Leona McMurtrey and Vardis Fisher

The great love of Vardis Fisher's early life was Leona McMurtrey—Neola of the autobiographical novels. Neola is indeed described in the image of Leona. "Her eyes were a deep dark brown, with depth upon depth lying in their softness, and with something in them that was haunting and sad," Fisher wrote in *In Tragic Life.*[9] He met Leona at school in 1908. Though he was smitten from the start, his approaches to her were awkward and inconclusive, and he did not court her until his visits home from college. While they were separated, Fisher's devotion became jealous and almost obsessive. Although many thought the couple an unlikely match—popular, well-liked Leona and bookish, introverted Vardis—they were married on September 10, 1917, at the Fisher ranch. This photograph was taken shortly after their marriage.

Courtesy of Grant Fisher.

Courtesy of Grant Fisher.

The Fisher Family, 1923

The newly married couple moved to Salt Lake City after their wedding, where Fisher resumed his studies at the University of Utah. Graduating in 1920 with a degree in English, Fisher moved on to the University of Chicago to pursue graduate studies. Leona joined him after spending several months in Idaho. This photograph was taken in Idaho on their sixth wedding anniversary, at the end of the family's summer vacation at the Fisher ranch. With them are their sons Grant, born in 1918, and Wayne, born in 1921. After their mother's death, the boys spent most of their childhood with their paternal grandparents in Idaho.

Leona McMurtrey Fisher

On September 8, 1924, Leona Fisher committed suicide. The crises that led to her death are documented in an extraordinary series of letters both Vardis and Leona wrote home to Vardis's mother, Temperance, in the spring and summer of 1924. The marriage had been troubled almost from the start. "The driving force of my life is to write," Fisher told his mother, and the role of husband and father, as well as his graduate work, interfered.[10] Fisher worked long hours, obsessively reading, writing, and studying. He drove himself to such states of fatigue and depression that he talked of suicide himself. Furthermore, he had fallen in love with Margaret Trusler. In the summer of 1924 he told both his mother and Leona that he was considering divorce. Driven to despair, the once vivacious Leona killed herself two days short of their seventh wedding anniversary. Fisher's grief was profound, for he blamed his failure to resolve the conflicts in his life for her death. He subjected himself to merciless self-examination, out of which came a resolution to explore, through literature, the human evasions that beget such tragedies. Photograph 1922.

Courtesy of T. Roberts Fisher.

Courtesy Boise State University Library, Special Collections Department.

Margaret Trusler

As Fisher's marriage with Leona was crumbling, he wrote to his mother, "I must have a woman...who understands me and what I want to do, who wants to do the same thing...who can intelligently sympathize with what I want to do and who can therefore help me do it. I must have that or I must do inferior work."[11] He found that woman in Margaret Trusler. A fellow writer and graduate student at the University of Chicago, Margaret shared Vardis Fisher's interest in literature and encouraged his intellectual pursuits. She accompanied him to Salt Lake City when, after receiving his doctoral degree in 1925, he accepted a teaching position at the University of Utah. They were married in 1928. A son, Thornton Roberts Fisher, was born to them in 1937. By then, however, the two were often separated, and in 1939 their marriage ended in divorce. This photograph of Margaret was taken in 1922, when she was a junior at Barnard College in New York.

Fisher's First Published Novel

Vardis Fisher's short career at the University of Utah was not a particularly happy one. He never fit in with the rest of the faculty, his style grated the administration, and his religious and political views offended the conservative Mormon leadership of Salt Lake City. By 1928, it was clear to him he would not be asked to stay. But at the same time, Fisher found a publisher for his novel *Toilers of the Hills.* Houghton Mifflin Company published the novel in the fall of 1928. Set in his native eastern Idaho, the book received critical acclaim, not only for the power of its story, but also for the new direction it set for Western literature. Vardis Fisher's first published novel also provided him a way out of Utah, for New York University was looking for young novelists to staff its English department, and they offered him a job.

Courtesy of Library of Congress.

Courtesy of Idaho State Historical Society (68-22.2).

Thomas Wolfe, 1937

Vardis Fisher left the University of Utah in 1928 and headed to New York to teach at Washington Square College of New York University. There he met another young assistant professor, Thomas Wolfe. "He was so huge, his stride was so long and loose, his dark hair so uncombed, his dark eyes so unhappy and suspicious, and his whole bearing so obviously that of one who felt himself called to an uncommon destiny that I stared at him, fascinated," Fisher wrote many years later. "I read your novel and liked it," were Wolfe's first words to Fisher, and the two became friends.[12] They had common interests; both were working on autobiographical novels (Wolfe on *Look Homeward, Angel;* Fisher beginning the tetralogy), and both preferred writing to teaching. They never saw each other again after Fisher left New York, but when Wolfe passed through Idaho in 1938, he tried to find Fisher but could not locate him.

Return to Idaho

In 1931, Vardis Fisher resigned from New York University. With two novels in print—*Toilers of the Hills* and *Dark Bridwell* (1931)—he wanted to devote himself full-time to writing, and he wanted to return home. With his wife, Margaret, he moved back to the Fisher ranch, and they made it their home for the next four years. Fisher also returned to Idaho in another sense, too. Unable to find an eastern publisher for *In Tragic Life,* Fisher turned to Caxton Printers in Caldwell, Idaho. Despite the frank sexual content that gave pause to other publishers, Caxton published *In Tragic Life* in 1932. It was the first volume of what is known as Fisher's autobiographical tetralogy, and the first of several Fisher books published by the firm. This photograph of the Caxton plant in Caldwell was taken in 1930.

Courtesy of Grant Fisher.

Courtesy of Boise State University Library, Special Collections Department.

The Federal Writers' Project

Vardis Fisher taught at the University of Montana during the summer of 1932 and part of 1933, and there he met Harold Merriam, one of the leading literary scholars in the West. Two years later, when the New Deal began looking for a director for the Federal Writers' Project in each state, Merriam recommended Fisher for the Idaho post. The job was offered to Fisher and he accepted, even though it meant leaving the family ranch and relocating to Boise. As Idaho director, it was Fisher's responsibility to produce the Idaho state guide. Fisher knew the first state guide to be published would be widely reviewed, so he worked furiously to earn that distinction for his effort. He was successful. *Idaho: A Guide in Word and Picture* (1937) was indeed the first state guide in print, and it was reviewed by the national press to near universal acclaim. In the *Saturday Review of Literature,* Bernard DeVoto called it a "triumph."[13] Under Fisher's editorial direction, the Federal Writers' Project in Idaho also produced *The Idaho Encyclopedia* and *Idaho Lore*. Vardis Fisher is pictured here on August 12, 1939, visiting Caxton Printers, who printed the Idaho guide.

Children of God

Fisher did not neglect his own writing while working for the Federal Writers' Project. He completed the novel *Children of God,* a fictionalized account of the Mormon migration to Utah, and it was published by Harper and Brothers in 1939. Though repudiated by the Mormon Church, the book was well received by literary critics, who found it to be an objective and compelling account of an authentic American saga. The book was also a commercial success, and it won the lucrative Harper Prize for Fiction in 1939. For Fisher, though, the greatest prize the book won for him was the freedom to begin a writing project he had long contemplated, the twelve-volume *Testament of Man* series. Ironically, Fisher claimed not to like *Children of God,* calling it "one of the poorest novels I have written."[14] This is the dust jacket of the Dutch edition.

Courtesy of Grant Fisher.

Courtesy of Idaho State Historical Society (69-4.68a).

Opal Laurel Homes and Vardis Fisher, Early 1940s

In 1940 Vardis Fisher married Opal Laurel Holmes. Eighteen years his junior, she had been hired to work as a researcher for the Federal Writers' Project in 1936. She became his third wife and lifelong companion. In Opal, wrote Fisher biographer Tim Woodward, Vardis Fisher found "the combination of temperament, intellect, and point of view he needed in a partner for the long pull."[15] After spending the winter together at the Fisher ranch in eastern Idaho, he bundled her off to a justice of the peace and, to her surprise, insisted they be married. They spent their married life together on a ranch near Hagerman, Idaho. Their marriage ended only with Fisher's death in 1968. Opal Fisher devoted the rest of her life to reprinting his books and defending his literary reputation. She died in Boise in 1994.

The Hagerman Valley, ca. 1940

The Hagerman Valley in south-central Idaho is famous for the "Thousand Springs" that seemingly come from nowhere to tumble down canyon walls into the Snake River. They actually are the many outlets of a vast underground river that flows beneath the southern Idaho desert. Vardis Fisher invested some of his earnings from *Children of God* in twenty-three acres of land here, and this is where he and Opal moved after their marriage in 1940. Over the years the Fishers transformed a wild wasteland into a working ranch. The crops and cattle they raised helped support them in later years when literary royalties were lean.

Courtesy of Grant Fisher.

Courtesy of Grant Fisher.

The Hagerman Home

Vardis Fisher took this photograph of his home in the Hagerman Valley, ca. 1962. Shown here are the main cabin, which Fisher built of lodgepole pine, and two of the smaller structures on the property. The Fishers surrounded the home with a dense stand of evergreens. They also utilized the springs to create a lake, which they stocked with rainbow trout. At this isolated homestead, so much like the river-bottom home of his youth, Vardis Fisher found a refuge where he could write and do the heavy physical labor he enjoyed.

Relaxing at Home

A relaxed Vardis Fisher at his Hagerman home, 1954. The Fishers often entertained relatives, friends from Idaho, and literary colleagues. They built a small guest house on the property for that purpose. Vardis and Opal Fisher made three long trips to Europe and the Middle East in the 1950s, but otherwise, only research trips took Vardis away from Hagerman for very long periods of time.

Alan Swallow Papers, courtesy of Syracuse University Library, Department of Special Collections.

Courtesy of Grant Fisher.

Alan Swallow and the *Testament of Man*

Vardis Fisher's most ambitious literary undertaking, the *Testament of Man,* is a series of twelve novels exploring man's psychological, spiritual, and social development from prehistoric times to the modern day. "We must look at human beings psychologically and realize that their sociology has been fashioned for thousands of years, impelled and directed, no matter how obscurely, by the emotional endowment of the race," he wrote in 1937. "We must know a lot more about ourselves and the way the ancient past has shaped us."[16] Fisher began that study with *Darkness and the Deep* (1943), a novel set in prehistoric times. It was received warmly by literary critics, but by the time the seventh novel of the series was issued in 1952, both critical and popular interest had waned. Fisher could not find a publisher for the eighth book, *Jesus Came Again* (1956). At that point, Denver publisher Alan Swallow stepped in. Swallow, pictured here in his study in 1961, believed in Fisher's work and, despite the series' commercial failure, saw the project through to its conclusion. Fisher paid tribute to Swallow for his help and friendship by dedicating *Orphans in Gethsemane* (1960), the final volume of the series, to him and Opal Fisher. More than his historical or autobiographical novels, or any other works, Fisher considered the *Testament,* his "backward look upon our path,"[17] to be his enduring literary legacy.

Vardis Fisher in His Study, 1958

Vardis Fisher used this den as his writing studio for more than twenty-five years. Here he wrote all twelve novels of the *Testament of Man* series, several historical novels and nonfiction works, dozens of essays and stories, and several hundred weekly opinion columns for Idaho newspapers. Fisher began writing newspaper columns in 1941. Among his fellow Idahoans he earned the nickname "Old Irascible" for the frank and sometimes biting manner in which he expressed his views. Photograph by Don Howard of the *Salt Lake Tribune.*

Courtesy of Grant Fisher.

Warner Brothers publicity photograph, courtesy of Boise State University, Special Collections Department.

Self-portrait at Age Seventy-Two

Over the course of a long and productive career, Vardis Fisher wrote or edited thirty-six books as well as poems, essays, stories, and newspaper columns. After completing the *Testament of Man,* he wrote three more books, *Suicide or Murder?* (1962; an investigation into the death of Meriwether Lewis), the novel *Mountain Man* (1965), and *Gold Rushes and Mining Camps of the Early American West* (1968), which he coauthored with his wife. Fisher died on July 9, 1968, from an overdose of pills and alcohol. The circumstances of his death—whether it was an accident or suicide—are unclear. Fisher left two works in progress, an autobiography and a book about the American West. He was seventy-three years old.

Celebrating the Work of Vardis Fisher, 1972

The stars came to Idaho in December 1972 for the American premiere of the Warner Brothers film *Jeremiah Johnson,* inspired in part by Vardis Fisher's novel *Mountain Man.* Pictured among the mountain men at the Boise gala are director Sydney Pollack, Opal Fisher, and the film's star, Robert Redford. How would Vardis Fisher have reacted to the hoopla?

Notes

1. Vardis Fisher, *Idaho: A Guide in Word and Picture* (Caldwell, ID: Caxton Printers, 1937), 77–78.
2. Elizabeth Nowell, ed. *The Letters of Thomas Wolfe* (New York: Charles Scribner's Sons, 1956), 768.
3. Fisher, *Idaho: A Guide in Word and Picture*, 77.
4. Vardis Fisher, *In Tragic Life* (Caldwell, ID: Caxton Printers, 1932), 26.
5. Ibid., 44.
6. Vardis Fisher, "Hometown Revisited," in *Thomas Wolfe As I Knew Him, and Other Essays* (Denver: Alan Swallow, 1963), 120.
7. Fisher, *In Tragic Life*, 381–82.
8. Ibid., 410.
9. Ibid., 221.
10. Quoted in Tim Woodward, *Tiger on the Road: The Life of Vardis Fisher* (Caldwell, ID: Caxton Printers, 1989), 85.
11. Ibid., 85–86.
12. Vardis Fisher, "Thomas Wolfe As I Knew Him," in *Thomas Wolfe As I Knew Him, and Other Essays*, 25, 27.
13. Bernard DeVoto, "The First WPA Guide," *Saturday Review of Literature*, February 27, 1937, 8.
14. Vardis Fisher, *God or Caesar? The Writing of Fiction for Beginners* (Caldwell, ID: Caxton Printers, 1953), 241–42.
15. Woodward, *Tiger on the Road*, 147.
16. Vardis Fisher, "Preface: In Defense of the Obvious," in David Rein, *Vardis Fisher: Challenge to Evasion* (Chicago: Normandie House, 1938), 4, 8.
17. Vardis Fisher, *Darkness and the Deep* (Caldwell, ID: Caxton Printers, 1943), 8.

2

Vardis Fisher and Dr. Edwin Stuart Robinson: A Friendship

Frederick R. Oyer

Vardis Fisher has been called a maverick, a man who stubbornly went his own way. In Idaho, he was sometimes dubbed "Old Irascible." Readers of his fiction might wonder if he was clubbable at all and what being his friend might entail.

Readers of Fisher's 1930s autobiographical tetralogy, and especially readers of its revised and expanded version as *Orphans in Gethsemane* (1960), will find the record of protagonist Vridar Hunter's friendships a revealing dimension of his personality. Vridar grows up almost pathologically suspicious of others. He is a graduate student before he finds anyone deserving the designation *friend*. Even in graduate school male friendships prove transitory. The only real bond Vridar makes in graduate school is with the woman who eventually becomes his second wife. Throughout Vridar's life, the pattern seems much the same. For the most part, the "friendships" in the novel disappoint Vridar. The truly memorable friendship Vridar forges is with Angele, his third wife. (Vridar demanded much from his wives, and only Angele was able to find satisfaction meeting that challenge.) At best, the theme of friendship is problematic in *Orphans in Gethsemane*.

Fisher may have given us a telling clue for understanding the pattern of the novel when in an interview on Fisher's *Testament of Man* novels Alan Swallow asked Fisher what he meant by the word *orphan* in the twelfth novel of the series:

> FISHER: I don't find it easy to define the word, though I think anybody would know at once what I meant who is familiar with the history of the father–son relationship. The dictionary says the word means to be deprived of one or both parents. A child can, of course, be as deprived of parents while actually living with them,

as when they are dead. But I think of the word more in a historical and philosophical perspective. Perhaps I can suggest it by saying that I see as the world's most unmistakable orphans that people who more than any other have praised the father (or Father), and more than any other have knelt in fear before the wailing walls.

SWALLOW: Do you think of yourself as an orphan?

FISHER: Oh, definitely—and all of my friends but two or three.[1]

Although Fisher highlights as the most obvious orphans those who are conventionally religious, the passage opens up other possibilities and provides a basis for seeing Fisher as an "orphan" and the reason he—who was certainly not conventionally religious—considered himself an orphan. The most telling hint is his statement that a child can be as deprived of parents with whom he is living as a child whose parents are dead—perhaps more so. Vridar Hunter often feels keenly deprived of his parents; it is no exaggeration to say that he never got over his unhappy childhood. If Fisher's parents made him feel "orphaned," his comments to Swallow also reveal that Fisher chose to be an orphan, someone who did not belong. Most people tend to define themselves in terms of family, ethnic group, nationality, or religion. Some people reject these more comfortable options and prefer to look at the world in their own terms. This decision usually leads to a far more tumultuous life because one is constantly having to reassess one's ideas rather than fall back on received answers to life's questions. In that sense, a person who is separate from and outside the mainstream of family, culture, ethnic group, or religion is an "orphan." Such persons would tend to find their friends outside the mainstream—persons who are orphans in this special sense.

As Fisher tells Swallow, he thought of himself as having several friends. Although a study of these friendships would be revealing, a look here at one provides insight into the nature of Fisher's friendships and his life. As we wait for the biography that might make such a study possible, this essay will describe the nature of a single friendship that came in the later stages of his life. It was with a dentist, Dr. Edwin Stuart Robinson. The relationship reveals that two orphans had found a companion.

Fisher, born to Mormon pioneers in virtually wild southeastern Idaho in 1895, grew up with little sense of community. For weeks on end, the boy saw only his family. He shied away from strangers. Robinson, born in New York City in 1902, was a friendly man who "never met a stranger." Fisher was a physically imposing man: tall, angular, with what has been described as an ashen, gray pallor.[2] To a select few Fisher was outspoken and argumentative, but to most, he seemed strange and reclusive. Robinson, a short, rotund, almost plethoric man, was president of the Idaho State Dental Association in 1938–39 and a member of many civic organizations. Yet the two seemed alike in some ways: readers, talkers, listeners, drinkers, opinionated, conservative, consumed by politics and world affairs.

Fisher bought twenty acres in the Hagerman Valley from W.G. Tupper in 1939 and moved there in 1940 with Opal Laurel Holmes.[3] They were subsequently married before a startled justice of the peace, as chronicled in *Orphans in Gethsemane*.[4] Vardis, with the assistance of Opal and young Bob Tupper, the son of W.G. Tupper,[5] then proceeded to build his own log home and outbuildings on the place. By the time Ellis Foote and his friends visited Vardis in 1942, the Fisher place was already known as Wit's End.[6]

Robinson graduated from the University of Southern California College of Dentistry on June 4, 1927, and opened his practice in Gooding, Idaho, the same year. On October 25, 1927, Dr. Robinson married Mildred Kern of Twin Falls, Idaho, and they set up housekeeping in the back room of the dental office. Thus as co-residents of Gooding County, the Fishers and Robinsons were practically neighbors. No one now knows when Fisher and Robinson first met. Henry Robinson, the youngest son of Dr. Robinson, surmised that they probably met in a bar. Considering their mutual fondness for scotch, this suggestion has some merit, although they may have met earlier during Fisher's tenure as the head of the Federal Writers' Project in Idaho. In that capacity, Fisher crisscrossed the state acquiring data for *Idaho: A Guide in Word and Picture* (1937), *The Idaho Encyclopedia* (1938), and *Idaho Lore* (1939). It is likely that Fisher met Robinson while visiting Gooding. Robinson was an outgoing, loquacious man who deftly learned the family history and significant events in the life of anyone he met, and Fisher, a stranger in town for a few days, would have been grist for his mill.

The growth of their friendship also remains shrouded in time but invites speculation. An undated inscription in the flyleaf of *Les Faux Anges* (first French edition of *Children of God*, 1950) may provide a clue:

> For Roby
> One of the Children of God
> Vardis
> P.S. He–I get drunk at Fisher Wit's End because
> of the intellectual Sahara Gooding County

Another flyleaf inscription in *Gods Eigen Kinderen* (first Dutch edition of *Children of God*):

For "Roby"
God bless and keep him
Vardis
Mar 4–1953
When Roby and I drank one fifth of Scotch
and I one fifth of Bourbon while cursing our mothers
VF

The genesis of Fisher's ambivalence toward his mother is chronicled in the autobiographical Vridar Hunter tetralogy when the three-year-old Vridar is taken to town for a studio portrait. He was encouraged by his parents and the photographer to watch for the white bird in the lens. He realized this was a lie and "during his childhood, he never fully trusted his mother again."[7]

Robinson's own feelings regarding his mother are more obscure but can be inferred from the fact that at the age of fourteen after the separation and ultimate divorce of his parents he ran away from the family home in New York City and headed west, hoboing on freight trains.[8]

Betty Emerson, the oldest daughter of Dr. Robinson, describes her father as a stern disciplinarian who required the children's presence at the family's nightly formal dinner, though he himself was chronically late. Further, Betty said, at times he would simply disappear for three or four days without explanation and when he would return without the family car he often had no idea where it was or what he had done. Was Fisher a participant in these binges? It is possible he was, in a few of them. For the most part, given the discipline of his occupation, Fisher probably avoided them except during weekends. In the earliest surviving letter in the Fisher correspondence with Robinson, dated September 28, 1944, Fisher chides Robinson for saying publicly that Vardis would not let them (the Robinsons) in his home:

> You lovable old bastard, why don't you tell the truth?—that you were drunk as a bureaucrat on his way to China, that Opal was sick, that you had promised to bring Millie [Robinson's wife] and didn't, and that I told you it would only put a strain on world affairs and the Republican chances to win if you went barging in on my little sick toots who would be in a mood to hit you over your coke with an unabridged Bible.

"Stu," as the young Robinson was known, won the Idaho State Tennis Championship at age sixteen, and in 1925, while a student at the University of Southern California, was one of four men who made the semifinals to vie for the B.H. Dyas Trophy in an all-university tourney. The mature "Dr. Roby" pursued interests in hunting and fishing. He bought his cabin on Baker Creek in the present Sawtooth National Recreation Area (a designated wilderness area) before investing in a family residence in Gooding. He would go on long pack trips in the Sawtooth wilderness area of Idaho for big game in the fall. Vardis Fisher would, on rare occasions, go on these pack trips, but not often since he was engaged in the research for his novels.[9]

After Fisher dammed the springs at his Hagerman place, enlarging a lake that he stocked with trout, Dr. Roby and his sons frequently fished there, and in the fall, as Fisher's guests, they would shoot ducks there, often forty or fifty at a time.[10] Fisher, on forays to Gooding, would often bring trout to the Robinsons, and if they were not home, would leave them in the refrigerator at the dental office. On one of these occasions when the Robinsons were gone, daughter-in-law Lela Robinson was housesitting and answered the phone. Before she could say "hello" a male voice shouted, "Mildred, where the hell's that damn refrigerator?" Vardis, chagrined to learn he was speaking to Lela, mumbled apologies and hung up.[11]

Another avid fisherman and mutual friend of Fisher and Robinson was Hy Berkowitz. Hy and his brother, Sam, owned the Old Mr. Boston Whiskey Distillery.[12] Hy also owned the Sand Springs Ranch near Wendell, Idaho, where the Robinsons and Fishers were often guests. Guests were required to remove their shoes before entering the elegantly appointed white brick ranch-style house built among sheltering trees adjacent to a controlled creek stocked with trout. The house was carpeted with custom handwoven Chinese carpets ranging in color from beige to white. For these dinner parties Berkowitz would have fresh seafood flown in from the coast in a private plane that landed at the Gooding airport, where it was picked up by the chauffeur and delivered to the ranch.[13] In a June 8, 1956, postcard to Robinson, complaining about *Time* reporters and photographers, Fisher said the fungus on his tongue was "as deep as the nap on a Berkowitz rug."

Besides these social gatherings at the Berkowitz ranch, where Vardis and Opal would sometimes stay for extended times ranging from seven to ten days,[14] the Fishers and Robinsons entertained each other at their respective homes. Much of the correspondence between them—now owned by Dave Gonzales, a used and rare book dealer in Nampa, Idaho—is in the format of postcards or brief typed notes on three-by-five cards, establishing or altering dates and times of getting together. A postcard dated March 18, 1957, had the following brief query:

> What time are we to come Sunday? Please write to us a long letter with lucubrations exacerbations meditations tintinnabulations unitednations and pemmicanrations not to mention the elations
> Vardis

One of the establishments in Gooding they frequented was a Basque boardinghouse run by Felix Gamboa and his wife in a three-story Victorian-style mansion originally built by Governor Gooding for his son. Vardis and Dr. Roby particularly enjoyed a spicy Basque dish prepared by Mrs. Gamboa that contained tripe.[15]

Dr. Roby was a conservative Republican. The many guests at his home in Gooding over the years included Senator William E. Borah, the "Lion of Idaho"; Senator Henry C. Dworshak; and Len Jordan, the former Idaho governor appointed to Dworshak's Senate seat after his death. Vardis and Opal Fisher occasionally attended these soirees. On October 20, 1952, at the Legion Hall in Gooding, Fisher spoke on the topic of McCarthyism. The notice by the Gooding County Republican Central Committee in the *Gooding Leader* was headlined, "What Is McCarthyism. Is Senator Joe McCarthy a Stinker or Is He Telling The Truth?" Vardis and Dr. Roby also discussed intelligence officer John Birch and his right-wing beliefs, but, according to Henry Robinson, Dr. Roby was never a member of the John Birch Society. He found it to be too secretive and on the political fringe.

Fisher and Dr. Roby were always betting each other on the outcomes of elections and other questions. In 1954, they had a bet of one case of scotch over the question, "Has the Mendelian Law of dominant and recessive characteristics been discredited?" To settle this bet they addressed the question to Douglas R. Drury, M.D., professor and chairman of the Department of Physiology at the University of Southern California, who replied that he had "no knowledge of any reason for discrediting the Mendelian Law," but suggested they contact the department of biology or zoology for the definitive answer. The bet was eventually settled in favor of Fisher, who wrote on June 29, 1955, as follows: "As far as the wager on Mendel, forget it—just let it teach you to be more prudent in wagering." Dr. Roby also appears to have been outclassed by Fisher on the political bets. Typed on the back of a First Security Bank of Idaho check dated November 28, 1960, and made out to Vardis Fisher in the amount of one dollar by Dr. E.S. Robinson, Fisher wrote:

> Dear Robby: As I recall it I said I had never lost a political bet and you said you had never won one. Out of my great compassion

I said we would put an end to that jinx and so offered to wager a dollar that Budge would lose. I'd have felt no more sure of losing if I had bet that the sun wouldn't come up or that Joe Kennedy would give a hundred million to charity. So your jinx still holds. Well, come next election we will break it, even if I have to bet that you or I will be president in 1964.

We have been getting some nice research done at the Huntington, a fine library, and are now off to Berkeley.

Love and Season's best to you and yours
Vardis and Opal

Always keenly interested in politics, Fisher found a forum to share his views in a weekly news column. In a May 19, 1955, column, Fisher proclaimed the existence of a conspiracy to prevent books critical of American foreign policy from reaching the public and, in particular, damned Perry Swisher, a book dealer in Pocatello, Idaho. Fisher invited Swisher to reply to these charges in his column. Swisher's four-page reply, dated May 23, 1955, is in the Robinson collection. Swisher concluded with a barb that challenged the use Fisher was making of his talent:

> To try to close on a note of candor, perhaps what irks me about Vardis Fisher is that today in Hagerman valley he seems to be living not in a writer's sanctuary but in his lair. His petulant criticisms of the political world are a waste of his time when you think of his capabilities, he only says in a little livelier language what other alarmists of the same school can say and do. Only occasionally does he come up with something as effectively humorous as his treatment on Nixon and the snooks, or as entertaining as his essay on bad hamburgers.
>
> Here is a master weaver who could produce the finest fabrics. Instead he gives us the warp, and the woof, of a bitter mind. A bad pun, that, but I'm serious.

In an April 26, 1959, letter to Dr. Felix Marti-Ibanez, president of MD Publications, Inc., Fisher offered to supply notes on the *Testament of Man* series for a proposed article in *MD* magazine. Fisher wrote:

> I look forward with particular pleasure to this for the reason that most of the readers of MD are medical men who have been thoroughly grounded in the sciences and who on that account are more likely to be sympathetic to what has been called my "vehement

> rationalism." Some of my closest friends are doctors...E.S. Robinson of Gooding, A.D. Gillespie, Twin Falls, O.F. Swindell of Boise, all in Idaho.... Indeed, I've had far more friends in the medical group than any other group in the nation.

In this same letter, Fisher also mentions Dr. Lyman West of Boise, "a close friend before he was killed in War II." Dr. West, an avid private pilot, may have served as the model for the physician pilot, Dr. Julian Horne, who is killed while testing a new plane, in chapter 18, book 2 of *Orphans.* The perceptive reader will note how ingeniously Fisher counts Robinson among his list of "medical men." Fisher is using a bit of flattery here, though the idea of luring such medical men through *MD* was doubtless attractive. Fisher's real feelings regarding the medical profession may be more accurately portrayed in *Orphans,* where following an unproductive visit to a physician, Vridar quotes Voltaire: "Doctors are men who prescribe medicine of which they know little, to cure diseases of which they know less, in human beings of which they know nothing" (800). Fisher's novels set in the twentieth century show more interest in psychiatry than in other medical professions. Of all of those in the healing professions, psychiatrists and psychologists would be the most likely to be drawn to Fisher's work.

In 1954, Robinson acquired the Shoshone Indian Ice Caves from the state of Idaho. This natural phenomenon formed in a one-half-mile-long section of lava tube eighty feet beneath the blistering surface of the southern Idaho desert. The ice formation is caused by a low-pressure wind-tunnel effect set up by the geographical lie of the cave and the prevailing westerly winds. The property originally belonged to the U.S. government. During the Depression, it became a W.P.A. educational project. After the property was inadvertently damaged by the Civilian Conservation Corps, the ice melted in the cave, and the property was abandoned by the government, thus reverting to the state of Idaho. Over a period of seven years, it was restored and subsequently managed by Robinson's son, Russell.[16] Fisher, in a letter of June 1, 1954, agreed to do the brochure for the caves. In a letter of June 14, 1954, Fisher assigned the resulting text to Robinson as his property.

As the friendship grew between Fisher and Robinson, Robinson became an avid Fisher collector. J.H. Gipson, the president of Caxton Printers in Caldwell, Idaho, wrote to Robinson at Fisher's request and offered to help him in acquiring a complete set of the works of Vardis Fisher.[17] Fisher also helped Robinson in this endeavor; on January 24, 1951, he wrote to him:

> Book collecting is I suppose a good hobby and a profitable one IF A PERSON CHOOSES THE RIGHT AUTHORS. If my new publisher is successful I feel that my reputation will grow quite enormously over the next half-dozen years, and if it does, first editions of my books *that appeared in small printings* may become pretty hard to get hold of. These include *Dark Bridwell,* of which Caxton still has a few copies; and the first five volumes of the Series. If you should want any of these five I can get them for you at 50% off list plus postage.

Over the years, Fisher sent Robinson correspondence from critics, fans, and autograph seekers, as well as other memorabilia for his collection, including three-by-five note cards filled with quotations from reference works and working dialogue for novels. One of the finished manuscripts in the Robinson collection was *Pemmican* (1956). Robinson had had a hand in the publicity for *Pemmican.* In a June 28, 1956, letter to Robinson, Fisher wrote:

> Doubleday are nuts about the idea of kits containing a plastic tube of sage, another of buffalo bush; a small square of buckskin; a tiny jar of huckleberry jam and 3 or 4 ounces of pemmican to give to each of the important reviewers and booksellers. So can you get pemmican for me? Time is short! If you can, order 15 pounds. I'll pay for it and the express. All I ask you to do is to write to your friends up there and tell them to get 15 pounds on the way if they can, and as soon as possible.
>
> We'll be over to the Gov. Lee thing. We may go in the afternoon so we can visit with you and Millie a bit, for I assume you two will be going. We might go together, if you are.
>
> If you have the time please get off the pemmican order pronto.
>
> Our best
> Vardis

Apparently Vardis did a "side piece" on trying to find pemmican, which was picked up by Pyke Johnson of the *San Francisco Chronicle,* who did a special feature on the Great Pemmican Hunt.

In another letter dated March 22, 1961, Fisher inquired:

> Do you want to trade a set of teeth for the ms of orphans? It weighs ten pounds and if sold for no more than scrap paper is worth a wad of money.

During the 1950s, Fisher experienced great difficulty finding a publisher for the *Testament of Man* novels. In a letter dated September 2, 1953, he shared his problem with his close friend and dedicated Fisher collector:

> Dear Roby:
> Thought possibly you might like a statement in writing of my problem. I have given the best part of my life to this series of historical novels and now find that apparently all publishers including Caxton are afraid of the Roman Church. I've been expecting this for some months. So it has seemed best to me and Opal to hike out and meet a lot of people including some editors and publishers abroad to see what we can do. We think we can swing the thing on what we would spend at home plus income tax deductions to me (not her) plus some articles which I may be able to sell back home. If nothing comes of our gamble we'll hole up at Hagerman and figure out some way to publish them ourselves. We're not discouraged yet. We're just fighting mad and we don't intend to say we're licked until we're out.

Vardis and Opal Fisher were not able to "swing the thing." Many months would pass before Fisher could report that the *Testament* would be published. Forced to abandon hope for a large commercial publisher, Fisher turned to Robinson for possible assistance. In a July 23, 1955, letter, Fisher wrote:

> Dear Robby:
> You once said that if I couldn't find a big commercial house for the remaining novels in my series but had to go to some small place or get them out myself you would want 50 copies of each. I am tired of shopping around and shall go, if he will have me, to Alan Swallow and his small press in Denver. He doesn't expect to get rich on me!
> If you still want 50 of each it occurs to me that we could put out a special limited, signed and numbered edition for the rare books trade (who buy and hold to speculate) of, say, 150 copies, of which you could have 50. They wouldn't cost you any such outrageous price as Gipson's but only trade price—I imagine 33% or 40% off list price, which might be $4.00, making them about $2.50 each to you.

But if the idea no longer appeals to you, forget it. And get your blood pressure down so we can have another drink before one of us goes off to the worms.

Regards,
Vardis

Robinson, true to his earlier offer, thus obtained signed limited editions of *Jesus Came Again* (1956), *A Goat for Azazel* (1956), *Peace Like a River* (1957), and *My Holy Satan* (1958) with the following printed opposite the title page:

A special printing of the first edition limited to fifty copies and made for
Dr. E.S. Robinson

On a promotional piece for the impending release of *Orphans in Gethsemane* sent out by Alan Swallow in 1959, Fisher had written:

Dear Robby:
Assume you want this. Also assume you want the 50. If not do let me know at once, or Swallow will have the thing done. As I recall it you get your 50 and I get Opal's at 40% off. God, I'll be glad when this job is done. Reading proofs now on 600,000 words. What a fool I am.

Best
Vardis

It is unclear if Robinson got his fifty of *Orphans,* but an August 21, 1967, letter reveals that he had six copies. In obtaining these books, Robinson provided a helping hand during a stressful time in the life of the Idaho author.

Fisher in turn dedicated certain editions to Robinson. In a postcard dated October 22, 1957, from Mandan, North Dakota, Fisher wrote:

I hear a fisher book is just out inscribed to you. I wouldn't know if that is true but I can tell you this, that poor old fisher has never oh never had a book dedicated to him. How important do you have to be?

Seriously, we are getting along without accident over the Lewis and Clark trail and send you our love and beer froth.

Robinson would have to wait some months for the dedication, but in a June 20, 1960, postcard from Hagerman, Fisher wrote:

> Dear Robby:
>
> You may not yet be aware of this astounding fact, that Almat Publishing Corp., 444 Madison Av., New York 22, has put peace like a river out in paper cover, and the dedication to you is there, as big as life. So I hope that a million people read it and see your name and say, he must be a hell of a good guy—probably did in a few virgins himself.

The Pyramid Books edition of *Peace Like a River* was also dedicated to Dr. Edwin Stuart Robinson.

Vardis and Opal took extended trips to Europe in the autumn and early winters of 1953–54, 1956–57, and 1958–59. The 1956–57 trip included the Middle East.[18] They arrived in Egypt in October 1956 and from there traveled to Jerusalem, arriving on October 23, 1956.[19] On these trips, Vardis and Opal corresponded regularly with the Robinsons. Opal's messages are neatly written and frequently seem to express concern about the expenses. Fortunately, Vardis typed most of the cards he sent, since his handwritten notes to the Robinsons are almost indecipherable. In a November 4, 1956, postcard to the Robinsons from Istanbul, Fisher related the following:

> After 3 nights of air-raids blackouts bomb shelters and hysteria (not ours) we got out of Israel at 3:30 in the morning in pitch black blackout-dark and are sitting here in Istanbul under a leaden sky with rain pouring and not a drop of bourbon in sight.

In a November 28, 1956, postcard from Rome with a photograph of the Castle of St. Angel on the reverse, Fisher wrote:

> The Roman Church changed it to the hut of the angel but it's really Hadrian's Tomb, which if you don't know we are ashamed of you. We hope to arrive in Gooding Jan 25, 100 lbs lighter and 100 years older. Hope everything is fine with you all and that the novel Goat did not make atheists of you...if you read it which of course you did not.

A postcard from Nice, France, dated December 8, 1956, followed up with:

> Out of the wars—up thru Italy...and into France where we are mellow on vin blancs. We'd rather have whiskey.

As they aged both men suffered from arthritis. Fisher had gout, which seems to have affected primarily his knees, although at times his whole body was wracked with pain. In a letter dated June 27, 1960, he wrote Robinson:

> The knees seem to be clearing slowly but steadily. I realize of course that this will be only what is called a remission; that other attacks will come until all of me is paralyzed but my eyeballs. And I do mean my *eye*balls.

According to his son Henry, Dr. Roby suffered from "five kinds of arthritis" including polyarthritis and gout. In the last year or two before he retired from active practice at age sixty-one he was so stiff in the mornings that he could not put on his socks and shoes.[20]

The last surviving letter from Fisher in the Robinson collection is dated April 17, 1968. In it Fisher wrote:

> For an old limping arthritic there is a lot of pressure on me now—reputations are a matter of simple contagion, like diseases, and in the past few years when a couple of persons decided to "promote" my books I have had quite a blooming. It makes the whole business of fame so trivial that it adds another welcome to death. But we shall get over to press your hand as soon as the pressure lets up.
>
> God help the nation (but I don't think he will) with an utterly stupid leadership that has got us into a hopeless war abroad and a civil war at home. Cremation when it comes is going to feel good.
>
> Our affectionate best
> Vardis

The friendship between Vardis Fisher and Edwin Stuart Robinson was primarily intellectual. According to Henry Robinson, they talked about anything and everything, from Karl Marx, world leaders, religion, and politics, to the stock market.[21] Dr. Robinson, to judge from conversations with his offspring, must have held his own in their debates. But Dr. Robinson was more than Vardis Fisher's intellectual foil. Robinson was someone he turned to for advice in business matters; someone to commiserate with over arthritic pains and advancing age; and someone with whom he could vent about a nation he thought had gone astray.

Henry Robinson believes that his father may have influenced Vardis Fisher's writing, citing *Pemmican*. Dr. Robinson made frequent hunting and fishing trips to British Columbia over the years, sometimes in the company of Hy Berkowitz. On one such hunting trip in the early 1950s when an attack of arthritis prohibited him from horseback riding, he contented himself with fishing, and in the process befriended some local Indians who showed him how pemmican was made. He brought some of the pemmican back to Gooding and no doubt shared it with Fisher. Henry Robinson thinks this may have served as the genesis of the historical novel.[22] He further maintains that *Pemmican* was one of the novels that Fisher would periodically turn out in order to pay the bills. As far as the subsequent publicity surrounding the publication of the novel (known as the Great Pemmican Hunt) was concerned, Dr. Robinson was able to obtain fifteen pounds of pemmican for Vardis Fisher from his sources in British Columbia.

But it is likely that the friendship met certain emotional needs for both men. This brief account can only make suppositions about the psyche of E.S. Robinson; he must have found something in Fisher's writing besides a shared political conservatism. Probably Fisher would identify him as another lonely orphan. Robinson may have been one who identified with the angst of Vridar Hunter. Fisher was always on the lookout for such people. Was Edwin Stuart Robinson an orphan? According to Henry Robinson, he was, both literally and philosophically: literally, since he left home at age fourteen, hopping freight trains across the United States, eventually coming to rest in Idaho; and philosophically, because of his independent, inquiring mind.

Vardis Fisher died at the age of seventy-three on July 9, 1968, from poisoning secondary to seconal ingestion in combination with alcohol ingestion.[23] Dr. Robinson was devastated by Fisher's death. Henry Robinson stated that his father had repeatedly warned Fisher about the lethal combination of sedatives and alcohol. Coming on the heels of the deaths of Hy Berkowitz and Felix Gamboa, the death of Fisher left Dr. Robinson deeply depressed. Henry Robinson said he never recovered from this depression.[24]

Did Dr. Robinson think Vardis Fisher had committed suicide? According to Henry Robinson, Dr. Robinson was not surprised by Vardis Fisher's death, but as far as suicide was concerned, he did not know. Suicide was another topic the two friends had discussed, but at the time of his death, Fisher was working on a book, so Dr. Robinson was inclined to think that his death resulted from an accidental overdose.[25]

In his remaining years, Dr. Robinson was housebound. He was usually dressed in pajamas and a bathrobe, sitting in an easy chair in the living room of his home where he read and watched sporting events on television. He died in 1975, also at the age of seventy-three.

Notes

1. Alan Swallow, "Alan Swallow Interviews Vardis Fisher on the Testament of Man Series," *A Way Out*, July 1965, 11–15.
2. Telephone interview with Dr. Thomas E. Kasper, April 17, 1997.
3. Interview, Bob Tupper, April 15, 1997.
4. Vardis Fisher, *Orphans in Gethsemane: A Novel of the Past in the Present* (Denver: Alan Swallow, 1960), 797.
5. Interview, Bob Tupper, April 15, 1997.
6. Ellis Foote, "The Unholy Testator," *American Book Collector* 14 (September 1963): 10.
7. Vardis Fisher, *In Tragic Life* (Caldwell, ID: Caxton Printers, 1932), 34–35.
8. Interview, Dr. Henry Robinson, January 25, 1997.
9. Ibid.
10. Ibid.
11. Interview, Lela Robinson, April 1997.
12. Telephone interview with Dr. Thomas E. Kasper, May 6, 1997.
13. Interview, Dr. Henry Robinson, January 25, 1997.
14. Telephone interview with Dr. Thomas E. Kasper, April 17, 1997.
15. Interview, Dr. Henry Robinson, January 25, 1997.
16. Russell Robinson, *The Story of the Shoshone Indian Ice Caves* (Twin Falls, ID: Ace Printing, 1978).
17. Letter from J.H. Gipson to Dr. Robinson, June 11, 1948.
18. Joseph M. Flora, *Vardis Fisher* (New York: Twayne Publishers, 1965), 14.
19. Postcard to Robinson from Fisher, October 23, 1956.
20. Interview, Dr. Henry Robinson, January 25, 1997.
21. Interview, Dr. Henry Robinson, September 11, 1997.
22. Ibid.
23. Autopsy No. A-74-68, MVMH, July 10, 1968.
24. Interview, Dr. Henry Robinson, September 11, 1997.
25. Ibid.

Bibliography

Fisher, Vardis. *In Tragic Life*. Caldwell, ID: Caxton Printers, 1932.

———. *Orphans in Gethsemane: A Novel of the Past in the Present*. Denver: Alan Swallow, 1960.

Robinson, Russell. *The Story of the Shoshone Indian Ice Caves*. Twin Falls, ID: Ace, 1978.

Swallow, Alan. "Alan Swallow Interviews Vardis Fisher on the Testament of Man Series." *A Way Out*, July 1965, 11–15.

3 "The Dim Immense Terror": Literary Naturalism in *Toilers of the Hills, Dark Bridwell,* and *In Tragic Life*

James H. Maguire

> It sometimes seems that the naturalists' "world" is constructed not according to indifferent laws but as a trap or even a torture chamber.
>
> —June Howard, *Form and History in American Literary Naturalism*

Temperance Fisher gave birth to Vardis in 1895, the midpoint of the decade that saw the beginning of American literary naturalism. Fisher's first publications did not appear until the late 1920s, after the end of the early phases of naturalism and during the beginnings of modernism, but he was nevertheless labeled a naturalist by some of his early critics.[1] Later critics agree that Fisher is a naturalist, and some of them point out the complexity of his naturalism. Joseph M. Flora, for example, writes that the "Antelope novels are themselves abundant evidence of Fisher's versatility. He is a Naturalist, yes; but he is not one who keeps working the same formula."[2]

If literary naturalism can be said to have a formula, it might be a very general one such as "Little person fights against huge forces and loses." Central to almost all definitions of naturalism is a stress on the genre's pessimism, the result of naturalists' fascination with the view that people are subject to the iron laws of materialistic determinism. In addition to its pervasive pessimism, a naturalistic novel can often be identified by its objectivity, by its reformist satire, and by its focus on lower-class characters. So pronounced are all these characteristics that, according to Louis J. Budd, "Within the protean genre of the novel, a sympathetic reader easily distinguishes a naturalistic from a realistic work, and either, through method as well as attitude, from any other mode."[3]

There can be pitfalls, however, in the easy recognition of a naturalistic novel. Having applied the label "naturalism" to Vardis Fisher's first three published novels, a reader might suppose that Fisher seeks only to tell the naturalist's story of protagonists who struggle against overwhelming forces that predictably defeat them. Such a reader might then miss all that *Toilers in the Hills* (1928), *Dark Bridwell* (1931), and *In Tragic Life* (1932) reveal about the Janus-faced nature of life: its "dim immense terror" and its "loveliness and light."[4] Viewing these novels as examples of naturalism, the reader might not see that Fisher struggled to escape from naturalism but found no effective exit from his dualistic view of the world.

Toilers of the Hills is clearly a work of naturalism. It tells the story of Dock and Opal Hunter, who begin their married life by homesteading in Idaho's Antelope Hills. They struggle year after year but gain a mere subsistence from the arid land, Dock never wavering in his conviction that he will eventually "conquer" the land, Opal agonizing in an ambivalence that has her half fearing they will be the conquered and half hoping that Dock may be right.

Dock and Opal's struggles certainly sound like the stuff of literary naturalism. The reviewers, as Flora has noted, compared Fisher with other writers who depicted "the farmer's battling nature on the frontier," writers such as "Hamlin Garland, Willa Cather, Erskine Caldwell—without sensing that Fisher's range was more varied, more profound, and, in short, richer."[5] A glance at a few passages in *Toilers* shows why Fisher's early critics saw him as just another naturalist depicting the plight of frontier farmers. Here, for example, Opal responds, early in her marriage, to Dock's declaration that "I ain't to be conquered by nature in all the life-long world."[6]

> She knew he would never yield, and she shuddered at a thought of what awaited them. Year after year of barren effort, springtimes of promise, of wild flowers and tall grass and rains, and summers of drouth and locusts and hawks. And as she thought of Dock and his ways, it seemed clear to her that he was pitting himself against a vast power, an unseen and ruthless power hidden in these hills and reflected in the passionless gray of this sky. Everywhere she looked there was something unfriendly and pitiless and hard, an unyielding force that would slowly crush them both to its will. This was to be the dream of a lone man's struggle against a power that was sinister and mighty and dimly seen.[7]

Until the last few chapters of the novel, Opal's fears seem well founded. Then Dock puts to work his years of observations of the land and the climate, and his accumulated knowledge leads to his mastery of dry-land farming just in time for him to profit from the outbreak of World War I, which has caused an increase in the demand for wheat.

Since the "unseen and ruthless power" fails to crush Dock, we encounter what seems to be the paradox of a naturalistic novel that has a happy ending. We might account for that paradox by taking Edwin H. Cady's view that American writers could never wholeheartedly accept pessimistic determinism; instead, they wrote novels depicting the world almost as it might be *if* philosophic naturalism were true.[8] Hence, Dock triumphs—but the world nevertheless seems at times a harsh battleground.

Donald Pizer, who views Cady's definition of naturalism as being "critically unproductive," says that "most nineteenth-century naturalistic novels are about people who seem to be going nowhere."[9] Looked at from the vantage point of Pizer's definition, *Toilers* remains an example of naturalism, for in spite of Dock's late success, he and Opal seem to be going nowhere. Dock's success arrives too late to change their lives much. Dock and Opal are thwarted not only by nature (including "the man-made 'second nature' of social forces," to use the terms of June Howard's definition of naturalism) but also by their *own* natures (including "the forces of instinct and heredity that embody nature within the very boundaries of the self").[10]

Wayne Chatterton discerned the conflict in *Toilers* in terms similar to Howard's (but years before Howard's book appeared). He wrote:

> Most critics have felt that the conflict [in *Toilers*] lies between struggling man and indifferent or antagonistic nature. But Fisher seems to have dramatized a conflict which is antecedent to the physical one, and which is its underlying cause. This basic clash pits the eternal Dream against stubborn Reality.[11]

Seen through the lens of Dock's "eternal Dream," the land holds the promise of abundance that will eventually be fulfilled through man's perseverance. Seen through the lens of Opal's naturalistic view, the land possesses so much ruthless, crushing power that it seems pitiless and invincible. Both views prove true, for Dock eventually does conquer the land, and Opal, after a life of lonely fear and regret, eventually closes "the door to her dreams."[12]

What meaning, if any, emerges from this conflict between dream and reality? If we see *Toilers* as nothing but naturalism, the conflict, ending as it does, simply leaves a bitter irony: even when luck allows Dock's dreams to come true, the end of it all is loss anyway, since reality has crushed Opal's dreams. If, however, we see *Toilers* as something besides just naturalism, as a blend of naturalism and western realism, then we can see something besides the irony. Max Westbrook says of western realism that its practitioners, writers like Fisher, "have a sacred as opposed to a profane mode of apprehension. Events are real or unreal according to whether or not they recreate the relevant original act, the primordial act which is the source of meaning."[13]

The primordial act that *Toilers* recreates is the myth of the Garden of Eden. Expelled from paradise, man fights to conquer the world of nature that once gave him sanctuary, solace, and an abundance of its fruits. To subdue nature, to force it to yield once again its Edenic abundance, Dock homesteads. Dock's war with nature terrifies Opal, since she generally sees the adversary as ugly and invincible, not beautiful and ultimately yielding, as Dock sees it. This western American Adam and his Eve have the intelligence and empathy to see nature sometimes as the other sees it. And they both come to accept the view of one of their neighbors, a woman whose children die stillborn: "Mary said it was God's way to mix the ugly and the beautiful the world over."[14] Nature, Janus-faced, reveals herself both as Eden and as exile, both as the mother and the destroyer, for she is, in fact, both. Fisher accepts the reality that nature destroys—hence, the naturalistic element in his fiction. He also accepts the truth that nature nourishes. He apprehends the sacrality of a nature that both creates and destroys, and this places him among western realists who possess a similar sacred mode of apprehension.

Unlike *Toilers, Dark Bridwell,* Fisher's second published novel, has nothing of happiness in its ending; it has, instead, catastrophe like that of Greek tragedy. When reviewers and early critics read *Dark Bridwell,* Flora says, they "labeled Fisher an American Hardy"; and if such early praise seems extravagant, consider John R. Milton's more recent assertion that *Dark Bridwell* may well be "one of the major accomplishments in modern American fiction."[15] As Flora also notes, *Dark Bridwell* continues Fisher's development of the theme *Toilers* sets up: "the loneliness, the isolation of the frontier."[16]

Like *Toilers, Dark Bridwell* tells a story of homesteading in Idaho's Antelope Hills. But these homesteaders, Charley and Lela Bridwell, are quite different from Dock and Opal Hunter, although the husband in both couples is the one who wants to homestead on the frontier. Dock never stops working, whereas Charley never ceases looking for ways to avoid work. Charley generally succeeds in avoiding it because he knows how to live off the land and other people. Lela resembles Opal in not seeking the isolation to which her husband brings her; but Charley manages for long periods to charm Lela into a kind of contentment with their lifestyle. He treats her like a princess, often doing her "woman's work" and finding ways to entertain and amuse her. For almost twenty years during their marriage, Lela does not recognize her own need for either a more active life or more people than just her immediate family.

Charley's idyllic existence might have continued for the rest of his life if he and Lela had not had children. Their first three—Thiel, Jed, and Beth—at first require few changes in Charley's way of life. Then, when Jed is still a small boy, he begins to try to outdo his father in trickery and cruelty; in the second part of *Dark Bridwell,* the narrative focus shifts from Charley to Jed, partly in order to show the father's effect on the son. When Jed is eight years old, he forces the clothes off Beth so that he can show the neighbor boys (Vridar and Mertyl Hunter) what a girl looks like. The Hunters tell their prudish mother what Jed has done, and she is shocked and outraged. Charley quickly guesses what has happened and brutally beats his sons to punish them. Such abuse leads to Jed's implacable hatred of his father. So strong is his hatred that some years later when Charley prepares to beat the boys for a prank that endangered a shepherd's life, Jed swears he will kill Charley if the beating takes place. Convinced of the boy's resolve, Charley does not follow through with the beating.

By the time Jed reaches the age of fourteen, he has tortured and killed many animals, but he is still sexually inexperienced. He loses that final vestige of innocence when one of Charley's old prospector pals arrives to hunt for gold, bringing with him his fourteen-year-old sexually abused and now promiscuous daughter. She copulates with Jed, and when she and her father leave, Jed runs away from home to follow her.

Except for the violence pervasive in the natural setting and the cruelties practiced by Charley and Jed, naturalism in the first two parts of *Dark Bridwell* does not seem to include much determinism, at least little that the narrator explicitly notes. Determinism emerges clearly in part 3, when the narrative focus shifts to Lela. The departure of her older children (Thiel and Beth soon follow Jed's example and leave home) leaves Lela anguished, and she awakens to her need for activity, for a purpose, and for more contact with other people. Left with a baby girl that she and Charley name Hetty, Lela heeds Prudence Hunter's advice that she labor in order to provide a good education for her fourth child. Lela begins to work with an intensity that scarcely slackens when she gives birth to her fifth child, a boy called Hamlin (Ham, for short).

Eight years after Jed has run away from home, his mother has driven herself, by bone-wrenching work, to earn enough money to begin to give her youngest children a good education, something denied to her oldest three. What she does not know is that Charley has taught Ham, still a little boy, how to chew tobacco and swear. In the novel's last scene, Lela finds out what Charley has done, and Jed returns home to kill his father. When Charley will not defend himself against Jed's attacks, the disgusted son and outraged mother leave with the younger children. After a night of drunken grieving, Charley leaves, too, heading eastward into the mountains, moving "steadily into the empire of solitude."[17]

Given Charley Bridwell's many animal-like characteristics, one might expect him to be a typical protagonist of a naturalistic novel. For example, when three-year-old Jed gets lost, the father finds his son in a way that makes Charley seem more animal than human:

> He dropped upon his hands and knees and followed Jed's trail. He barked, in an absurd way, like a dog, and he smelled of the earth; he fell back on his haunches and howled like a coyote, and again went forward, hopping like a great beast. (35)

Charley finds Jed by using the same animal-like methods he later uses to find the bodies of people who have drowned in the river near his cabin. Such animal instinct seems remarkably like that possessed by McTeague, the eponymous protagonist of Frank Norris's 1899 novel. When a posse pursues McTeague after he has killed his wife, he instinctively senses their approach. Charley and McTeague are also alike in their large size and power and in their lack of formal education.

But Charley possesses greater intelligence than does McTeague, who sometimes seems mentally retarded, so slow and faulty is his thinking. In contrast to McTeague's dim wit, Charley exhibits a keen, albeit usually cruel, sense of humor, as well as an ability to coax loans and gifts out of reluctant neighbors. In fact, the narrator says Charley is so shrewd and quick-witted that people said of him "that he was a philosopher who had read all books and had built a home for his mind among the wisdoms of the world" (9). Besides not finding evidence that he has read any books, let alone all of them, we can see that only Charley's intelligence creates the impression that he is wise, for he manifestly lacks wisdom in his treatment of his wife and children.

What, then, is Charley? He is a frontier Diogenes with strong instincts attuned to the natural world. Like the ancient Greek philosopher Diogenes, Charley can see no sense in working. Like Diogenes, he begs and "borrows" from others, even though he has the ability to get by on his own, and then, after begging and "borrowing," scoffs at the very workers who have just given him what he asked for. Unlike Diogenes, Charley chooses not to live in a city or town, and he encumbers himself with responsibility when he marries and has children. Nevertheless, Charley's outlook strongly resembles the philosophy of his ancient counterpart. In effect, when the novel begins, Charley tries to force his way back into the Garden of Eden by refusing to accept the punishment (i.e., work) that God has given humankind for the transgression of Adam and Eve.

The author's naturalism is not played out in Charley's tragic fate, for it is not the natural world that dooms Charley. Instead, he falls by his own folly, for he believes that he can ignore the nature of his wife and children, that he can control their lives without suffering any of the consequences of stifling their natural desires. Intelligent though he is, he never understands the reason for his downfall:

> He turned the pages of his history, but they were meaningless and dark, meaningless and dark. (316)

Not understanding the cause of his calamity, he explains it to himself by adopting a naturalistic view:

> He stared at the bitter wind, whipping its fury and greed over a depth that it had already paralyzed. Life, it came to him now, was like that: it conquered, and then, still unsated, it drove the blade of its will through age and into death. (369)

It was not, however, life or the bitter wind that made Charley trick Lela and keep her and their children isolated and subject to his will.

On the one hand, had Charley Bridwell been willing to forgo the joys of marriage and family life, he could have spent his life without working and without a care among the beauty and bounty of the mountains. Much like the lone Adam in the Garden of Eden, and more self-reliant than even Henry David Thoreau, Charley possessed human intelligence and animal instincts that fitted him ideally for life in the wilderness. On the other hand, had he been willing to work and to live among people, he could have helped Lela and his children to pursue their dreams. Yet he could not keep both Eden and Lela's love, because Lela, given her nature, could never rest happy in Charley's Eden. By revealing Charley's dilemma, Fisher shows that life places before someone like Charley a choice between the natural world and the human world. Charley's tragic flaw consists of thinking he can have both.

In telling the stories of Charley and Lela Bridwell, and of Dock and Opal Hunter, Fisher had, it is true, written naturalistic novels about the lives of homesteaders in the American West. As Louie W. Attebery sums it up: "In the two novels he had rendered the effects of environment upon the shaping of human life."[18] As readers, we are, to use Louis J. Budd's words, "manipulated to regret the fate" of poor farmers on a thinly populated frontier.[19] Moreover, instinct sometimes overpowers the conscious will of some of the characters in *Toilers* and *Dark Bridwell*. Regardless of hard-won victories over the land and their economic circumstances, these characters seem to be going nowhere, and the novels end on a note of pessimism as many of the characters close the door on their dreams.

In the midst of all their naturalism, *Toilers* and *Dark Bridwell* also rework the myth of Eden. Max Westbrook explains why the Edenic myth exerts such a pull on American writers. He says that in earlier myths, insensitive forces like the giant Titans of Greek mythology bring order from chaos and are then displaced by more sensitive powers like Zeus. In America, however, both the "sensitive" and "insensitive" participated in settling the country, and the former allowed the latter to kill or displace Indians. Westbrook adds:

> Since the founding of the American world was thereby left to the insensitive, our founding does not satisfy. We constantly seek to do it again and to get it right this time. The American West has provided a series of second-chances, the possibility of meeting honestly and without Puritanical tyranny the extraordinarily difficult task of doing the Titan's job while maintaining fidelity with a premature love of individual human beings and with a culturally precocious knowledge of democratic rights.[20]

Fisher's pessimism about our chances of "getting it right this time" stands out in the endings of his first two published novels; at least he shows that whatever dreams people manage to achieve, the costs of achievement can sometimes crush the dreamers.

In *In Tragic Life*, Fisher's third published novel, the protagonist seems crushed by fear before he is even old enough to have any dreams. Vridar Hunter (Fisher's fictional self-portrait) comes from pioneer stock so accustomed to violence and pain that when young Vridar cuts his foot, Prudence, his mother, tells him to hush because "It don't help none to cry" (130). Stoic, taciturn, and unaware of Vridar's fears, his parents tell him little about life, and what they do tell him comes mostly from ill-informed or bowdlerized wives' tales and from Prudence's puritanical beliefs.

Trying hard to be his mother's "brave little man," Vridar does not tell either of his parents how frightened he is of the world around him. And he has ample reason to be frightened. In just one of dozens of scenes of violence, Vridar watches as a horse impales itself on a fence post, and then the boy sees his father stuff the horse's guts back into its abdominal cavity. In that instance, Joe Hunter exhibits some kindness, but on other occasions he flies into a rage and beats and injures farm animals. Reading scene after scene like these is like reading the first half of Upton Sinclair's *The Jungle* (1906), except that the blood and guts in Fisher's novel cannot be blamed on the Beef Trust or any other reformable institution, for the source of the violence in *In Tragic Life* is either individual humans or nature itself.

As in *Toilers* and *Dark Bridwell,* however, nature in *In Tragic Life* is not just violent and frightening. At frequent intervals, Vridar experiences the beauty and tenderness of nature. These moments of relief, however, scarcely begin to counterbalance his long periods of fear. In fact, when Vridar looks back over his first four years on his parents' isolated homestead by the Snake River, "He saw the four years as one moment, bound with one uninterrupted terror, drawn into one nightmare" (46). Nor does the nightmare go away when Vridar leaves the isolation of the homestead and begins attending school. Now, however, instead of experiencing terror caused by forces outside him, Vridar comes to fear what is within him. He learns to masturbate, regards it as a sin, though he cannot quit, and lives in mortal dread that his sinning will damn him to hell or drive him crazy. Only in the novel's last few pages, as Vridar approaches the age of eighteen, does a teacher save him from his dread of the world and himself. By laughing at the boy's obsessive fears, the teacher frees Vridar from their grip.

Telling the story of Vridar's life from his earliest years until he reaches late adolescence, *In Tragic Life* shows Fisher to be as much a master of the Bildungsroman as was Charles Dickens. Like Dickens's Pip, David Copperfield, and Oliver Twist, Fisher's Vridar Hunter has great expectations. Dickens's young protagonists, however, look only to be restored to wealth or to their true station in life, whereas Vridar expects to be a prophet. Even before he reaches the age of ten, he tells his mother: "I'll be a prophet and talk to the Lord" (102). Since the narrator is an older Vridar, a reader can see that as a novelist, Vridar does indeed possess prophetic powers.

As prophet, Vridar reveals the nature of life in the Garden of Eden that is his parents' homestead. Joe and Prudence toil incessantly in their Eden, yet unlike their relatives Dock and Opal Hunter, Joe and Prudence do so not for themselves but for their children. Vridar also bears witness to Charley Bridwell's refusal to toil. From these adults and from his own experiences, the young Vridar learns: "There was sin in the world, there was guilt, and it was decoyed in everything of loveliness and light; and virtue, upon which God alone smiled, was to be found in the stern and austere" (364). Then the teacher's laughter awakens Vridar to the possibility of joy, and although he still lacks understanding of joy, Vridar ends the novel on a note of hope.

Vridar's story continues in the next three novels of Fisher's tetralogy; in his later years, Fisher revised and expanded the narrative and titled it *Orphans in Gethsemane* (1960). Flora writes, "In *Orphans* the protagonist is often a satirist judging society, but he is more understanding than his predecessor in the tetralogy."[21] According to Thomas J. Lyon, though the Vridar of *Orphans* is more understanding, in "the tetralogy, *Orphans,* and the late novel *Mountain Man,* a dualistically framed emotional extremism is common. Nature is either wondrously benign or the opposite, freezing cold and heavy with the threat of death."[22] Like Dock and Opal Hunter, like Charley Bridwell, and like his parents, Vridar sees that nature has two faces, and he is like the adults, too, in failing to accept the essential unity under that appearance of duality.

Who can blame them? They had to struggle in the face of the cold indifference of a nature they saw crush life often and easily. Although they knew at times they were within the Garden of Eden, they also knew from the death and violence all around them that this Eden was no walled paradise like the one in the Bible. Certainly, "what is false within" betrays Dock and Opal, Joe and Prudence, and Vridar, too. But no inner betrayal thrusts the very young Vridar into an Eden full of terror. He is born into Eden as nightmare. The beauty and tenderness he later experiences—even the hint of joy at the end of *In Tragic Life*—may move the mind to think that nature is mother as well as destroyer; but one feels the incommensurability of those benign traits after experiencing through Vridar's narrative a world full of "the dim immense terror, of the infinite" (149). Fisher is the prophet of that terror.

Notes

1. Joseph M. Flora, *Vardis Fisher* (New York: Twayne Publishers, 1965), 29.
2. Ibid., 106.
3. Louis J. Budd, "The American Background," in *The Cambridge Companion to American Realism and Naturalism: Howells to London,* ed. Donald Pizer (Cambridge: Cambridge University Press, 1995), 43. In addition to Budd's essay and Pizer's "Introduction: The Problem of Definition," *The Cambridge Companion* includes (on pages 278–80) a list of sixty-three studies of American realism and naturalism. To the list should be added Donna M. Campbell's *Resisting Regionalism: Gender and Naturalism in American Fiction, 1885–1915* (Athens: Ohio University Press, 1997).
4. Vardis Fisher, *In Tragic Life* (Caldwell, ID: Caxton Printers, 1932), 149, 364.
5. Flora, *Vardis Fisher*, 99.
6. Vardis Fisher, *Toilers of the Hills* (Boston: Houghton Mifflin, 1928), 27.
7. Ibid., 128.
8. Edwin H. Cady, *The Light of Common Day: Realism in American Fiction* (Bloomington: Indiana University Press, 1971), 24, 48–49, 51.
9. Donald Pizer, *Realism and Naturalism in Nineteenth-Century American Literature,* rev. ed. (Carbondale: Southern Illinois University Press, 1984), 40.

10. June Howard, *Form and History in American Literary Naturalism* (Chapel Hill: University of North Carolina Press, 1985), 44.
11. Wayne Chatterton, *Vardis Fisher: The Frontier and Regional Works* (Boise: Boise State College, 1972), 13.
12. Fisher, *Toilers*, 360.
13. Max Westbrook, "Conservative, Liberal, and Western: Three Modes of American Realism," in *The Literature of the American West,* ed. J. Golden Taylor (Boston: Houghton Mifflin, 1971), 16.
14. Fisher, *Toilers*, 165.
15. Flora, *Vardis Fisher*, 99; John R. Milton, *The Novel of the American West* (Lincoln: University of Nebraska Press, 1980), 140.
16. Flora, *Vardis Fisher*, 102.
17. Vardis Fisher, *Dark Bridwell* (Boston: Houghton Mifflin, 1931), 376.
18. Louie W. Attebery, "Vardis Fisher," in *A Literary History of the American West,* ed. J. Golden Taylor et al. (Fort Worth: Texas Christian University Press, 1987), 870.
19. Budd, "The American Background," 43.
20. Max Westbrook, "The Ontological Critic," in *Interpretive Approaches to Western American Literature,* ed. Daniel Alkofer et al. (Pocatello: Idaho State University Press, 1972), 65.
21. Flora, *Vardis Fisher,* 66.
22. Thomas J. Lyon, "Revisionist Western Classics," in *Reading the West: New Essays on the Literature of the American West,* ed. Michael Kowalewski (Cambridge: Cambridge University Press, 1996), 151.

Bibliography

Attebery, Louie W. "Vardis Fisher." In *A Literary History of the American West,* ed. J. Golden Taylor et al., 862–86. Fort Worth: Texas Christian University Press, 1987.

Budd, Louis J. "The American Background." In *The Cambridge Companion to American Realism and Naturalism: Howells to London,* ed. Donald Pizer, 21–46. Cambridge: Cambridge University Press, 1995.

Cady, Edwin H. *The Light of Common Day: Realism in American Fiction*. Bloomington: Indiana University Press, 1971.

Campbell, Donna M. *Resisting Regionalism: Gender and Naturalism in American Fiction, 1885–1915*. Athens: Ohio University Press, 1997.

Chatterton, Wayne. *Vardis Fisher: The Frontier and Regional Works*. Boise: Boise State College, 1972.

Fisher, Vardis. *Dark Bridwell*. Boston: Houghton Mifflin, 1931.

———. *In Tragic Life*. Caldwell, ID: Caxton Printers, 1932.

———. *Mountain Man: A Novel of Male and Female in the Early American West*. New York: William Morrow, 1965.

———. *Orphans in Gethsemane: A Novel of the Past in the Present*. Denver: Alan Swallow, 1960.

———. *Toilers of the Hills*. Boston: Houghton Mifflin, 1928.

Flora, Joseph M. *Vardis Fisher*. New York: Twayne Publishers, 1965.

Howard, June. *Form and History in American Literary Naturalism*. Chapel Hill: University of North Carolina Press, 1985.

Lyon, Thomas J. "Revisionist Western Classics." In *Reading the West: New Essays on the Literature of the American West,* ed. Michael Kowalewski, 144–56. Cambridge: Cambridge University Press, 1996.

Milton, John R. *The Novel of the American West*. Lincoln: University of Nebraska Press, 1980.

Pizer, Donald, ed. *The Cambridge Companion to American Realism and Naturalism: Howells to London*. Cambridge: Cambridge University Press, 1995.

———.*Realism and Naturalism in Nineteenth-Century American Literature*. Rev. ed. Carbondale: Southern Illinois University Press, 1984.

Westbrook, Max. "Conservative, Liberal, and Western: Three Modes of American Realism." In *The Literature of the American West,* ed. J. Golden Taylor, 9–22. Boston: Houghton Mifflin, 1971.

———. "The Ontological Critic." In *Interpretive Approaches to Western American Literature,* ed. Daniel Alkofer et al., 49–66. Pocatello: Idaho State University Press, 1972.

4 A New Light in the Canyon: Vardis Fisher's *Dark Bridwell* and American Literature of Inhabitation

Peter Blakemore

Our landscapes not only provide physical sustenance through clean air, pure water, and fertile soil; the places where we live also reflect back to us our identity and offer a source of stable grounding for our sense of the present, the past, and the future. Yet we rarely pay much attention to this fact, and our general disregard for specific locations may, in the long run, put us at risk. In his book *Place and Placelessness*, geographer Edward Relph considers the psychological association between people and the physical landscape and decides that "the means of experiencing, creating, and maintaining significant places...are disappearing and that 'placelessness'—the weakening of distinct and diverse experiences and identities of places—is now a dominant force."[1] Recognizing that places are "literally fields of care, settings in which we have had a multiplicity of experiences and which call forth an entire complex of affections and responses,"[2] Relph points to the psychic disarray and emotional damage we suffer from the homogenization of our common fields of perception. He suggests that the Heideggerian concept of "sparing" might provide an antidote. Sparing will teach us that we owe our grounds of perception "a tolerance for them in their own essence...a willingness to leave places alone and not to change them casually or arbitrarily, and not to exploit them."[3] Of course, all human societies have had to alter their landscapes somewhat in order to survive. But the degree of transformation and the speed at which these changes now occur, combined with the loss of our ability to affect the process, add up to form a deeper sense of alienation.

This increasing disconnection from landscapes is not solely a human concern. The way we talk and think about places can have an immediate effect on other life-forms. In "The Loss of Floral and Faunal Story: The Extinction of Experience," Gary Paul Nabhan and Sara St. Antoine show how such common things as childhood stories and local lore change our consciousness of the land. Removing species of flora and fauna from the communal imagination increases the chances of their real loss in the biosystem. Without stories about animals or plants, how will people keep track of things, and how will the children learn of such species in the future? Out of sight, out of mind, out of existence is a chain reaction, and the galloping pace of development means that the world relies on human attention and perception now more than ever.

To spare our places and the diversity of life-forms dependent upon them, these places must exist in our imaginations and emotions. Aldo Leopold understood this fifty years ago when he wrote in the "Land Ethic" section of *A Sand County Almanac,* "It is inconceivable...that an ethical relation to land can exist without love, respect, and admiration."[4] Leopold recognized the subtle interconnections that exist in a place, and he developed the concept of a "land community" in order to unify the apparently separate parts of an environment. He offered this vision because he knew that people needed a new way of imagining the land. He knew that how we encounter landscapes lies at the very heart of who we are, and that the marks we leave on places, in our stories of them and in our actions, are memorials to the past and signposts to the future.

To understand how far we are from Leopold's vision and to gain a sense of the possibility of affiliation with place, we can compare the modern American approach to landscape with that of the White Mountain Apaches, who use stories set in specific locations as tools for moral and ethical memory. Through a practice known to this eastern Arizona tribe as "speaking with names," many among them can illustrate an important social tenet or offer ethical guidance to a wayward or perplexed tribal member by telling the story of what happened in a certain place. As anthropologist Keith Basso explains, "[A] single place-name may accomplish the communicative work of an entire saga or historical tale, and sometimes, depending on the immediate social circumstances, it may accomplish even more."[5] Such emphasis is put on the historic past residing in place that one might simply mention the name of the crucial location and let the listeners make the connection and draw the relevant conclusions for themselves. In his study of this method of oral healing, *Wisdom Sits in Places,* Basso explains how "speaking with names" gives the Western Apache "the power to establish enduring bonds between individuals and features of the natural landscape."[6] A reciprocal relationship has evolved out of this practice; the people depend upon the land, and, as part of this exchange, "the landscape in which the people dwell can be said to dwell in them."[7] The historical or legendary past is called to life in the individual imagination and activated by the existence and stability of a place. One practitioner described the process in this way: "We gave her clear pictures with place-names. So her mind went to those places, standing in front of them as our ancestors did long ago. That way she could see what happened there long ago. She could hear stories in her mind, perhaps hear our ancestors speaking. She could recall the knowledge of our ancestors."[8]

Such deep history residing in place is a mark of inhabitory identity. People who see stories in the surrounding landscape become interwoven with their places. They live out reciprocal, evolving relationships, whether they be nomadic hunters and herders, or sedentary agriculturalists and city dwellers. It is this perceptual phenomenon that philosopher Edward S. Casey refers to when he writes of place as "the generatrix for the collection, as well as the recollection, of all that occurs in the lives of sentient beings, and even trajectories of inanimate things. Its power consists in gathering these lives and things, each with its own space and time, into one area of common engagement."[9] As the background, foreground, and underground of the recent and the deep past, and as the site of the future, place stands at the center of perception.

What are our American stories of place? How far removed are we from them? How much attention do we pay them? Which places do we focus on? If scholars are the "shamans of the intellectual tribe," as E.O. Wilson claims—if it is the critic's job to "interpret knowledge and transmit folklore, rituals and sacred texts"[10]—how are we increasing consciousness concerning these vital questions of person in place? Michael Kowalewski believes that "critics still seem to feel that landscape and nonhuman environments do not crucially influence writers or their characters."[11] Kowalewski points out that the criticism generated by the concept of literary regionalism includes almost no actual discussions of the physical world itself.[12] Regional labels—the "South," "West," and "Midwest"—seem vacant of any environmental meaning. The terms generally stand for nothing more than political boundaries to territories or as convenient (though shaky) grouping mechanisms for specific (though questionable) cultural characteristics. Such dearth exists that Kowalewski has come to believe that critics have avoided meaningful discussion of this subject because they "lack a vocabulary with which to ask engaging philosophical, psychological, or aesthetic questions about what it means to dwell in place."[13] If Kowalewski is right, as I think he is, then we must lay a path back into place.

A first step on the path returning us to place might be to start the important task of bringing long-neglected stories back into the light. One of the most remarkable works focusing on inhabitation is Vardis Fisher's novel *Dark Bridwell* (1931). As the tale of one family's attempt to settle an Idaho canyon, the book explores questions of relationship to landscape and the phenomenon of realizing the self in place as thoroughly as any I can think of. And like many novels in the genre labeled "regionalism," *Dark Bridwell* reminds us that there are more pressing reasons to read about place than nostalgia or local color. Paying close attention to a book such as *Dark Bridwell* warns us that we should no longer simply dismiss or marginalize a work because it focuses itself on a distant location. Fisher's novel reminds us that our intentions as we approach the land, and our ability to perceive what we find there, will have a profound effect on how we live and survive.

Considering the complexity involved in developing a relationship with place, *Dark Bridwell*'s plot is remarkably simple. We too often think of ourselves as entirely portable—the places where we settle seem less important than the tools we carry. In Fisher's novel, a family hoping to settle in a remote area of the West experiences immediate success, which continues at a level pace, but the story ends with the protagonist's failure to endure upon the land. It is an old American story, to be sure. And from this summary it might seem that *Dark Bridwell* is just another example of what Wallace Stegner claims is present in "any book that is western in its feel" —that they are books "not about place but motion, not about fulfillment, but about desire. There is always a seeking, generally unsatisfied."[14] And the novel does match Stegner's description in that it speaks to desires that remain unfulfilled: In this case, the central character, Charley Bridwell, wants to protect his family from what he sees as a fallen, degenerate civilization—a hope that is dashed by novel's end. But Fisher never for a moment forgets the importance of place, and, because of this, *Dark Bridwell* runs counter to Stegner's claim—as a novel that will not allow us to sink into a blinkered interiority of human enclosure. From start to finish our attention is kept clearly focused on the physical properties of an east Idaho canyon. In fact, the physical environment is so thoroughly evoked that one could say *Dark Bridwell* "becomes" a place.

As we engage in an imaginative recreation of the Bridwells' river bottom, we are reminded how the landscape actively shapes its characters. Just as a real canyon keeps one's mind constantly aware of the surrounding walls and draws the gaze downward to the ever-moving river, our attention is pulled inward to the canyon's topography. Like many other notable works that settle the mind in the physical world, we get a large-scale, geological sense of place: "[L]eaving its source, some beautiful Wyoming lakes, the stream flows quietly through the Jackson Hole country; but in spring and summer it gathers, creek by creek, the white wintry acres of Teton peaks, and becomes broad and deep before it passes Jackson City and plunges into the mountains flanking east and south."[15] Fisher carefully channels our perceptions down into the drainage as the river disappears "into sunless foam between two mountain walls," and he lays down the terraces of horizon formed in this type of arid, high-altitude border plateau spreading out beneath the range:

> The entire Antelope benchland was once its bed. But little by little, through countless centuries of toil, the river has narrowed its shores and cut downward, until to-day it lies four hundred feet below those hills, where it moved in a wide lake, and left its gravel to be buried by wind and dust. In sinking its channel, it has eaten away the flesh of earth and left curious skeletons of rock. It has left tablelands of stone, long since bedded again with soil, some of which now lie in long shelves, two hundred feet above its passage, and some of which are small bottomlands only a little above its present level. (4)

Clearly, Fisher enjoys a western sensibility for exposed, semi-arid country and well-defined changes in landscape. His attention to uplift faulting, subsidence, scouring, and continuous visible weathering as rocks crumble, fall, and reshape the land reveals a mind schooled by its surroundings.

Readers who are at all familiar with such geophysical motion will likely see the hills and tablelands and the winding canyon of the South Fork moving in their own imaginations. Inhabitants, residents, and visitors to western canyons will recognize the experience of shifting layers of humidity and warmer air from rim to river, the sudden cooling caused by an entering creek, the wafting of cedar and sage at the turn of a corner. Those who have never experienced the sensation of standing in the depths of the earth at the bottom of a great canyon will have their imaginations activated and the canyon created in the mind's eye. Thus *Dark Bridwell* transcends the shallow sense of mere "setting" that Lawrence Buell has rightly criticized. Instead of the typical, simplistic "prefatoriness...dramatic intensification...and symbolic doubling" by which landscapes have so often been subsumed in order to highlight the human psyche,[16] *Dark Bridwell* reverses the focus to show us how the land draws attention and displays order. Fisher's canyon centers the story. We have begun with a reminder through geologic history that the land lives its own life, that it, too, is in motion.

Landscapes also hold human history. Until the how and why and when of former inhabitants are activated, until we attend to the marks they have left in orchard remnants, stone walls, cabins, and diggings, we cannot know the canyon's true depth. Realizing this, Fisher moves us still further into the landscape by going beyond the scientifically active description of the countryside to give motion to its human past. We experience the first sense of this place through the eyes of a woman who has preceded the Bridwells here. We learn that seven years before the Bridwells had bought their small tract of bottom land from Silas Bane, he and his wife, Miranda, had entered the canyon at night. The first opportunity readers have to see a personality interpreting the landscape comes through Miranda Bane's eyes as she awakens to find herself enclosed by the surrounding mountains. Her attention is drawn downward to the river, which "broke upon innumerable tons of rock: mammoth gray piles, scrags and boulders and ledges: and recoiled upon itself in an appalling fury of boiling mud and clouds of spray, of black shoulders of water rearing and crumbling and falling down like avalanches of shattered glass" (5). The phenomenon causes her to imagine a future spent "down in a hole" (6), and she never gets over the fact. Our first psychological perceptions in the novel offer a dismal prospect and the "enormous loneliness of this world" (7).

These perceptions of the landscape will soon change. Charley Bridwell's wife, Lela, begins her time in the canyon with a slow, phenomenally gradual ride down into her home. As her new place is revealed to her from a variety of perspectives, she obtains distinct ideas of distance, proportion, and where precisely she has landed. For Lela, the South Fork seems to promise relief from the squalor of a Pocatello apartment house. In this sense the novel stands in the fine American tradition of pastoral escape. But, more important, the juxtaposition of these two views makes us party to the dynamics of physical space and psychological life. We know that this place has been tried—the enclosed horizon, the continuous roar and shifting roil of the river, the short days and intense, concentrated sense of being down inside of something—all of this is given before the Bridwells' story even starts. Though Fisher never develops a deeper human past in this section of the canyon—for instance, we have no sense of the pre-European, indigenous human population—we are made mindful of the fact that to at least one white American settler's eyes a western canyon is a specific kind of place to live. The novel's opening seems to say, "Are you ready for this?"

Such a carefully constructed representation of place is, by itself, an aid to protecting and keeping landscapes. To settle our places in literature is to put them into consciousness, to remind and introduce. If everybody read this book, whatever canyons remain along the eastern Snake River and its tributaries would certainly stand a better chance of our sparing them. And creating the landscape in this way sets Fisher in that relatively small group of novelists who have recognized and played upon the reciprocal relationship between person and place. Hamlin Garland, Sarah Orne Jewett, William Faulkner, Willa Cather, Eudora Welty, H.L. Davis, Ken Kesey, and others—many of whom have been marked for good or ill as regionalists—have tried to point us toward the expression of landscape via story and the imagination. But few of these authors keep us focused on the acute interaction between psyche and land in the way that Fisher does. Such a phenomenal—or what Edmund Husserl would call "kinesthetic"[17]—experience transports the reader from mimesis to sensing. In *Dark Bridwell* we are rarely asked to know a phenomenon in the abstract. In the same way that a good naturalist describes physical nature through sensations, we understand the physical, phenomenal reality through its effect on the psyche. All through the novel, the objective physical world shifts toward an active role of making meaning in characters' minds.

Once we have been introduced to the South Fork of the Snake and situated on the Bridwell place at Rattlesnake Point, we learn why this location has been chosen and how Charley Bridwell conceives of his life here. The South Fork is remote enough that he has only two neighbors, one family miles downstream and the other across the roaring river. Here he can keep his clan safe from the corrupting influences of society, which as far as he sees it is made up of nothing but "lustful hoodlums, knaves ...hellcats and harlots" (40). In short, Charley thinks he has escaped civilization.

Unlike many western settlement narratives, *Dark Bridwell* does not have hardship as its main focus. There is enough difficulty to lend credibility to the experience of homesteading in such a remote and wild area, but Charley seems more than capable of eking out a living here—otium, a life without toil, is easily arrived at on this section of the South Fork. And judging from Charley's view of the world as a comically chaotic playground overseen by a childlike trickster God, he seems to fit a character-type that Joseph Meeker celebrates in his groundbreaking study of literature and environment, *The Comedy of Survival*. It would appear from his philosophy and his opportunistic, ursine feeding habits that Charley Bridwell is a classic example of the "nature-accepting picaro" for whom "sanity is recognition of the world's madness, not approval or emulation of it."[18] In several important passages, we hear of Charley's philosophy, an ethic closely attuned to the rambling picaresques Meeker uses to make his point that our environmental problems can be seen to derive, partly, from the exalted though ecologically divisive view of human as tragic hero. Indeed, for the first half of the novel, little upsets Charley: "He could grow indolently ripe and full, letting the mad world spin toward its catastrophes, letting other men spend their years for broad estates. The seasons of his life would march in quiet cycles. His body would soak up sunshine, drowse through the warm months, and sheathe itself in fat against the cold" (136–37). Unlike the earlier inhabitant of Rattlesnake Point, Miranda Bane, who, as her name itself suggests, could not bear to look out upon the canyon walls any longer, Charley is undaunted by his surroundings. In fact, all might have gone well for him had he lived like a male bear—alone, searching for food when his stomach moved him, eating, sleeping, and only occasionally meeting a mate. But having a wife and three children with him means necessary contact with humanity, and, as Charley is forced to discover, social organization is also part of one's place. Charley seems not to have accounted for this fact as he laid plans for the future.

Like so many actual grand adventures of human encounter with the land, a story that begins as a comically hopeful, even picaresquely careless, narrative of blithe pastoral bliss shifts by its end to misapprehension, discord, and blight. The family scatters, and all of its members seem to despise both the land and the man who has brought them to it. As the novel transforms from comedy into tragedy, *Dark Bridwell* asks us to consider what went wrong. Though Charley, the self-reliant fell hunter, powerful swimmer, and encyclopedia of woodcraft and animal lore, seems a remarkably well-evolved animal in the canyon, he fails. Why? It is this descent that makes the novel such an important work of environmental literature and a vital story of American inhabitation. Charley's experiment in pastoral otium is destroyed, not by external forces, Indians, the weather, or legendary packs of ravenous beasts, but from within. The Bridwell family disintegrates because Charley lacks wisdom. His foresight looks only to satisfying his immediate appetite, and as Fisher's novel darkens, sending the family into its decline, the lesson becomes clear: simply possessing the knowledge of how to extract material substance from the world, which Charley owns, is not enough.

The best explanation of how and why Charley fails can be found in Paul Shepard's *Nature and Madness*. In this foundational work of ecological psychology, Shepard lays out a compelling argument for the view that Western culture's shift toward agriculture and domestication has resulted in our alienation from the natural world. Shepard claims that the course our Middle Eastern and Greek philosophical forebears chose has led us to a pathological state of cultural immaturity. Whether or not you agree with Shepard's belief that most in the industrialized West exist in general states of arrested adolescence toward nature, our current serious environmental degradation is indisputable. Fronting the facts of washed-up medical waste, vanishing wildlife, fishkills, red tides, clearcuts, silted streams, and Superfund sites makes it hard to dispute the conclusion that we live out of balance with our landscapes. The general environmental decline ought to serve as a constant reminder that establishing healthy, secure home environments requires an awareness of the linked causal network of actors and systems within the land. We need to know that dumping spent motor oil down the storm drain might harm the local cutthroat trout. If killing all the snakes in a place leads to an increase in mice, we need to question how this will affect the general stability of a specific area before we kill the snakes. Will the mice eat our food stores? Will their feces carry disease? What part do our own decisions and actions play in such subtle relationships? What frame of mind, what approach, is necessary to see probabilities and possibilities? And most important of all, those who consider these issues need to know how to pass this awareness on to other members of their society. Societies ought not to have to rediscover environmental principles with each new threat and each new generation. Societies need foresight.

Charley has none of this. He is, in effect, a meat-making machine, packing away kegs full of salted elk, deer, bear, and fish, living quite literally off the fat of the land, and merrily propelling his wife and children down a road to psychic ruin. In spite of his legendary ability to survive, the pathological social dynamic he has created within his own family turns to defeat him. His Arcadia on the South Fork becomes an abomination—a basin full of hatred and discord—and instead of ending as a comic celebration of the survival instinct, the story concludes in bitter tragedy.

As the linchpin to the family's decline, Charley's second son, Jed, is also a perfect fictional representation of Shepard's arrested adolescent. Following a terrifying incident when Charley nearly strangles his three-year-old son to death, the child "lived and grew in darkness" (151). Jed evolves into a kind of deconstructionist of his land community. All can be broken down into a simplistic code of binary abstraction—there is good and there is evil. Subtle distinctions, organic affiliations, and relationships do not exist for him. By adolescence, Jed's cruelty has become a regional legend for its creativity and imagination: he beats a skunk "until the flesh [is] soft as jelly" (157) because he cannot get the trapped animal's lifeless eyes to stop watching him. Like Descartes practicing on the beasts he thought of as insensate machines, Jed toys with a variety of creatures whose instinctual behavior ensures that they will inflict pain upon themselves: a dog who must advance when commanded, he sets upon a porcupine; a mule who must kick when barbed, he digs a pit behind and goads to madness; billy goats who inherently butt heads, he corrals together until they batter themselves senseless and bloody. And in what may well be one of the strangest images of this novel full of bizarre scenes, after practicing a kind of genocidal rampage against woodchucks and finding them an "unequal struggle" (168), Jed turns to rattlesnakes, girding himself in a suit of armor lovingly fashioned out of discarded tin cans. In the snakes' eyes Jed reads a "malignant hatred" and makes his battle into a legend fit for such a knight: "[S]itting by the fire, moody and silent, he envisioned himself as a mighty warrior piling dead reptiles mountain high" (168). His war ends predictably. As has so often been the case in Euro-American settlement, the animal that has lent its name to, or stood as the mascot for, a place, vanishes entirely. Jed's special hatred renders meaningless the place-name Rattlesnake Point, since after his reign of terror no snakes remain. Like towns named Buffalo or California's wild emblem—its golden bear that strides across the state flag—the animal's significance fades along with its reality.

In *Nature and Madness,* Shepard provides a compelling explanation of how such killers form. Without the "framework of nature as metaphoric foundation for cosmic at-homeness," writes Shepard, a developing youth will "always lack true reverence for the earth." He goes on to explain that "infantile fantasies" lead to incapacitation and eventual needs to control the outer world. "To be helpless is, to the modern mind, the worst of all fates."[19] This state of childish fear that would, of course, result from a father's trying to kill his child, as Jed experienced, leads to a pathological nightmare world where, according to Shepard, "[n]ature has lost its magical capacity to reveal that an ultimate symbiosis holds the universe together." Jed cannot see the relational nature of himself to his place—how the water he drinks, the flesh he consumes, and the firewood he burns to keep warm become parts of himself. Instead, the external, physical world "becomes the enemy for those who cannot face their own unconscious assumption that all other people are hostile."[20]

In Jed Bridwell, Fisher creates precisely the character Shepard describes. We learn that Jed "divided the world sharply into the good and the bad.... He liked flowers and birds. He liked certain trees, such as the maple and the fir; but the spiked hawbush drew his wrath. Thorns and briars and thistles, like rattlesnakes and skunks, seemed to him to be symbols of that power for evil which he saw in life.... Once he decided that a thing was his enemy, he found no peace until he had destroyed it. At everything he met, whether animal or plant, he stared with sober eyes, searching its power for evil or good. If he decided it was evil, he at once laid plans against it" (197). The list of hated organisms is long: hornets, hawks, sheep, cactus, vultures, badgers, mules, shepherds, and greenhorns come up against his wrath. The sink-or-swim method of child rearing, which Charley and so many others practice, leads to a perception in the child's mind of the world as opponent; places mean us harm. The description fits Jed Bridwell perfectly, and if we follow the implication that his psychological epigenesis has led him to this view of existence, there is only one place that our search can lead.

Of course, as it turns out, Charley himself has such a puerile fascination with cruelty, for though he generally eats what he kills, we do recall the pleasure he takes in tormenting animals for the sake of comedy, as when he ties bones to mice's tails, or shows complete disregard and cruelty by starving his pack animals, then butchering the emaciated carcasses and using the flesh to bait his traps. The tricks he plays on unsuspecting greenhorns and shepherds is further proof of his view of the world as opponent. If we have read closely, we will have learned that Charley's outlook on the canyon itself amounts to a childish dissatisfaction with the way nature has organized itself. Charley conceives of the river, which brings them sustenance and is the centering force of life in the canyon, as "an absurd thing...the stormiest idiot among all the headstrong fools of life" (44). His dissatisfaction with it leads to an infantile wish that rather than the river "there should be a blue lake, deep and still; a calm mirror of water that would hold the sky and the white cotton piles of its bedding. The river annoyed him" (44). From early on we might have expected something to go wrong when we hear that Charley views his world as a clash of divided forces. This imagined view of place is carried on into the lives of his children, all of whom discover at some point in the novel their hatred for the canyon.

Though Charley never recognizes how his immature, materialist view of the canyon destroys his chance at permanent settlement, his son Jed does experience a rebirth of sorts when he turns toward the romantic other in the person of Bonnie Adams, a wayfaring miner's daughter. Bonnie serves as the catalyst to Jed's final decision to leave the canyon. Jed and Bonnie may simply be made for each other—"I like men drink whiskey and kill things" (248), she explains to Jed, and at least in the killing we can see a mutual interest—but it is hard to say whether practically any girl near his own age might not appeal to him in the same way. In the depths of the canyon, isolated as they have been all their lives, Jed and his brother, Thiel, almost instantly set up a rivalry for Bonnie's attentions. Jed wins out, as he must in all things. The change his newfound affection brings over him is remarkable, not for the fact that his common adolescent urges are fulfilled, nor because it represents a side of him we have not seen before, but because Fisher uses this episode to clarify how precisely our sense of place, world, and affiliations with nature are affected by internal moods and what phenomenological philosophers call "intentionality." A single kiss from Bonnie unlocks a flood of experience: "He heard...the rich woody cry of a flicker, the cool trilling of a warbler, and the clear tinkling lute-notes of a canyon wren. All the birds were gathering around him, singing into the old empty room of his heart; and the trees were taking the wind from the sky, drenching their boughs with it, and whispering out over him in a great wide breath; and flowing under their leafy sound, under the spilling bird-cries, was the wet wave-wash of river waters, lifting into the sky a gray cloud of music, beating their hunger into mountain walls" (242–43). It is one thing to equate a storm-swept evening with moodiness and Sturm und Drang—such clichés of pathetic fallacy have flowed from the poet's pen since the Romantics and before—it is another thing entirely to create a character who divides his world between the good and the evil, and who sets about on sustained campaigns of species extinction, and then, with the arrival of an adolescent love interest, sees the world anew. But it is not projection; it is perception that changes:

> He looked at the sun, like a yellow pool in the sky, like a hole in the golden depth of space; at the pale blue far away; and he felt as if both the blue and the gold were in his breath and mind. He was part of this vast enchantment, this blue and green wilderness.... The silver body of the river was part of it, too; and this tangled garden of light and the bosom of this earth.... It was more than his mind could grasp, more than his blood could hold; and it spilled out of him in a sigh, as if he flowed in rivers of emotion from an inexhaustible source. But it was also intense, as if he had drawn into himself all life, all ecstasy and meaning, and would henceforth burn like a thing of flame. In one moment it was a knot, a handgrip half of rage and half of joy; but in the next moment it was a softness spreading forth, a hungry vale of light that opened and drew the world in. (243)

In this Fisher has created a marvelous subtlety of philosophical distinction. Jed's shift in intentionality—his predisposition toward the landscape—does not remake the world into an image of his choosing. His newfound connection and sudden sense of security and peace show him finally perceiving his true relationship with the canyon. The birds, the trees, the river—he now recognizes the whole land community as the ground of his being. As he dissolves into the world, or as the world, the canyon, and life within it enter into him to form an interconnected self, Jed sees for the first time an inkling of what it might be like to feel at home. He has discovered a world in which he belongs. The tormented son suddenly finds that his long-despised place mirrors back wholeness, sustenance, and the complex beauty of order.

It would be fine if Jed had been able to take some kind of permanent solace out of this experience, but such attachments without a fundamental grounding in the sense of place cannot last. A love of the sort Jed feels for Bonnie is transitory. And what is more important for the sense of place and identity in the novel, Jed is incapable of seeing this landscape as a secure home for the future. Though the canyon may be the location of his first love, it is also the place of all his pain. Everywhere along the paths around the Bridwells' cabin, through the canyons, and by the river's edge lie the historic landmarks of his tortured childhood. He vanishes to find a world where he can live, and soon after him all of Charley and Lela's children also escape. Bearing a fourth child only confirms for Lela that Charley is a terrible father. Lela finds her own psychological passage away from Charley and the land by taking the familiar path of mindless, driven toil, production, and accumulation. Lela Bridwell finally breaks the spirit of the place where she finds herself, struggling to turn a semi-arid benchland into a productive farm. Her scheme of raising chickens proves worthy, and she is finally able to squirrel away enough money to safely escape from Charley after a final confrontation over his child rearing. Though she has shuddered at his cruelty and poor handling of their children in the past, she cannot bear to see it happen a fourth time, and Lela takes their child and vanishes like all the rest.

Joseph Flora has found that most of Vardis Fisher's works "deal with the theme of uncovering man's evasion."[21] *Dark Bridwell* certainly upholds this assessment, since it is fundamentally about evading responsibility to the future—the future of settlement, the future of a family, and the future of eternity itself. But in its focus on evasion, Fisher has also created a lasting story of human encounter with—and misapprehension of—the land. At its heart, *Dark Bridwell* deals with the way a landscape and a group of people interanimate each other—how the place makes its people and what the people make of the place. The Bridwells' life as a unified identity exists in the physical marks they have left on the land—extinct species, shelter, clearings, and discarded tools and trash—and in the stories that turn to legend. Like the place-centered stories of the White Mountain Apaches, Charley Bridwell's misprision, avoidance, and exile ought to serve as a warning and a cautionary example of how not to live. As we revisit the canyon of the South Fork, Charley's evasion can be our gain.

In his desire to understand how landscape, place-names, and story work together among the White Mountain Apaches, anthropologist Keith

Basso asked Dudley Patterson to explain what the concept of wisdom means to his people. After some days of mulling it over, Patterson replied:

> The trail of wisdom—that is what I'm going to talk about. I'm going to speak as the old people do, as my grandmother spoke to me when I was still a boy.... "Do you want a long life?" she said. "Well, you will need to have wisdom. You will need to think about your own mind. You will need to work on it. You should start doing this now.... Your life is like a trail. You must be watchful as you go. Wherever you go there is some kind of danger waiting to happen. You must be able to see it before it happens. You must always be watchful and alert. You must see danger in your mind before it happens.... How will you walk along this trail of wisdom? Well, you will go to many places. You must look at them closely. You must remember all of them. Your relatives will talk to you about them. You must remember everything they tell you. You must think about it, and keep on thinking about it, and keep on thinking about it. You must do this because no one can help you but yourself. If you do this your mind will become smooth. It will become steady and resilient. You will stay away from trouble. You will walk a long way and live a long time.
>
> "Wisdom sits in places. It's like the water that never dries up. You need to drink water to stay alive, don't you? Well, you also need to drink from places. You must remember everything about them. You must learn their names. You must remember what happened at them long ago. You must think about it and keep on thinking about it. Then your mind will become smoother and smoother. Then you will see danger before it happens. You will walk a long way and live a long time. You will be wise. People will respect you."[22]

How many of us in our wanderings through canyon country in Idaho, New Mexico, Montana, Utah, Oregon, Arizona, California, or Nevada have come upon the abandoned cabins where the Bridwell families of the West have fallen apart and vanished from the land? Do we think of them and how their lives transpired? Do we note another's passing and draw the connection between our own town or city and this small reminder of what has been? Do such places of pain and the stories we imagine there act upon us to make us wise?

The story of Charley Bridwell and his canyon cannot be too far from the realities of a thousand little family sagas of getting and losing a living on the western landscape—but we need to touch them again. We need to see that novels like *Dark Bridwell* are more than just quaint pictures of regional life in times past. We can read our way into various modes of emplacing ourselves in the landscape; we can learn as the White Mountain Apaches have to see stories about places as the collecting pools of wisdom—the Bridwells' disastrous canyon, Faulkner's vanished Big Woods, Woody Guthrie's and John Steinbeck's Dust Bowl, Leslie Marmon Silko's mesa lands. "To return to things themselves," writes philosopher Maurice Merleau-Ponty, "is to return to that world which precedes knowledge, of which knowledge always *speaks,* and in relation to which every scientific schematization is an abstract and derivative sign-language, as is geography in relation to the countryside in which we have learnt beforehand what a forest, a prairie or a river is."[23] Perhaps, as we read our ways into these and other landscapes, as the stories like *Dark Bridwell* return us to places themselves, we can remember what a canyon might be and how we might approach a life there. From the vantage point of storied landscapes, we will see a more vital reason to rediscover place and the authors who have kept it for us. Our literature is full of such deep roots—the places await our reenactment of them. Lighting up Vardis Fisher's dark canyon, and a thousand other places like it, can lead us back into our own relationships with the places we call home.

Notes

1. Edward Relph, *Place and Placelessness* (London: Pion Ltd., 1980), 6.
2. Ibid., 38.
3. Ibid., 39.
4. Aldo Leopold, *A Sand County Almanac* (New York: Ballantine, 1966), 261.
5. Keith Basso, *Wisdom Sits in Places: Landscape and Language among the Western Apache* (Albuquerque: University of New Mexico Press, 1996), 89.
6. Ibid., 40.
7. Ibid., 102.
8. Ibid., 86.
9. Edward S. Casey, "How to Get from Space to Place in a Fairly Short Stretch of Time," in *Senses of Place,* ed. Steven Feld and Keith Basso (Santa Fe: School of American Research Press, 1996), 26.
10. E.O. Wilson, *Biophilia* (Cambridge: Harvard University Press, 1984), 58.
11. Michael Kowalewski, "Writing in Place: The New American Regionalism," *American Literary History* 6 (Spring 1994): 174.
12. Ibid., 176.
13. Ibid., 174.
14. Wallace Stegner, "The Sense of Place," in *Where the Bluebird Sings to the Lemonade Springs* (New York: Penguin, 1992), 138.
15. Vardis Fisher, *Dark Bridwell* (Boston: Houghton Mifflin, 1931), 3. [Subsequent references to this text are given in parentheses.]

16. Lawrence Buell, *The Environmental Imagination: Thoreau, Nature Writing, and the Formation of American Culture* (Cambridge: Harvard University Press, 1995), 254.
17. Edward S. Casey, *The Fate of Place: A Philosophical History* (Berkeley: University of California Press, 1997), 219.
18. Joseph Meeker, *The Comedy of Survival: In Search of an Environmental Ethic* (New York: Scribner, 1974), 100.
19. Paul Shepard, *Nature and Madness* (San Francisco: Sierra Club Books, 1982), 99.
20. Ibid., 100.
21. Joseph M. Flora, *Vardis Fisher* (New York: Twayne Publishers, 1965), 20.
22. Basso, *Wisdom Sits in Places,* 126–27.
23. Maurice Merleau-Ponty, *The Phenomenology of Perception,* trans. Colin Smith (New York: Routledge, 1996).

Bibliography

Basso, Keith. *Wisdom Sits in Places: Landscape and Language among the Western Apache.* Albuquerque: University of New Mexico Press, 1996.

Buell, Lawrence. *The Environmental Imagination: Thoreau, Nature Writing, and the Formation of American Culture.* Cambridge: Harvard University Press, 1995.

Casey, Edward S. *The Fate of Place: A Philosophical History.* Berkeley: University of California Press, 1997.

———. "How to Get from Space to Place in a Fairly Short Stretch of Time." In *Senses of Place,* ed. Steven Feld and Keith Basso, 13–52. Santa Fe: School of American Research Press, 1996.

Fisher, Vardis. *Dark Bridwell.* Boston: Houghton Mifflin, 1931.

Flora, Joseph M. *Vardis Fisher.* New York: Twayne Publishers, 1965.

Kowalewski, Michael. "Writing in Place: The New American Regionalism." *American Literary History* 6 (Spring 1994): 171–83.

Leopold, Aldo. *A Sand County Almanac.* New York: Ballantine, 1966.

Meeker, Joseph. *The Comedy of Survival: In Search of an Environmental Ethic.* New York: Scribner, 1974.

Merleau-Ponty, Maurice. *The Phenomenology of Perception.* Trans. Colin Smith. New York: Routledge, 1996.

Nabhan, Gary Paul, and Sara St. Antoine. "The Loss of Floral and Faunal Story: The Extinction of Experience." In *The Biophilia Hypothesis,* ed. E.O. Wilson and Stephen Kellert, 227–50. Covelo, CA: Island Press, 1993.

Relph, Edward. *Place and Placelessness.* London: Pion Ltd., 1980.

Shepard, Paul. *Nature and Madness.* San Francisco: Sierra Club Books, 1982.

Stegner, Wallace. "The Sense of Place." In his *Where the Bluebird Sings to the Lemonade Springs,* 199–206. New York: Penguin, 1992.

Wilson, E.O. *Biophilia.* Cambridge: Harvard University Press, 1984.

5

The Mothers, Yes; The Feminists, Maybe Not

Doris Betts

Today's tourists, after a short drive west of Truckee, California, on Interstate 80, will come to a state park in which stands an emigrant statue with its base twenty-two feet above ground, marking the snow's depth during 1846–47 when some members of the trapped Donner Party barely survived a record freezing winter here by eating their own dead. Against one flat-sided granite boulder where the Murphy family built its lean-to, fire marks can still be seen.

Of the eighty-one in that wagon train, snowbound in early November, only forty-six made it months later through the blizzards to Sutter's Fort near present-day Sacramento.[1] Visitors to park headquarters today may read the index cards on which are recorded the names of more than 150 site visitors who are descendants of those Murphy, Reed, Breen, and Donner survivors. The central museum offers artifacts and a film, and its bookstore stocks most of the histories available to Vardis Fisher while he was writing *The Mothers* in the early 1940s. He could have consulted, for instance, C. F. McGlashan's *History of the Donner Party* (1880), *The Expedition of the Donner Party and Its Tragic Fate* (1911) by Eliza Poor Donner Houghton, who was only three years old when carried to safety by the third rescue team, or what seems to have been Fisher's main source and is still the most popular account, *Ordeal by Hunger: The Story of the Donner Party* (1936), by George R. Stewart.

My own stunned reaction to visiting Donner Memorial State Park led me to read these and many other histories as well as Fisher's novel, *The Mothers* (1943), until all this saturation eventually produced a novel of my own, *The Sharp Teeth of Love* (N.Y., A.A. Knopf, 1997). Fisher himself, though he took research seriously, seldom read other writers' novels.[2] Among fellow novelists he did not read who tried their hand at fictionalizing the grim drama are Hoffman Birney, Homer Croy, George Keithley,

Jeannette G. Maino, Joseph Pigney (though Dutton marketed this book as history), and Richard Rhodes. Joseph M. Flora says Fisher probably "paid the price for reading less fiction in his later years."[3]

Not only did Vardis Fisher prefer to read nonfiction, but by the time he published *The Mothers* in 1943, he was already concentrating less on the historical Western novels that had earned him fame, except as interim moneymaking books to be sandwiched into the twenty-year project that had by then claimed his almost fanatic attention. This twelve-volume *Testament of Man* (1943–60), launched in the same year as *The Mothers,* depended not so much on storytelling as on abstract ideas and didactic theses, tracing the evolution of the human soul from the Stone Age to Christianity.

In fact, Fisher has said his inspiration for *The Mothers* was also an intellectual one, and did not arise as did my own novelistic impulse from a strong emotional reaction to standing on the very spot where desperate pioneers ate human flesh. Instead, Fisher wrote in a letter to George Frederick Day that a work of nonfiction, Robert Briffault's three-volume anthropological work also titled *The Mothers,* had actually inspired him.[4] Briffault's work, subtitled "The Matriarchal Theory of Social Origins," even when approached in its abridged one-volume version, is no gripping story, but a scholar's weighty comparison of man—and especially woman—with the lower animals of both genders: Briffault includes chapters on social relations, motherhood, exogamy, matrilocal marriage, and sex. Briffault considered maternal love an "older, more primitive, and more fundamental sentiment than affection between the sexes" and noted that among most animal species "the female is the more cautious, wary, ingenious, and sagacious."[5] In the animal kingdom, matriarchy rules, and no real societies exist below the human species.

When matched to the historical facts about the ill-fated Donner Party (two-thirds of the men died early, with unmarried male adults dying first; one-third of the children died and most frequently the boys; but only one-fourth of the women died, surviving until very late in the winter entrapment), Briffault's ideas can be seen to underlie the thesis of Fisher's novel, which does not focus on cannibalism, unlike most of the yellow journalism of the day and most of the treatments since. Fisher is primarily interested in the survival skills of the women, especially those women who headed the only two families that came through intact: the nine Breens and six Reeds.

When William DuBois reviewed Fisher's novel in the *New York Times,* he wrote that those women displayed "she-wolf tenacity."[6] Such an animal comparison is apt since here, as in other works, Fisher peels off layer after layer of civilization until most of the starving emigrants have been gradually stripped down to their lower selves.

Fisher's male characters, however, receive his harshest animal comparisons. Mary Graves and Peggy Breen may display "fierce motherhood,"[7] Lavinia Murphy "could be an Irish tigress" (205), and each mother strongly defends "her brood" (206), but Pat Breen is like "a serene donkey" (237), Lewis Keseburg's hands are "talons" (283), and eventually he becomes "a dog in man's clothing" (233). Augustus Spitzer is "a sly stray fox" (237), a "trapped beast," a "homeless but very cunning dog" (238), and "a beast facing winter" (239). One of the strong women, Peggy Breen, stares at Spitzer "as she might have looked at a female beast who had eaten her young" (234). It is Keseburg who initiates cannibalism by summoning the others down to their animal natures, saying that if they do not dig up and devour their dead fellow travelers, the wolves will eat the corpses first. And even in starvation's late extremity, after the injured George Donner has lost all ability to speak and must grunt and gesture like an ape, his skeletal but artistic wife, Tamsen, still ventures into the "pure" outdoor air, where she still manages to create paintings of the snowy landscape that is killing them all.

Themes similar to this human/subhuman split are ongoing in Fisher's work and may only have received a new stimulus from Briffault's anthropology. Certainly dichotomy finds other guises in Fisher's earlier and autobiographical tetralogy about Vridar Hunter (1932–36). If the Donner Party members seemed to Fisher split between those whose natures predetermined who would live or die, Vridar's divided internal nature is a smaller mirror of the same split. Vridar, too (and Fisher?), felt pulled between his selfish ego drives and the larger, more unselfish goals aimed at the greater good, as Flora has noted in analyzing the tetralogy.[8] Vridar sees his teenager self as "a jungle thing"[9] and cannot decide whether humans are "generous and warmhearted" or "a vast spawn of apes with the jungle in their hearts...more ferocious than the tiger and more venomous than the snake."[10]

Fisher expresses another polarizing in *God or Caesar?* (1953), his handbook on the art of fiction that defends the goal of writing for posterity and contributing to the good of art and of the human race, versus the ego drive of writing for immediate success. Again, Fisher's philosophical template is overlaid differently on many of his books where it may function as immature/mature, selfish/selfless, primitive/evolved, art/commerce, male/female, sun/moon, flesh/spirit, or matriarchy/patriarchy. The tenacity of this approach and its variations, Flora writes, are rooted in ideas Fisher gleaned early from Carl Jung as well as from his psychologist brother, Vivian.[11]

One might also ascribe these views to a simpler, experiential origin—Fisher's childhood. He certainly grew up in hot proximity to the opposites lived out in his parents' marriage. His mother, Temperance Thornton Fisher, hated her primitive cabin life in the Snake River Canyon at Burns Creek, hated keeping house on dirt floors where the doors were hung on shoe-sole hinges. She drove her two sons to achieve, to seek mind-over-body success in a larger world outside that Idaho wilderness. His father, Joseph Fisher—a silent, almost brutal man—struggled so harshly against a harsher natural world that he had no tenderness or humor for his family. For all her ambition and high standards, Mrs. Fisher, a devout Mormon, made sex seem to her sons wicked, animalistic; and their father's personality may have lent credence to her view. Finding matriarchy an older and stronger pattern than later and atypical patriarchy, Briffault noted that all carnivorous animals and rodents eat their own, and sexual attraction itself he called "a form of voracity."[12]

Some form of superior womanhood, and especially maternal womanhood, distinguishes many of Fisher's fictional female characters from their male counterparts. Examples might include: Opal Hunter, June Weeg, and Emma (Mrs. Joseph) Smith among the Mormons; Eilley Bowers's social climbing in the Comstock Lode; and what Wayne Chatterton calls the "primal Mother mystique" of Kate Bowden in *Mountain Man* (1965).[13] One of these women, Prudence Branton Hunter, certainly resembles Temperance Fisher; Prudence praises her son Vridar as precocious much as Mrs. Fisher praised Vardis, but both mothers also misled their sons about sex and by portraying all women as always more noble and virtuous than men.

For Vardis Fisher, Briffault's anthropology may have merely rationalized a pattern already emotionally in place.

Beyond setting forth a thesis about the stalwart Donner Party women, Fisher's subtitle for *The Mothers: An American Saga of Courage*, by specifying "American" also emphasizes the patriotic spirit of the World War II 1940s during which the novel first appeared. This 1942–44 context may have contributed to Fisher's ideas; it certainly contributed to what Tim Woodward calls the novel's "relative popularity."[14]

During 1942, the German army reached Stalingrad, and the news was full of the heroic resistance of Russian women. Among popular films, *Mrs. Miniver* won three academy awards, with Greer Garson exemplifying the brave survival of women during the bombing of Britain; *Madame Curie* memorialized an earlier gifted woman. Pearl Buck's novels made heroines of Chinese matriarchs, and the leadership of a woman was paramount even in the lighter story, *Anna and the King of Siam*. American women for the first time were serving in the military and also working long shifts in wartime factories, while their radios blared "Rosie the Riveter" and "Pistol-Packin' Mama," and sturdy Kate Smith belted out "God Bless America." Even art exhibitions benefited war causes, such as the Dutch Masters show for the Queen Wilhelmina Fund. Eleanor Roosevelt was a vivid, if controversial, First Lady at a time when gallant self-denial by those female heads of households left behind on the home front was being preached everywhere.

If valiant women were often prominent in both the news and propaganda, so was America's national anger against the Axis forces. Although Fisher had Germanic origins on his father's side, *The Mothers* characterizes Rinehart and Spitzer as sly Germans, depicts the Wolfingers as rich and haughty, and is quick to make Keseburg, a German Lutheran, the primary evil villain in the Donner wagon train. Although he omits details of Jim Reed's rescue team struggling back across the Sierra Nevada, Fisher does praise and admire Reed, who was Polish. Keseburg's hands with their long talons "crawl like beasts" (284). He has "enough strength to beat his wife but never enough to leave the cabin and gather wood" (136). Philippine Keseburg is "not a bold fighting mother like the other five" (203), but exhibits a "fatal softness in her character" (203) and lacks "the stuff of which American pioneer women have been made" (204). And Rinehart, the short-legged German, has the "long predatory face of a night prowler" (121). The descriptions of both men as sly and crafty, chilling in appearance, with eyes like those of a monkey, almost suggest the comic-book simplicities of the day. Like cartoon enemies, the Germans betray trust: "It was as if he offered a hand in greeting and you grasped it and closed on a knife" (41). Noting this slant, some readers have also observed that Fisher—like his source George Stewart—almost dismisses the lives of Indians and Mexicans as less important than those of other ethnic types in the Donner Party. Both writers are also hard on the Irish Catholics in the group, Fisher accepting Stewart's view that Patrick Breen was a lazy, prayerful lout and Peggy Breen an Irish harridan.

Although Stewart was probably Fisher's main source for facts and chronology, the shape (three parts, thirty-seven chapters) and all invented scenes and dialogue in *The Mothers* were his own. After an opening alphabetical list of twenty-eight travelers in his cast of characters and after omitting the early journey and the fateful decision to follow the Hastings cut-off, part 1 of *The Mothers* opens where most novelists would choose, *in medias res*—by skipping the departure of the overly optimistic Donner Party from their very different Midwestern homes (though Fisher will later emphasize their naiveté), by only summarizing in retrospect their increasing difficulties in the journey across the plains, but zeroing in on page 6 as the emigrants face the imminent and central crisis of Fisher's story: the ominous sight of early snow in September, already showing ahead of them on the mountain peaks.

During the previous spring, five hundred wagons had moved in relative safety toward Oregon and California and, two years before, the first wagon party had crossed the Sierras to Sutter's Fort with no loss of life. But this Donner Party (eight to ten babies, thirty or more children under ten, men who were greenhorns or disabled or lacked strong leadership) contains within its wagon train special problems and rivalries. By chapter 2, John Snyder dies in a fight and his killer, Jim Reed, banished, moves out alone toward California. As the others round the bend of the Humboldt River, near where Winnemucca is today, conflicts between Reed's critics and supporters mount.

By chapter 4, mother-love, as expressed through Peggy Breen and Mrs. Graves, is showing its ruthless side in defense of the young, while Indians keep killing or driving off livestock. Snow falls October 28. At Truckee Lake "it was the mothers...who were finally resolved to fight against death" (89). Fisher counts up the pioneers, Indians, mules, cows, and dogs like a death toll in advance, all of them stranded together now in camp as the party digs in, still hoping a break in the weather will let them press through the pass to California.

By chapter 10, they are eating the only animal they have been successful in hunting—one grizzly—their starved oxen are already dead and lost under the deepening snow, and a small group (known both here and historically as the "Forlorn Hope") plans to make snowshoes out of the wagon bows and cross the mountains for help. Although the unmarried males with no offspring have already sunk into deep despair, parents—especially the mothers—do not falter. Instead, they "tend their children" (117).

Of the fifteen who make up this "Forlorn Hope," more women than men set forth through huge and smothering drifts to cross the mountains for help, while back at the lake camp Peggy Breen guards her meager food supply ("Her eyes were full of her children" [191]). Early in the trip, Staunton goes snow-blind and dies. Bill Eddy discovers that his wife, Eleanor, has secretly packed him a small portion of bear meat along with an encouraging note. He wonders "how the notion arose that women were physically weak" (161).

By Christmas Eve, the "Forlorn Hope" has been reduced to thirteen. Fisher emphasizes that the dying Frank Graves urges the others to eat his body, but survivors resist until chapter 16, after five of the men have died but "the women are all alive" (172). Then they finally cook and eat Pat

Dolan, the exhausted men pressed to this exigency by the "five clear-headed and determined women here" (176) who, once the taboo has been broken, are "resolved to be guided only by intelligence and duty" (176). No one in this group will eat a family member (though in reality the Donner girls back in camp appear to have eaten their uncle). They dry and pack the human meat with "the desperation of mothers" (177).

Here, and also when cannibalism occurs back at the lake camp or among the separate Donner family camped a few miles away at Alder Creek, Fisher plays down the usual sensationalism about the Donner Party, emphasizing instead the willpower and survival instincts of the women who are driven to decide cannibalism is necessary.

By the time they stagger into the Sacramento Valley, members of the "Forlorn Hope" have eaten the thongs of their shoes, the first leaves and grass that emerge above the snow, one deer, and two Indians. After thirty-three days of flailing through deep drifts and slogging through heavy snowstorms, seven of the original fifteen have barely survived.

In part 3, Fisher shifts his narrative back to the six families left behind at the lake camp where "eight mothers had forty children to care for" (206) with "all their energy, cunning, and devotion" (206). Here the men are also dying off, but the mothers have survival work to do.

On Christmas Eve, the prospect of cannibalism is first introduced to the traveling "Forlorn Hope" by Frank Graves. On the same Christmas Eve back at the lake camp, Margaret Reed exhibits almost magical power when she performs a miracle not unlike that of Jesus feeding the five thousand. She so transforms a few beans and fragments of dried apple that her children feel they have savored a holiday feast.

Chapter 24 also has World War II resonance. After Dutch Charlie dies, Spitzer (German and a confessed murderer) and Keseburg (German and a wife beater) steal his clothes and money. In the meantime, the women feed the pet dog to their children and one of them leads another futile rescue foray into the snows but is forced back with frozen feet.

In camp now, the mothers are boiling animal hides to eat the resulting glue-soup. Peggy Breen keeps children alive by parceling out scant but extra nourishment to the weakest. Everyone stays in bed all the time to conserve warmth and strength. Patrick, father of the Breen family, ill with kidney stones, contributes little more than prayers and homilies—not a contribution ex-Mormon and atheist Fisher would be inclined to value. February brings more snow, more dying babies.

In chapter 31, still glorifying mothers, Fisher invents one of his least believable episodes by having Tamsen Donner, who is still nursing her husband during his slow death from gangrene, carry her brushes and oils outdoors daily at Alder Creek to "paint the magnificent winter" (289). Students of Donner Party history who recall their earlier horrible trek across the Salt Desert, how everyone lightened every wagon of superfluous personal property while thirst-crazed oxen dropped in the traces and died, will not find it credible that Tamsen could have retained her art supplies, much less that she could boil a mouse for George's breakfast, then go out to commune with the very Nature that was destroying all her hopes of starting a girls' school in California.

Once the first rescue party arrives February 16, a few relatively able-bodied survivors leave with it toward California and encounter Jim Reed's long overdue second party coming in. The wife Reed had left behind five months before, now unrecognizable and emaciated, feels her "invincible spirit" (301) give way, and she faints in the snow. This second party reaches the lake camp March 1, where "the foul and selfish Keseburg" (307) has instigated cannibalism. Two of these supposed rescuers (male) cheat Tamsen Donner of the gold she pays them to carry out her daughters; then they leave both girls behind in the second camp. These scenes, too, are largely Fisher's invention.

In late March 1846, and on Fisher's last page, before the third rescue party can reach the camp with food, George Donner has finally died and Keseburg finds Tamsen Donner dead on the floor of his hut. Many newspaper and interview reports during the late nineteenth century accused the real Keseburg of murdering and devouring her; some claimed the rescuers found him a demented fiend stirring pots of human blood on the boil. Richard Rhodes's 1973 novel *The Ungodly* goes so far as to have Keseburg kill her with an ax, rape what's left, and then eat both Tamsen and her husband, George. But Fisher, while omitting Captain William O. Fallon's fourth and last relief party, gives Keseburg the benefit of the doubt, instead driving home his point: "Eight mothers had been left in the two camps. In devotion to their children, four of them had given their lives" (334).

Though Fisher has omitted from his novel the first eighty and the last forty-five pages of George Stewart's *Ordeal by Hunger,* he obviously accepted that account as largely accurate. In 1992, a revisionist book, *Winter of Entrapment: A New Look at the Donner Party* by Joseph A. King, took serious issue with Stewart's version, which King considers a pseudohistory, "heavily researched indeed, but a fictional account nevertheless."[15] King argues against Keseburg as arch villain, noting that Eliza, the surviving daughter of George and Tamsen Donner, as an adult interviewed Keseburg herself and believed he had been unfairly vilified. McGlashan's history also attempted a more balanced view.

King also notes Stewart's bias against certain racial groups, less strong in Fisher but not entirely absent. Stewart calls John Baptiste Trudeau a "little mongrel," and "a little Mexican with bad qualities"[16]—which King disputes with evidence of his good character. Stewart's version portrayed the Indians as cowardly. He also praises William Eddy, also one of Fisher's rare male heroes; King makes the case that Eddy was a self-important liar who inflated his heroism in bragging interviews. King's book includes a full bibliography, photographs, maps, reproductions of diaries from Donner Party emigrants, a follow-up on the later lives of survivors who made it to California, and survivor testimony, some of it contradictory. One chapter, "Whom to Believe?," deals with these uncertainties.

King's book is helpful to those of us far from the Bancroft Library in Berkeley, the Huntington Library in San Marino, Sutter's Fort Historical Museum, and the Gleeson Library at the University of San Francisco, where most of the relevant documents are archived.

Readers might think that feminist scholars would by now be poring over these documents to match the real Donner Party heroines with Fisher's Tamsen, who for twelve days and nights sleeps by her husband until certain he is dead and then, having "done her duty," buries him and crawls away through the snow, "a picture of her children waiting at the far end" (333).

Despite Fisher's emphasis on the "unquenchable spirit" of women (161), any requirement to be a "superwoman" has gone out of fashion in feminism. His own portrait in *Tale of Valor* (1958) of Sacajawea, a figure first taken up by the woman's suffrage movement and then in later feminist works, is of a promiscuous Shoshoni girl who happened to be in the right time and place to guide and interpret for Lewis and Clark—however bravely.[17] His Western women in general are usually brave but some are too mythic to be believed or easily to become role models.

In his personal life, too, Fisher may seem an unlikely women's advocate. His marriage in 1917 to a childhood sweetheart, Leona McMurtrey, ended with her committing suicide in 1924 by drinking a Lysol-type disinfectant. He always blamed himself for her depression and death, and many female readers of his biography will be inclined to agree. His second marriage in 1928, to Margaret Trusler, a fellow student at the University of Chicago, ended in divorce in 1939 after he had brought her back to the very ranch in Idaho from which he had fled. Here, like Robinson Jeffers, he began constructing buildings and improvements to the home place with his own hands, including a new dwelling for his parents. In 1940 he married Opal Laurel Holmes and they moved to twenty-three acres of mountainside near Hagerman, Idaho, in Thousand Springs Valley. There he attacked the wilderness with some of his father's feverish grim drudgery, built his own house, piped his own irrigation system from the dam he also built, erected buildings and fences, and gave Opal the opportunity of surviving an uncomfortable rural life not all that much easier than the one Fisher's mother had despised. After his return to the ranch, for the rest of his life, Fisher alternated between writing in the mornings and hard physical labor in the afternoons; he was working on books thirty-seven and thirty-eight when he died.[18]

Searching for writer-disciples Fisher might have influenced, and noting that he briefly taught freshman English to Wallace Stegner at the University of Utah, readers may scan Stegner's essays, seeking a tribute to Fisher, but will find only a brief mention: "I was almost glad that Fisher left after my first year, for he had a caustic tongue and a great contempt for time-wasters."[19] In contrast, Stegner devotes an entire chapter to Donner historian George R. Stewart, whom he liked and admired, and says of *Ordeal by Hunger* that Stewart chose to find "no scapegoat, though he finds several heroes."[20]

Romance and teaching aside, what were Fisher's connections to fellow writers? He also taught briefly at the Washington Square College of New York University, along with Henry T. Volkening (later to found with Diarmuid Russell a leading literary agency in New York City) and Thomas Wolfe—but these literary figures seem more his acquaintances than friends. Wolfe did recognize Fisher's talent and ambition, did complain to him when *Look Homeward, Angel* angered his Asheville friends, and later praised Fisher's *In Tragic Life* as containing some of the most "powerful and magnificent writing" in recent American literature.[21] Wolfe also said of Fisher that the terrain around Boise "explains a lot about him"; Fisher felt Wolfe never understood the riddle of himself and kept writing the same story.[22] Fisher had a strong antipathy for the other giant at Scribner's and became increasingly annoyed that Ernest Hemingway's brief stays in Ketchum made him better known as an Idaho novelist, and he dismissed William Saroyan and numerous other writers as Hollywood sellouts.[23]

In his later years Fisher worked vigorously on his *Testament of Man*—two volumes of which are about life in a matriarchal society—wrote part of a volume about the western United States, circulated regular newspaper columns across the state criticizing President Roosevelt, the New Deal, the American presence in Vietnam, and almost everything else; he was known by some as a resident curmudgeon. At seventy-three, having mixed alcohol with valium (whether by accident or suicide is unclear), he collapsed in a home that had no telephone, sending his wife rushing away for help, and died in a hospital in Jerome, Idaho.

No, Fisher's is not an easy biography for women to warm up to, and neither is the majority of his published work.

Although for his last twenty years he expected his twelve-volume *Testament* to be his crowning achievement, the Western historical novels he felt he had outgrown have earned a far greater readership. His stubborn devotion to his final massive project may be one reason Chatterton closes his Fisher monograph by saying, "Currying no favor, still on his own terms, he has triumphed."[24]

But Fisher's own terms may have been mistaken; the Western historical novels seem far more likely to last.

In the year before his death, Fisher said his earnings averaged about $2000 for each book he had published, but *The Mothers* was still in print and was still selling in the 1980s.[25] The novel remains what is usually called a "good read," skillfully written, in which Fisher makes accessible a story that has long haunted Western history and continues to generate treatments on stage and television, and in fiction, historical writing, and poetry. Appearing when it did, during America' s "good" war against the Nazis, *The Mothers* may even have met a timely social need.

George R. Stewart certainly believed this particular history turns easily into legend for that very reason, ending his own account of the Donner Party this way: "[T]heir story may even be said to meet the demands of some that literature should serve an extraneous social purpose. For though despair is often close at hand, it never triumphs, and through all the story runs a sustaining bond, the primal force which humanity shares with all earthly creatures, the sheer will to live."[26]

Notes

1. Joseph A. King, *Winter of Entrapment: A New Look at the Donner Party* (Toronto: Meany, 1992), 44–45. (Author's note: The number in the Donner Party fluctuates, depending on who counts, and at what point in the trek. In his listing, Vardis Fisher puts the number at eighty-seven. Joseph King lists by name those actually marooned in the snow; his count has been used here.)
2. Tim Woodward, *Tiger on the Road:The Life of Vardis Fisher* (Caldwell, ID: Caxton Printers, 1989), 201.
3. Joseph M. Flora, *Vardis Fisher* (New York: Twayne Publishers, 1965), 98.
4. George Frederick Day, "The Uses of History in the Novels of Vardis Fisher" (Ph.D. diss., University of Colorado, 1968).
5. Robert Briffault, *The Mothers: The Matriarchal Theory of Social Origins*, abr. ed. (New York: MacMillan, 1931), 45, 21.
6. William DuBois, "Death in the Woods," review of *The Mothers*, by Vardis Fisher, *New York Times Book Review*, October 3, 1943, 6.
7. Vardis Fisher, *The Mothers: An American Saga of Courage* (New York: Vanguard, 1943), 204. (Author's note: All other references to this novel are cited parenthetically in the text.)

8. Flora, *Vardis Fisher,* 65.
9. Vardis Fisher, *In Tragic Life* (Caldwell, ID: Caxton Printers; Garden City, NY: Doubleday, 1932), 394.
10. Vardis Fisher, *We Are Betrayed* (Caldwell, ID: Caxton Printers; Garden City, NY: Doubleday, 1935), 320.
11. Flora, *Vardis Fisher,* 34–35.
12. Briffault, *The Mothers,* 47.
13. Wayne Chatterton, *Vardis Fisher: The Frontier and Regional Works* (Boise: Boise State College, 1972), 38.
14. Woodward, *Tiger on the Road,* 157.
15. King, 158.
16. Ibid., 133.
17. Chatterton, *Vardis Fisher,* 42.
18. Ibid., 5.
19. Wallace Stegner, *Where the Bluebird Sings to the Lemonade Springs,* rev. ed. (New York: Random House, 1992), 17.
20. Ibid., 165.
21. David Herbert Donald, *Look Homeward: A Life of Thomas Wolfe* (Boston: Little, Brown, 1987), 117.
22. Flora, *Vardis Fisher,* 27.
23. Woodward, *Tiger on the Road,* 197.
24. Chatterton, *Vardis Fisher,* 46.
25. Woodward, *Tiger on the Road,* 157.
26. George R. Stewart, *Ordeal by Hunger: The Story of the Donner Party* (New York: Henry Holt and Co., 1936; rev. ed., Lincoln: University of Nebraska Press, 1986), 298.

Bibliography

Briffault, Robert. *The Mothers: The Matriarchal Theory of Social Origins.* Abr. ed. New York: MacMillan, 1931.

Chatterton, Wayne. *Vardis Fisher: The Frontier and Regional Works.* Boise: Boise State College, 1972.

Day, George Frederick. "The Uses of History in the Novels of Vardis Fisher." Ph.D. diss., University of Colorado, 1968.

Donald, David Herbert. *Look Homeward: A Life of Thomas Wolfe.* Boston: Little, Brown, 1987.

DuBois, William. "Death in the Woods." Review of *The Mothers,* by Vardis Fisher. *New York Times Book Review,* October 3, 1943, 6.

Fisher, Vardis. *In Tragic Life.* Caldwell, ID: Caxton Printers; Garden City, NY: Doubleday, 1932.

———. *The Mothers: An American Saga of Courage.* New York: Vanguard, 1943.

———. *We Are Betrayed.* Caldwell, ID: Caxton Printers; Garden City, NY: Doubleday, 1935.

Flora, Joseph M. *Vardis Fisher.* New York: Twayne Publishers, 1965.

Houghton, Eliza Poor Donner. *The Expedition of the Donner Party and Its Tragic Fate.* Chicago: McClurg, 1911.

King, Joseph A. *Winter of Entrapment: A New Look at the Donner Party.* Toronto: Meany, 1992.

McGlashan, C.F. *History of the Donner Party: A Tragedy of the Sierra.* Rev. ed., ed. George Henry Hinkle and Bliss McGlashan Hinkle. Stanford: Stanford University Press, 1947.

Stegner, Wallace. *Where the Bluebird Sings to the Lemonade Springs.* Rev. ed. New York: Random House, 1992.

Stewart, George R. *Ordeal by Hunger: The Story of the Donner Party.* New York: Henry Holt and Co., 1936. Rev. ed. Lincoln: University of Nebraska Press, 1986.

Woodward, Tim. *Tiger on the Road: The Life of Vardis Fisher.* Caldwell, ID: Caxton Printers, 1989.

6 Vardis Fisher and the Mormons

Stephen L. Tanner

Children of God: An American Epic, published in 1939, was the most successful of Vardis Fisher's novels in terms of favorable recognition and commercial success. It won the Harper Prize for Fiction and outsold all of his previous novels put together. Unlike most of his novels, which went out of print after selling a few thousand copies, *Children of God* persisted in print through more than twenty editions over more than fifty years.

As a fictional rendering of the founding of the Church of Jesus Christ of Latter-day Saints (the Mormons) and the first seventy years of its history, the novel provoked controversy that remains unresolved after sixty years. A battery of questions invites consideration. How accurate is the book as history? How successful is it as imaginative literature? How objective was Fisher in writing about a religion from which he had apostatized? To what extent was he ever really a Mormon or influenced by his Mormon background? What, after all, was his attitude toward religion in general? As a lifetime Mormon and a professor of American literature for thirty years with a special interest in Western American writers, I wish to examine these questions.

I was reared in the same region as Fisher, like him a descendent of maternal and paternal Mormon pioneer ancestors. Like Fisher I attended the University of Utah and later earned a doctoral degree in English at a Midwestern university, one just 150 miles from the University of Chicago, where Fisher studied. These similarities in culture, geography, and academic field naturally sparked my interest in this extraordinary Idaho author.

The nature of Vardis Fisher's relationship with the Mormons remains a matter of considerable disagreement. The basic facts are that his parents were members of the Mormon Church, but the family lived in an isolated area without opportunity for church affiliation. As teenagers, Vardis and his brother lived on their own in a small, predominantly Mormon town in order to go to school. He was baptized at age twenty and apostatized very soon afterward. His first wife was a member of the Church, and they were married by a Mormon bishop in 1917. She committed suicide in 1924, a year before Fisher received his doctoral degree and began teaching at the University of Utah. At this university in Salt Lake City, his open hostility toward the Church created tensions within the university and the community, and his departure after three years to take a position at New York University was a relief for everyone concerned. He remained a vocal critic of the Mormon Church throughout his life.

Joseph M. Flora provides, from a non-Mormon perspective, an informed consideration of Fisher's ties with Mormonism and concludes that, despite his overt rejection and criticism of the Church, "Fisher's Mormonism ran deep. It was not merely something that Fisher revolted against; it was also something that helped form his life style and code."[1] A similar conclusion, from a Mormon perspective, is reached by Leonard J. Arrington, long-time official historian of the Church. His essay, "The Mormon Heritage of Vardis Fisher," written in collaboration with Jon Haupt, argues that Fisher was significantly influenced by his Mormon background. Arrington and Haupt emphasize that "there was no actual parting of the ways between Vardis Fisher and the church he joined at the very outset of his career of writing. He was never excommunicated; the Church did not at any time officially or publicly criticize or repudiate *Children of God.*" Then they add in wry understatement: "[A]lthough it could also not be said that the Church made a cult of Fisher." They acknowledge that Fisher "was only on the fringes of Latter-day Saint culture" and that his comments on the Church remained "tart and crusty" to the end. In answer to their query in 1967 regarding his connections with Mormonism, Fisher ironically replied, "I am, as the simple minds in the hierarchy in Salt Lake could tell you, a member in good standing, but shamefully behind the past fifty years in all assessments." "Nevertheless," Arrington and Haupt insist, "it is clear that as he grew older he came to a greater harmony with his background. He was able to look at Mormon values and appreciate them." Their explicit purpose is to establish that "(1) Fisher was not an apostate; he never renounced his religion nor did Mormonism renounce him. (2) Fisher's outlook on life and history was religious, definitely Judeo-Christian."[2] Similarly, in *The Mormon Experience,* a history of Mormonism, Arrington and Davis Bitton devote a short paragraph to Fisher in which they remark that "his Mormon upbringing had a powerful influence not only on *Children of God*...but on his other novels."[3]

On the other hand, Fisher's widow, Opal Laurel Holmes, took angry exception to these statements linking her husband with the Mormons and threatened legal action. In a press release, she quotes the paragraph from *The Mormon Experience* and follows it with this statement in oversized bold letters: "This is a lie." She explains that "although Fisher's parents had been baptized into the Mormon Church as children, they did not practice the faith; and cared so little about Mormonism, that they never bothered to have their own children baptized. Mormon influence was negligible during Fisher's formative years, almost non-existent." She acknowledges that Fisher was voluntarily baptized at the age of twenty because he was looking for direction in his life, but claims that he apostatized within the year without experiencing a religious conversion. She insists that there was no Mormon bias in his thinking, except in a negative way: "Fisher never made any secret of the fact that he had nothing but contempt for the Mormon hierarchy, the Mormon 'religion' (which, in his opinion, was not *religion* at all), and for the Mormon way of life, which he considered stultifying in the extreme." In that same press release she announces that she will publish a book using Fisher's own words to refute the claims that he had sympathetic feelings toward the Mormons. (As far as I know, no such manuscript or book exists.) She also includes an open letter to Spencer W. Kimball, then president of the LDS Church, demanding that he put a stop to the promulgation of claims that Fisher was a Mormon.[4] In addressing the American Atheists Convention in Salt Lake City in 1981, she took the opportunity to debunk furiously the "Mormon heritage" attributed to her husband.[5] For years after her husband's death, she continued to act as his publisher, and at the end of each book she placed a statement denying claims that he was a Mormon. Her position is reflected in Tim Woodward's biography of Fisher: "Fisher was an atheist and a critic of Mormonism to his dying day, and his widow has spent years fighting what she sees as attempts by the Mormon Church to reclaim in death the man who, in life, was one of its most caustic detractors."[6] Levi Peterson reports that Fisher's widow told him "that regularly, once or twice a year during their married life, Fisher instructed her that should he die before she did, she must not allow the Mormons to reclaim him. In no wise, she said, was Vardis Fisher a Mormon."[7] Fisher's hostility toward the Mormon Church, in fact toward religion in general, was particularly apparent during the three years he taught at the University of Utah. Opal Laurel Holmes said that at that time he was "very forthright about the fact that he was not a Mormon and not a Christian." And Wallace Stegner, who was one of his students, said, "Since Vardis was outspoken in his contempt for Mormon theology and belief, and both in class and out made a point of his apostasy, there must surely have been some pressure from conservative Mormon elements to get him out."[8]

Wherein lies the truth? Predictably, both sides are substantially right, depending on what aspects of Mormonism are emphasized. In relation to the Mormons Fisher was both an insider and an outsider. In attempting to reconcile these opposing claims, we must be aware that the term *Mormonism* denotes two quite different concepts.

On the one hand, it describes a social-historical phenomenon, a distinct religious group that also formed together as a society, experienced repeated persecution, migrated to the Salt Lake Valley, and then systematically colonized the Great Basin region. These communities in the West developed their own social customs and traditions, their own culture, shaped by both region and religion. Mormon theology was eminently practical and made practical differences in Mormon communities. Brigham Young taught: "The religion of Jesus Christ is a matter-of-fact religion, and taketh hold of the every-day duties and realities of this life.... I reduce the Gospel to the present time, circumstances and conditions of the people.... My desire is to teach the people what they should do now, and let the Millennium take care of itself.... We are to be taught with regard to our every-day life in a temporal point of view.... Our religion is not merely theory; it is a practical religion, to bring present enjoyment to every heart."[9] Vardis Fisher was an insider in the sense that he grew up in an environment of social values and patterns colored by the practical effects of Mormon beliefs. He had a regional Mormon heritage in the way that a New Englander or Southerner might have a regional heritage—patterns of speech, family relationships, political inclinations, and attitudes toward work, self-reliance, and the natural environment. In this sense, Flora, Arrington, and others are correct in attributing a Mormon heritage to Fisher.

Mormonism, on the other hand, refers to a particular body of theological doctrine independent of region or social milieu; being a Mormon means having faith in that doctrine and participating regularly not only in worship services but in various activities and callings. The LDS Church has no professional clergy; its elaborate organization requires service and responsibility from every member. In this view of Mormonism, Fisher was a complete outsider. Soon after the publication of *Children of God,* Fisher wrote, "I was reared a Mormon and from early childhood heard many stories, variously told, of early Mormon history and legend, and particularly of the persecutions. At about the age of eighteen I left the Church."[10] This statement was probably intended to explain and support his qualifications for writing such a book, but it must not be taken at face value. For one thing, he was not baptized into the Church until he was twenty. For another, he was not reared a Mormon in any significant sense. To be so reared would typically mean that a boy begin regular attendance in junior Sunday school at age four, be baptized at eight, be ordained to the Aaronic Priesthood at twelve, serve in the offices of Deacon, Teacher, and Priest by age twenty, and then be ordained to the Melchizedek Priesthood. This process involves attendance on Sundays and some weekdays, and constant instruction in auxiliary organizations in addition to sermons from the pulpit. Fisher, for several reasons, including his parents' marginal connection with the Church and the isolation of the family homestead, experienced very little of this kind of rearing.

Joseph Flora compares Fisher to James Joyce in that both left their religions, but not completely: "Fisher is to Mormonism as Joyce is to Catholicism."[11] This analogy is appealing, but will not bear scrutiny. Fisher knew a regional Mormon society, but he knew little about Mormon faith and doctrine from an informed and believing perspective. From an early age he was temperamentally averse to religious belief. He had a seemingly innate secular disposition that inhibited any deep interest in or sympathetic appreciation of theology. He wrote: "Mormon theology is as naive as its first prophet."[12] This is a nice turn of phrase, but devoid of substance, as an enormous body of history, biography, and commentary attests. Fisher's own knowledge of theology was restricted by his antitheological bias. In *Children of God,* for example, he describes the first converts to Mormonism as having visions of the Virgin Mary, but Joseph Smith and his first converts were New England Protestants to whom Mariolatry was anathema. Fisher tended to lump Protestant, Catholic, and Mormon theology together in a hellfire-and-damnation caricature. Mormon leaders in *Children of God,* for instance, frequently threaten damnation in hell for those who resist their wishes, but, as a matter of fact, Mormon theology has no usual notion of hell. According to Mormon doctrine, life on earth is followed by three degrees of glory: the telestial, terrestrial, and celestial. Even the wicked are consigned to a glory surpassing life on earth. Similarly, Vridar, Fisher's autobiographical character in *In Tragic Life* (1932), goes to a Mormon Sunday school to find answers to his problems and there hears only a "thundering denunciation of joy in life."[13] But in reality, one of the passages from the Book of Mormon best known to LDS Sunday school children is "Adam fell that men might be; and men are, that they might have joy" (2 Nephi 2:25). And, as quoted above, the burden of Brigham Young's teaching was that Mormonism is a practical religion intended "to bring present enjoyment to every heart." Fisher researched the Mormon religion extensively and even describes in *Children of God* the temple ceremony, which members consider too sacred to be made public, even too sacred to discuss among themselves outside the temple. Yet he says through his characters that one of the purposes of going to the temple is to receive the Holy Ghost. This misconception would be surprising to anyone with the least familiarity with Mormon doctrine. The Church's thirteen Articles of Faith, widely distributed on small cards from the early days of the Church, clearly state that in Mormon doctrine and practice the gift of the Holy Ghost is bestowed by the laying on of hands at the time of baptism. This ordinance, which includes the words "receive the Holy Ghost," is not part of the temple ceremony.

Such examples could be multiplied. The point is that although Fisher possessed a thorough and comprehensive knowledge of Mormonism, his secular disposition led him to a hostility toward religious faith that hampered any genuine interest in the intricacies of doctrine and theology and kept him essentially an outsider. He was interested in religion as a psychological phenomenon, an aberration of human imagination in the direction of unreason. The trajectory of his career was to begin, in autobiographical novels, an unflinching scrutiny of his own life that exposed religion as a chief source of frustration and unhappiness, and then to extend that scrutiny, in novels treating the breadth of human history, to expose human self-delusion in general. He wrote about Mormons early in his career because he had grown up among them; they were a familiar subject. After studying and writing about the psychology underlying the emergence and early development of the Latter-day Saints, he went back to examine the beginnings of man and the naturalistic origins of religion in general. He was well acquainted with the Bible. It was one of the few books in that isolated Fisher home, and, according to Woodward (drawing on information from the author's sister), Fisher had read it "several times by age eleven" and found the reading decidedly unedifying: "Though it fascinated him, it seemed to him to be a book neither of hope nor inspiration, but of baffling parables and barbarous cruelty." The Old Testament, read in that lonely wilderness environment, gave him nightmares, and "before he ever saw the inside of a classroom, he had rejected forever the god of the Old Testament, whom he saw as a symbol of vengeance and cruelty." Woodward bolsters his point by quoting a passage from Fisher's essay "My Bible Heritage" in which Fisher describes the negative psychological effects of his childhood reading of the Bible. Nevertheless, throughout his career, Fisher continued to study and analyze the Bible, trying to come to terms with it. "Fisher knew the Bible as well as most priests or ministers," says Woodward, "but he remained an atheist."[14]

A clue to Fisher's relationship with Mormonism is suggested in his essay "The Novelist and His Background": "As I see it, the chief task of the novelist is sufficiently to liberate himself from his background to be able to see it in some kind of perspective." Thomas Wolfe, he points out, was unable to do this. In varying degrees, he says, we all are unable to do this. "We have in some manner to break free, without on the one hand losing touch with the stuff that made us, without on the other mistaking our self-protective illusions for truth. And the threat of a deeper and deeper schizophrenia broods over the struggle."[15] He speaks elsewhere of his preparations for writing *Children of God:* "I felt that first of all I should thoroughly disabuse my mind and disgorge any Mormon cant and dogma that possibly, and quite probably, remained in it. To do that, it seemed to me best to read all the rabidly anti-Mormon books I could find; and I read a great many of heaven knows how many have been published."[16] These statements reflect the two senses of Mormonism mentioned above. His family and regional connections with Mormonism—the external culture of Idaho Mormon communities—constituted what he speaks of here as "the stuff that made us." On the other hand, Mormon doctrine and belief constituted what he refers to here as "self-protective illusions" and "cant and dogma." Again, Fisher both was and was not a Mormon.

Flora and Arrington and Haupt insist that Fisher's outlook on life and history was religious. How can such assertions be justified when Fisher himself, his widow, and others who knew him well explicitly state that he was an atheist? The answer, as in the case of Fisher's Mormon connection, is a matter of specifying precisely what is meant by "religious." Fisher was a religious writer in the sense that he was preoccupied throughout his career with the moral nature of human beings and the phenomenon of religion. And there is no doubt that he subscribed to Judeo-Christian values and admired the moral earnestness of peoples like the Hebrews and the Mormons. In writing of the influence of the Bible in his life, he said that we must "accept the Bible humbly as the noblest effort of our ancient forebears to come to terms with the problem of evil and to overthrow it" and that "many of its pages" still provide truths that, "if not eternal, are still as eternal as any that man has uttered."[17] But, as Flora points out, Fisher neither grasped "the dynamism of Christianity" nor appreciated its "poetic mysticism and beauty."[18] It is probably misleading to call Fisher a religious writer; although he wrote much about religion, he wrote of it always from the outside, never conceding to it a supernatural reality. Religion interested him because he was fascinated, perhaps to the degree of obsession, with the human capacity for illusion and self-deception, and in his view religion provided the most numerous and interesting examples.

Richard M. Andrews praises Fisher as an "Atheist intellectual" who "never failed to talk and write about Atheism. He never failed to say he was an Atheist and was proud of his Atheism." Andrews is an atheist activist who was named Atheist of the Year in 1993 by the American Atheists organization and who was a personal friend of Fisher's widow, another member of that organization. In his estimation, Fisher's *Testament of Man* series was "a bold attempt by a lone Atheist to popularize his Atheism," and although Fisher was not completely successful in this attempt, his books "could still be used as a tool for the advancement of atheist philosophy."[19]

It seems as misguided to claim Fisher as an atheist crusader as to claim him as a Mormon, but certainly he did not keep his disbelief in God to himself. His inability to do so created problems in his first two marriages. In describing the deterioration of Fisher's second marriage, Woodward points out that "the primary sources of tension were philosophical differences. Vardis, the ex-Mormon and atheist, had a dim view of virtually all religions. Margaret, on the other hand, was determined to remain a Christian. There appeared to be no way their views could be reconciled, and Vardis seldom was content to let things lie. By most accounts, he was forever probing, criticizing, and provoking arguments." On the other hand, Opal, the third wife, was drawn to him specifically because of a shared point of view concerning religion. "I was attracted most by his intelligence, by his way of looking at things," she said. "That was one of our strong points. Vardis, of course, was an atheist long before I met him. When we were dating, he asked me what religion I had been brought up in." She told him she had been brought up a Gnostic (probably she meant *agnostic*), a fact that did not threaten Fisher's atheism. "That was a very significant factor in our relationship. In fact, that may have been the big thing that made it possible for us to stay together as long as we did."[20]

Fisher's attitude toward God and religious faith calls to mind the attitudes of other expansive American novelists, notably Herman Melville and Theodore Dreiser, novelists impelled by a volatile mixture of doubt and curiosity to wrestle on a grand scale with the complexities of human nature and destiny. As Nathaniel Hawthorne said of Melville, such men are unable to believe, but are restlessly dissatisfied in unbelief. They are great ironists unable to smother completely within themselves volcanic metaphysical yearnings. Mick McAllister may be near the truth when he says that Fisher's voice as a novelist "is an essentially tragic voice, in that his rationalist philosophy aligned him with the reductionism of the sociobiologist who is convinced that behavior can be explained by the accumulation of detail, but his emotional upbringing promoted a nearly pathological mysticism."[21]

The foregoing considerations can orient our exploration of how objective and accurate Fisher was in narrating Mormon history. His portrayal of the rise of Mormonism has been praised and denounced by Mormons and non-Mormons alike. For some it has aroused a sympathetic interest in the Mormon religion that in a few cases led to conversion. For others it has confirmed their worst suspicions about the motives and behavior of Joseph Smith and his "polygamous cult." The majority of readers have been swept along by the sheer variety and multiplicity of incidents and personalities that constitute the Mormon story, without troubling themselves about theology. As Clifton Fadiman puts it in his review of the novel, "What Brigham Young believed may have been twaddle. What Brigham Young did was titanic."[22] As Bernard DeVoto points out, the story of the Mormons is one of the great stories of American history:

> It has everything: mobbing and martyrdom, lust and murder and the vision of eternal life, tenderness and brutality and the deepest faith, frenzy and despair and prophecy, the drive Westward that is the basic experience of the American race, humble folk, adventurers, criminals, traitors, villains, great men, men drunk on cruelty, men drunk on Godhead, great bravery, great suffering, great betrayal, insanity, starvation, massacre—all perfumed with heaven and highlighted by the fires of hell.[23]

This statement bears the imprint of DeVoto's characteristic rhetorical boldness and his own distinct conception of Mormonism, but his point is sound. Fisher had a lot going for him in his subject alone. In fact, the question arises as to whether the Mormon story as embodied in *Children of God* succeeds because or in spite of Fisher. As one reviewer observed, "You can't spoil the Mormon story."[24]

How objective and accurate was Fisher in his portrayal of the Mormons in *Children of God*? This question cannot be answered to everyone's satisfaction. There are no objective measures of objectivity in such cases. But several points should be kept in mind in seeking an answer. First of all, the claims regarding Fisher's impartiality found in reviews and critical discussions of the book are, on the whole, unauthoritative. Most of the reviewers' knowledge of Mormon history and belief is confined to what the book itself provides. One, for example, who makes a special point of praising Fisher's objectivity, states as evidence that Fisher used Mormon documents "and even portions of the Book of Mormon describing Joseph's vision." But simply opening the cover of the Book of Mormon and glancing at the table of contents will reveal that it does not include Joseph's vision. Others rely on notoriously biased and unreliable sources. Fred T. Marsh, for example, who presents himself as an authority on

Mormonism and pronounces Fisher's book the gospel truth as near as one can get at it, bases his judgment on sources now at the margins of Mormon scholarship.[25] Of course, the remarkable abundance of solid scholarship by Mormon and non-Mormon historians was not available until more recently. At the present time, Mormon history is a much studied area of American history, with an active and prolific professional association devoted to it. Neither Fisher nor his reviewers had the benefit of such information. To a large extent, the strides made in developing a more accurate and balanced history of Mormonism since 1939 make considerations of the accuracy and objectivity of Fisher's history beside the point. There are simply much better histories available now. Similarly, extensive study of the literary aspects of the Book of Mormon in recent years makes obsolescent Fisher's characterization of it as "wordy and rather illiterate," "ungrammatical, poorly written, often redundant and sometimes pompously rhetorical."[26]

Another consideration regarding the question of objectivity is Fisher's own conception of and capacity for impartiality. He said that in writing *Children of God* he "was resolved above all to be impartial, to see the whole matter in reasonably clear perspective, and to avoid all editorializing and all moral implications." He started out by reading "rabidly anti-Mormon" books written by "very virulent anti-Mormons" and then balanced this reading by "the most pious and unreflecting books by Mormons." He kept these extreme positions ready at hand as he wrote in order to walk "the middle path." He measured his success by the fact that he received abusive letters from both Mormons and non-Mormons.[27] There may be something to be said for this method, but on the whole it is naive and misguided. Impartiality cannot be construed simply as a hypothetical point equidistant from two extremes. Impartiality is actually a matter of discounting extremes. The highest degree of objectivity or impartiality is achieved by discerningly identifying the most informed and accurate attempts at impartiality and making cautious use of them, not by indiscriminately imbibing extreme views and expecting thereby to arrive at an ideal middle. And the best indication of success is not that you offend people at both extremes but that you bring moderate views on each side closer together.

But Vardis Fisher was not a moderating or compromising sort of person. As his friend Ellis Foote says of Fisher's responses to other people and ideas, "[A]ction, with him, becomes excess of action; statement becomes overstatement; and truth becomes excess of truth." John R. Milton similarly notes Fisher's "paradoxical condition of rationality and excessiveness." Fisher furiously insisted on rationalism. "The argument for rationalism may well have been valid," concedes Milton, "but as it was carried to its extremes it became emotional—perhaps the final irony."[28] Part of Fisher's achievement as a novelist is his portrayal of extremes, contrasts, and conflicts in human behavior. Therein lies much of the vitality of *Children of God*. But impartiality in that portrayal is of a qualified sort: it never extends beyond the parameters of Fisher's version of rationalism. For instance, Louie W. Attebery says that Fisher "set out neither to prove nor disprove Mormon theology and claims about revelation but to dramatize and narrate Mormon history."[29] This is true, but only in a trivial way. Such proving or disproving was simply outside the realm of consideration for Fisher because revealed religion for him was by definition irrational.

This qualified impartiality or objectivity is characteristic of *Children of God* as a whole. Beginning with the novel's first page, religious people are described as either crazed and witless or cynically hypocritical. Fisher's fiction in general probes human nature relentlessly, stripping away self-delusion. But, unfortunately, Fisher's atheistic rationalism prevented him from appreciating religious needs and motives. He had a keen eye for violence—in word and action—and for the dramatic in suffering. He was a vigilant detector of selfish ambition and human meanness. But he had little appreciation for nondramatic goodness, spiritual conviction, altruistic motives, and genuine humility—in short, for the transcendent in human experience. His is a crippled objectivity because it lacks a religious sense. George Day claims that "what is often assumed to be Fisher's deep cynicism is in fact a salutary insistence on objectivity and evidence."[30] There may be more truth in the exact reverse of this: what is assumed to be a salutary insistence on objectivity and evidence is in fact a deep cynicism. What might appear to one person to be an evenhandedness in Fisher's portrayal of Joseph Smith can seem to another to be a cynical indifference to religious claims of any kind.

A final point regarding objectivity in *Children of God* is a caution that we must not mistake artistic inconsistency for impartiality. Fisher portrays Joseph Smith and Brigham Young in contradictory ways. Of course complex personalities embody contradiction, but that is not what I have in mind. I am thinking of the contradictions and inconsistencies that grow out of Fisher's method of historical fiction. As several critics have pointed out, Fisher was preoccupied with research and facts in telling the Mormon story. The novel's construction is episodic and the focus always changing; there are flurries of action and intermittent thematic exposition. The result is diminished coherence in characterization and imaginative vision. In trying so hard to get at facts and valuing them so highly, he sometimes slighted artistic truth and plausibility in characterization and motivation.

His chief fault, according to John R. Milton, was an excessive reliance on scholarly sources because "the historical novel which stays close to the information of its sources and tries hard to achieve historical accuracy is likely to be less satisfactory as fiction, as art, than the novel which allows freer use of the imagination."[31] History never provides adequate information, and each historical source has its own slant. If the gaps in information are not filled in and the diversity of perspectives is not melded by the imagination, incoherencies and contradictions result. It is these inconsistencies that we must not mistake for objectivity. Edward Weeks, remarking on *Children of God* as editor of the *Atlantic,* points out that readers like himself, who do not know Mormon history well, must ask more of the novelist than imperfectly assimilated historical data: "[W]e question not the accuracy of his source material, but rather the degree of skill with which that source material has been heated and fused into the semblance of life." Lacking that kind of fusion, Fisher's portrayal of Joseph Smith, in Weeks's view, is a muddle: "This Joseph to me seems an obdurate faker, with a stubborn capacity for giving and receiving pain."[32]

These observations lead to a final question: How successful is *Children of God* as a novel, as a work of imaginative literature? To some extent, this question has been deflected in the past by the fact that the Mormon story in itself is so compelling to readers. But even among the reviewers, Weeks is not alone in pointing out artistic failings. Clifton Fadiman, while praising the book's general appeal, calls it "repetitious, wordy, freighted with interminable dialogue. Cast in the form of a novel, it is apt at any moment to do a quick-change act and appear as a straight historical chronicle. The prose is often careless, often tumid.... He never suggests when he can explain, and he will explain at the drop of a semicolon." Another reviewer allows that by modern standards the novel "may be said to have a quality of a certain kind. But as a meritorious work of art it is atrocious."[33] Wallace Stegner says that Bernard DeVoto had written a piece damning all Mormon novels. "Then came out *The Children of God,* which had won the Harper Prize. Benny had to concur, it was a good book; and so he ate crow publicly and wrote another piece in which he, I think, overpraised *The Children of God.*" Stegner himself, while expressing gratitude for what Fisher did for him as a teacher, admits, "I never had the highest respect for Vardis's novelistic skill." He says of *Children of God,* "It wasn't good prose. It hurt my ears, it seemed so blunt. It was made with an axe." He liked the man but could not admire the writing.[34] Dale L. Morgan says that "with all its merits, and it should be understood that they are many," the novel does not succeed as an effective blending of history and fiction. Despite the fact that the book "was the Harper prize novel in its year, that it sold well, and that it attracted a considerable measure of critical acclaim, *Children of God* is by no means a front-rank novel."[35] Levi Peterson, reconsidering the achievement of the novel in 1979, concludes that "*Children of God* is a good book, a suspenseful book, but it demonstrates in its author a lack of the largest, most comprehensive kind of imagination."[36]

Fisher himself said, "I received a Harper award for one of the poorest novels I have written."[37] He may have been playing down the importance of literary prizes here, or the statement may be an instance of his sardonic bluntness, but we cannot discount it without impugning the credibility of his literary judgment in general. He thought his novel *April: A Fable of Love,* published two years before *Children of God,* was much better, and in terms of artistic skill he may have been right.[38] In any case, he was disturbed by winning a prize for a book he considered inferior to much of his other work. Kenneth Hunsaker reports that at a meeting of the Western Literature Association in Salt Lake City in 1966, Fisher "made the acid comment that the reason *Children of God* won the prize was that the judges thought the manuscript belonged to Bernard DeVoto."[39] In a letter to George Day in 1967, Fisher admitted that one of his reasons for writing the novel was financial: "[A]fter a lot of lean years I hoped to do a book that would sell better."[40] There were undoubtedly a variety of motives that prompted the book: the desire to come to terms with Mormonism; the recognition that the subject was marketable; and the fact that he was heavily and professionally engaged in historical research in the late thirties (the Idaho guides and encyclopedia) and, consequently, was in a research-history mode when he undertook the novel. It is possible that among these motives artistic expression and richly imagined fiction were not paramount considerations.

In *Children of God* content takes precedence over presentation, theme over characterization, historical sources over imaginative plausibility. Consequently, the artistry of the novel will not bear close scrutiny. Sometimes the problem is carelessness. For example, page 359 tells us "Brigham told the band to play waltzes, polkas and quadrilles," while page 360 tells us Brigham refused to allow the band to play waltzes: "No, the waltz is sinful." This is a trivial inconsistency, but also telling and representative. There are two themes here ineffectively juxtaposed: (1) Brigham Young as pragmatic leader who kept pioneer spirits up by having his people dance and sing in their camps as they crossed the plains, and (2) Brigham Young as puritanical fundamentalist. A similar example occurs on page 327, where Brigham is described as having lost twelve inches around his middle, his cheeks are sunken, and his eyes had drawn back in his skull. This is his emaciated condition in the flight from Nauvoo. The theme is trial and suffering. Yet, a few pages later, in his sickly condition and with his people in such cold and misery that a woman must bear her child on the ground unsheltered from pouring rain, Brigham asks two sisters to marry him. We have now shifted abruptly to the polygamy motif. Such inconsistencies are particularly common in Fisher's portrayal of Joseph Smith, in which theme and circumstance dictate whether Joseph will be courageous or cowardly, naive or cunning, honest or dishonest, peaceful or militant, ignorant or eloquent, a sincere visionary or an ambitious fraud.

Such examples suggest that Fisher addressed Mormon history as separate units of events and information from which he extracted patterns of attitude and behavior and some basic themes. Throughout his career he had great faith in his version of scholarship, which largely emphasized quantity over discrimination of sources and authority. He often bragged of the two thousand books he had read for the *Testament* series, as though the sheer amount of reading would compensate for his rural background and justify his rejection of religious superstition. In the case of *Children of God,* he relied too much on scholarship and too little on literary imagination. The episodic chronicling of events is not complemented by a coherent imagining of his main characters.

This failure of imagination is manifest particularly in the basic sameness of the novel's voices. Fisher had grown up on the frontier and was gifted in portraying a vernacular frontier type, but in this book he overuses the type. As Dale Morgan points out, a kind of lifeless repetition in the novel is a consequence of Fisher's clothing "the bones of history with Mormon flesh of the kind he knew in the Snake River Valley." Dock Hunter, a character in one of his earlier novels, was the product of Mormon society interacting with the desert environment. "In peopling his pageant with a congregation of Dock Hunters, Mr. Fisher achieved a flavor of the frontier but lost qualities of personal fulfillment and deep spirituality that were profoundly important in the inception and growth of Mormonism."[41] Mormon converts came from all walks of life and levels of education and culture. The majority of them came from Europe. Yet no hint of this diversity appears in the novel. The same ring-tailed roarer personalities and vernacular idioms ("hit the grit," "mouth-almighty," "sock 'em away") characterize all Mormons from 1820 in New York to 1890 in Utah.

Children of God can provide an introduction to the frontier period of Mormonism, but it is of little use in understanding the present worldwide church of ten million members. Vardis Fisher envisioned Mormonism in decline at the end of the nineteenth century when polygamy was discontinued. In reality, the growth and influence of the LDS Church since that time is a singular phenomenon in the religious world. Fisher's antitheistic bias and stultifying rationalism prevented him from understanding the vital forces of emotion, imagination, and intellect underlying religious doctrine and practice. His biases prevented him from recognizing the most important qualities in Joseph Smith, Brigham Young, and their associates—the qualities that made all the difference. For all his probing of human nature, Fisher's understanding of the human psyche was neither broad nor deep enough to enable him to capture the essence of the Mormon experience. As an historical document, *Children of God* can only become increasingly inaccurate as Mormon historiography inevitably grows and changes. Unfortunately, as a literary achievement, the novel has little vitality beyond its historical subject—few characters to cherish, few scenes to reread for pleasure, few passages to rehearse and savor. If the book endures, it will do so because of the force of its author's character, his courage in confronting the human predicament without comforting illusions, and his compassion—often obscured by his methods—for the creatures he scrutinizes so unsparingly.

Notes

1. Joseph M. Flora, "Vardis Fisher and the Mormons," *Dialogue: A Journal of Mormon Thought* 4 (Autumn 1969): 48.
2. Leonard J. Arrington and Jon Haupt, "The Mormon Heritage of Vardis Fisher," *Brigham Young University Studies* 18 (Fall 1977): 45, 46, 28.
3. Leonard J. Arrington and Davis Bitton, *The Mormon Experience* (New York: Alfred A. Knopf, 1979), 330.
4. Opal Laurel Holmes, "Vardis Fisher Was Not a Mormon," press release, Vardis Fisher Collection, Boise State University, n.d. (ca. 1979).
5. Richard M. Andrews, "Vardis Fisher: An American Atheist Author," *American Atheist: A Journal of Atheist News and Thought* 35 (Summer 1997): 11.
6. Tim Woodward, *Tiger on the Road: The Life of Vardis Fisher* (Caldwell, ID: Caxton Printers, 1989), 149.
7. Levi Peterson, "Vardis Fisher's *Children of God:* A Second Look," *SunStone* 4 (January–February 1979): 31.
8. Woodward, *Tiger on the Road*, 107.
9. *The Teachings of the Presidents of the Church: Brigham Young* (Salt Lake City: The Church of Jesus Christ of Latter-day Saints, 1997), 23, 25.
10. Vardis Fisher, "*Children of God*," *Oregon Historical Quarterly* 41 (June 1940): 126.
11. Joseph M. Flora, *Vardis Fisher* (New York: Twayne Publishers, 1965), 48.
12. Vardis Fisher, "The Mormons," *Transatlantic*, May 1944, 40.
13. Vardis Fisher, *In Tragic Life* (Caldwell, ID: Caxton Printers, 1932), 446.
14. Woodward, *Tiger on the Road*, 40–41.
15. Vardis Fisher, "The Novelist and His Background," *Western Folklore* 12 (January 1953): 3.
16. Fisher, "*Children of God*," 126.
17. Vardis Fisher, "My Bible Heritage," in *Thomas Wolfe As I Knew Him, and Other Essays* (Denver: Alan Swallow, 1963), 166.
18. Flora, *Vardis Fisher*, 142.

19. Andrews, "Vardis Fisher," 11, 13.
20. Woodward, *Tiger on the Road,* 143, 145, 153–54.
21. Quoted in Andrews, "Vardis Fisher," 12.
22. Clifton Fadiman, "Books," review of *Children of God,* by Vardis Fisher, *New Yorker,* September 2, 1939, 53.
23. Bernard DeVoto, "Millennial Millions," *Saturday Review of Literature,* August 26, 1939, 3.
24. Fred T. Marsh, "A New Novel by Vardis Fisher," review of *Children of God,* by Vardis Fisher, *New York Times Book Review,* August 27, 1939, 1.
25. George Frederick Day, *The Uses of History in the Novels of Vardis Fisher* (New York: Revisionist Press, 1976), 91; Marsh, "A New Novel," 1.
26. Fisher, "The Mormons," 38; Vardis Fisher, *Children of God* (New York: Harper, 1939), 44. The most comprehensive consideration of the Book of Mormon as literature is Richard Dilworth Rust, *Feasting on the Word* (Salt Lake City: Deseret Book, 1997).
27. Fisher, "Children of God," 126–27.
28. Foote is quoted in Wayne Chatterton, *Vardis Fisher: The Frontier and Regional Works* (Boise: Boise State College, 1972), 8; John R. Milton, *The Novel of the American West* (Lincoln: University of Nebraska Press, 1980), 119.
29. Louie W. Attebery, "Vardis Fisher," in *A Literary History of the American West,* ed. J. Golden Taylor et al. (Fort Worth: Texas Christian University Press, 1987), 871.
30. Day, *The Uses of History,* ii.
31. Milton, *The Novel of the American West,* 131.
32. Edward Weeks, editorial comment on *Children of God, Atlantic,* October 1939, preliminary pages.
33. Fadiman, "Books," 53; A. L. Byron-Curtiss, review of *Children of God,* by Vardis Fisher, *The Churchman,* December 15, 1939, 23.
34. Wallace Stegner and Richard Etulain, *Stegner: Conversations on History and Literature,* rev. ed. (Reno: University of Nevada Press, 1996), 29–30.
35. Dale L. Morgan, "Mormon Storytellers," in *Rocky Mountain Reader,* ed. Ray B. West, Jr. (New York: E. P. Dutton, 1946), 409–10.
36. Peterson, "Vardis Fisher's *Children of God,*" 31.
37. Vardis Fisher, *God or Caesar: The Writing of Fiction for Beginners* (Caldwell, ID: Caxton Printers, 1953), 241–42.
38. Woodward, *Tiger on the Road,* 150.
39. Kenneth Burnice Hunsaker, "The Twentieth Century Mormon Novel" (Ph.D. diss., Pennsylvania State University, 1968), 12n.
40. Day, *The Uses of History,* 143 n. 1.
41. Morgan, "Mormon Storytellers," 409.

Bibliography

Andrews, Richard M. "Vardis Fisher: An American Atheist Author." *American Atheist: A Journal of Atheist News and Thought* 35 (Summer 1997): 9–14.

Arrington, Leonard J., and Davis Bitton. *The Mormon Experience.* New York: Alfred A. Knopf, 1979.

Arrington, Leonard J., and Jon Haupt. "The Mormon Heritage of Vardis Fisher." *Brigham Young University Studies* 18 (Fall 1977): 27–47.

Attebery, Louie W. "Vardis Fisher." In *A Literary History of the American West,* ed. J. Golden Taylor et al., 862–86. Fort Worth: Texas Christian University Press, 1987.

Byron-Curtiss, A.L. Review of *Children of God,* by Vardis Fisher. *The Churchman,* December 15, 1939, 23.

Chatterton, Wayne. *Vardis Fisher: The Frontier and Regional Works*. Boise: Boise State College, 1972.

Davis, David B. "'Children of God': An Historian's Evaluation." *Western Humanities Review* 8 (Winter 1953): 49–56.

Day, George Frederick. *The Uses of History in the Novels of Vardis Fisher*. New York: Revisionist Press, 1976.

DeVoto, Bernard. "Millennial Millions." *Saturday Review of Literature*, August 26, 1939, 3–4, 14.

Fadiman, Clifton. "Books." Review of *Children of God*, by Vardis Fisher. *New Yorker*, September 2, 1939, 53.

Fisher, Vardis. *Children of God*. New York: Harper, 1939.

———. "*Children of God*." *Oregon Historical Quarterly* 41 (June 1940): 126–28.

———. *God or Caesar? The Writing of Fiction for Beginners*. Caldwell, ID: Caxton Printers, 1953.

———. *In Tragic Life*. Caldwell, ID: Caxton Printers, 1932.

———. "My Bible Heritage." In *Thomas Wolfe As I Knew Him, and Other Essays*, 160–66. Denver: Alan Swallow, 1963.

———. "The Mormons." *Transatlantic*, May 1944, 37–41.

———. "The Novelist and His Background." *Western Folklore* 12 (January 1953): 1–8.

Flora, Joseph M. *Vardis Fisher*. New York: Twayne Publishers, 1965.

———. "Vardis Fisher and the Mormons." *Dialogue: A Journal of Mormon Thought* 4 (Autumn 1969): 48–55.

Holmes, Opal Laurel. "Vardis Fisher Was Not a Mormon." Press Release. Vardis Fisher Collection, Boise State University.

Hunsaker, Kenneth Burnice. "The Twentieth Century Mormon Novel." Ph.D. diss., Pennsylvania State University, 1968.

Marsh, Fred T. "A New Novel by Vardis Fisher." Review of *Children of God*, by Vardis Fisher. *New York Times Book Review*, August 27, 1939, 1.

Milton, John R. *The Novel of the American West*. Lincoln: University of Nebraska Press, 1980.

Morgan, Dale L. "Mormon Storytellers." In *Rocky Mountain Reader*, ed. Ray B. West, Jr. New York: E. P. Dutton, 1946, 404–13.

Parkinson, Linda Frances Lamb. "Wider Than Mormonism: Vardis Fisher's Prophets and His Vision of Man." Masters thesis, University of Idaho, 1964.

Peterson, Levi. "Vardis Fisher's *Children of God:* A Second Look." *SunStone* 4 (January–February 1979): 30–32.

Rust, Richard Dilworth. *Feasting on the Word*. Salt Lake City: Deseret Book, 1997.

Stegner, Wallace, and Richard Etulain. *Stegner: Conversations on History and Literature*. Rev. ed. Reno: University of Nevada Press, 1996.

Taber, Ronald W. "Vardis Fisher: New Directions for the Historical Novel." *Western American Literature* 1 (1967): 285–96.

Teachings of the Presidents of the Church: Brigham Young, The. Salt Lake City: The Church of Jesus Christ of Latter-day Saints, 1997.

Weeks, Edward. Editorial. *Atlantic*, October 1939, preliminary pages.

Woodward, Tim. *Tiger on the Road: The Life of Vardis Fisher*. Caldwell, ID: Caxton Printers, 1989.

7 Father to the Man: An Apology for Fisher's Indians

Mick McAllister

It is unpleasant to return to Vardis Fisher's frontier novels with a mature understanding and appreciation of the complexity of American Indian cultures. In all of Fisher's work, the Indian is a malicious child, victim of his own avarice, a windmill of emotions, cruel with the thoughtless solipsism of a four-year-old swinging a kitten by its tail. His Indians are above all filthy people, alcoholics by nature, incapable of loyalty, transparently contemptuous of people from other cultures. They are ruled by superstition and driven by covetousness; the men treat their women like property and treat the aged as worthless refuse. Fisher's Indians are, in a word, the ugliest stereotype of their race that the white man has imagined.

This stereotype is especially evident in the two frontier novels of the fifties, *Pemmican* (1956) and *Tale of Valor* (1958). A typical passage from *Pemmican:* "Though Indian faces were impassive, once in a while you saw in them a delight that was infernal."[1] Later: "The Cree were woods Indians, which meant that they were lazy as hell" and "next to the Saulteurs they were the worst drunkards in the country" (225). *Tale of Valor* (Fisher's novelization of the Lewis and Clark expedition) ends with this description of the Sioux: "How like small children they were! Lewis reflected. They were full of wind and brag and bluff. Would they have dared, four of them, to go up Maria's River into Blackfoot country? Not one of them—not even a hundred of them."[2] Earlier Fisher describes a war party from another tribe as "children acting upon impulse" (248), and at the beginning of the novel the Sioux chiefs behave like sullen children: "They pouted and sulked. They were so completely childlike in their behavior" (42).[3]

Indians do not figure significantly in Fisher's frontier books of the thirties and forties, although they do appear in *The Mothers* (1943) and *In Tragic Life* (1932). Beginning with *Pemmican* and continuing through

Fisher's last published book, *Gold Rushes and Mining Camps of the Early American West* (1968), the descriptions of the Indian "race" are as one-sided as anything in his published work. There are four significant sources for Fisher's view of the Indian: his relationship with Leona McMurtrey,[4] more general elements of his personal history,[5] his research in journals and history books for the frontier fiction,[6] and the voluminous research for the *Testament of Man.*

The last source offers an important alternative to dismissing Fisher's attitude toward the Indian as simply racist. Between 1943 (publication of *The Mothers*) and 1956 (publication of *Pemmican*), Fisher's intellectual perception of the American Indian underwent a radical transformation. It is significant that the seven *Testament* novels on the pre-Christian history of Western man were published precisely during that period.[7] Three of those novels are set in roughly Stone Age cultures, and Fisher's research on those cultures is the key to the stereotype that appears in the two frontier novels that follow those on Western man's prehistoric roots.[8]

I do not intend to excuse the racial stereotype or to deny its presence in Fisher's work. I must confess that I would not give a Fisher novel with significant Indian content to a new reader without warning that his picture of the Indian people is distorted and one-sided, just as I would warn the innocent reader that elements of Mark Twain's picture of Jim are products of its time. However, I would like to examine the stereotype in the context of Fisher's work and the few relatively certain details of his biography. His Indians evolved from a complex of sources and motives, and their nature is a product of the whole process of Fisher's thinking, not merely the thoughtless reaffirmation of a racial prejudice. Fisher's idea of history was recapitulative and hierarchical. A child of his own intellectual climate, he accepted the notion that cultures could be identified in terms of human maturation and thus be ranked qualitatively.[9] In *Mountain Man* (1965), although his limited and ethnocentric view of Indian cultures is still evident,[10] Fisher leavens his intellectual position with some understanding that the life of the American Indian was richer and far more complex than his reading of anthropologists and archaeologists had suggested.

Racism is a violent word, and I expect some readers to come away convinced that I regard Fisher as a racist, and others to conclude that he was a racist and I am making excuses for him. Still others will take away as their share of the elephant the idea that I have a distorted, "romantic" view of the Indians, who were roughly as horrible as Fisher's work suggests. Of course, I think all three groups will be mistaken, but this is not to say that Fisher's view of the Indians is "true" or that it is not "bad." Before looking at Fisher's work, let me establish the meanings of the terms *racist* and *stereotype* in my contexts.

I adopt the position that "race" is no more than a heuristic concept (if heuristic can be used to describe a term invented to a negative purpose).[11] Common sense suggests that race is nothing more than prolonged limitation of a gene pool interacting with a fixed environment. In this sense, finches on the Galapagos Islands eventually evolved into a genetically unique group, or "race." So did Celts isolated on a hostile island off the coast of France. Race exists, and it consists of difference. Some commonly identified differences among humankind become charged with judgmental freight. A race with different eating habits may smell different (i.e., bad). A race may adapt to the climate by evolving a broader nose, paler skin, longer legs (i.e., ugly).[12]

Common sense may go so far as to say that some of these races must be superior to others, simply because all things can be ranked (Faulkner is better than Capote, Manfred is better than Hemingway, Wharton is better than Garland, and so on) or because some characteristics are obviously undesirable. A chorus of dissent will immediately ask a series of key questions: Superior by whose standard? Superior in what regard? Undesirable in what context?

So far, no methodology has emerged that can demonstrate the innate, objective superiority of any race. Are the nut-crushing finches of one climate "superior" to their bug-hunting relatives a thousand miles distant? Even if you put a bug-hunter to work in nut country, its lack of success would hardly be considered proof of innate inferiority. Stephen Jay Gould identifies the Western need to measure and rank as the snake in our intellectual garden. It may actually be true that one race is less intelligent or less graceful than another; certainly anyone who denies even the possibility is flying in the face of both logic and biology. The question, however, is not whether races differ but whether those differences matter qualitatively in the particulars of day-to-day life.[13]

Fisher himself constantly ridicules the concept of racial superiority and the related concept of cultural superiority, whether expressed by the people of Adom's village in *The Divine Passion* (1948), who are convinced that all other villages are degenerate both morally and physically in a direct ratio to the distance from their own,[14] or by the civilized jingoists from *Orphans in Gethsemane* (1960), who march into two world wars armed with the conviction that their adversaries are subhuman.[15] His free trappers in *Mountain Man* are all philosophically racists, however egalitarian their behavior. Accurate reflections of their era, they are convinced of their self-evident superiority to blacks, Indians, and "Mexicans."[16] Sam Minard is carefully distanced from their intellectual limitations, just as Fisher distanced Bill Eddy from the racist point of view at the end of *The Mothers*. Like Fisher's views on feminism, his racial views were progressive for his own era, however badly dated in our time.[17]

By "stereotyping" I mean that extension of racism that presumes because one is a member of a "race" one has all the generalized characteristics of that race. Black Africans with no admixture of other genetic material can be described in terms of their uniqueness. Therefore, they have "racial" characteristics. Those characteristics may be both appealing and unappealing, both to the members of the genetic group and to outsiders. They are, however, a fuzzy set. That is to say, most members have most of them; some members have all of them; and no members have none of them. However, if *race* is a genetic term (as, strictly speaking, it must be), then as soon as the black African leaves Africa and begins a century of forced intermarriage, her descendants cease to be members of the race. If environment is a factor in racial character, then of course that abduction to the Americas also contributes to their separation from that race.[18] The concept of race as a genetic template retained during "racial mixing" is, in scientific terms, nonsense. The concept of racial characteristics as something identifiable scientifically and retained (or lost) through this evolutionary process is a fabrication.

The problem surrounding stereotypes has always been that in some sense they are "true"; often they are hasty generalizations. A stereotype may take the form of an observation of a physical detail (Paiutes and Asians are smaller than white people—that is, white North Americans) or a judgment (observing that Plains Indian men did not work the way Anglos did, Anglos judged them lazy). The most pernicious stereotypes are those that disguise judgment as observation, often beginning from flawed observation.[19] At its least offensive, a stereotype is a faulty generalization about a fact with no judgmental loading. That, of course, is a rare enough *avis* to constitute little more than a thought experiment. Even as superficially innocuous an overgeneralization as that regarding the size of Asians and Paiutes (consider the Ainus and Wayne Newton) carries the connotative charge of white American males' preference for large things, whether in their buildings, their heroes, their trophy rooms, their driveways, their girlie magazines, or their trousers.

The most characteristic observation Fisher makes about his Indians is that they are "children." The term is the key to understanding the intellectual roots of Fisher's idea of the Indian. Cultural anthropologists beginning with Herbert Spencer and Edward B. Tylor have espoused the view that cultures, like species, evolve and mature, with the tacit assumption that the goal of this linear and inevitable process is whatever those white Victorian men perceived as the nature of Western man. Generalizing from the progressive development of animal species,[20] they take the position that prehistoric cultures are less mature cultures. The metaphors of cultural history are indicative of how thoroughly this judgmental point of view pervades anthropological thought: "The Birth of Religion," "The Cradle of Civilization," "The Evolution of Legal Doctrine," and Peter Farb's witless, unwitting caricature of the thesis, *Man's Rise to Civilization as Shown by the Indians of North America from Primeval Times to the Coming of the Industrial State* (1968).

Stephen Jay Gould distinguishes carefully between the anthropological theorists who hold that ethnic groups are inferior genetically and those who hold that culture types are immature. Both groups operate from a subjective and ethnocentric model of human history but with a politically significant difference. While the first justifies racial inequality, the second leaves room for the achievement of racial equality. Fisher is clearly of the second camp. His viewpoint is not racist but evolutionist. His investment in the religion of progress was whole, and his Indians are not racially inferior but culturally immature. If his solution to the "Indian problem" would be unpopular with today's cultural relativists, his point of view is, nonetheless, more misguided than malicious. The distinction between racial inferiority and cultural immaturity may seem pedantic. However, I think we will find that our own views, carefully examined, are less different from Fisher's than we might prefer to admit, and none of us, surely, is a racist. Consider some basic premises of cultural evolution: A culture that cannot cure tuberculosis is less desirable than one that can. A culture that has a high incidence of starvation is less desirable than one that does not. A high rate of infant mortality is an undesirable cultural trait. Humans need cars, TV sets, artificial hearts, newspapers, antihistamines and analgesics, freeways, and sound teeth. Should we choose to deny these self-evident truths, seated complacently as we are among the privileged, I will not have to search far to find "primitive" parents eager to reduce infant mortality, "primitive" hunters covetous of the latest high-powered rifle, "primitive" village elders willing to compromise environmental impacts for less hunger, and "primitive" shoppers waiting at the doors of international K-Marts and Kresges. And if we write their desires off to ignorance, how is that patronizing dismissal any different from the dismissive superiority of the Victorian pundit?

Fisher's Indians are covetous and superstitious not because they are Indians but because they are primitive and human. The Crees of *Pemmican* are no different from the prehistoric Europeans of *Intimations of Eve*

(1946) and *Adam and the Serpent* (1947). The Sioux and Blackfeet of *Tale of Valor* are the intellectual brothers and sisters of the prehistoric Semites of *The Divine Passion* (1948). Significantly, Fisher does not place his prehistoric cultures geographically until he arrives at the vaguely identifiable period of *The Divine Passion.* In the preceding novels of the series, the people's skin color suggests that they are "white," and their climate, flora, and fauna suggest a locale somewhere between the Atlantic and India, south of Finland and north of the Sahara. The religious practices of the prehistoric people of *The Divine Passion,* set in the pre-Sumerian Middle East, are similar, in the broad strokes, to those of the Indians of *Tale of Valor* and *Mountain Man.* Unlike anthropologist and fiction writer Björn Kurten, Fisher feels no need to localize the milieu of his prehistoric novels. Localizing them would be contrary to Fisher's basic assumptions. The "primitives" of his *Testament,* like the "primitives" of the frontier novels, are intellectual concepts, not "races" but immature cultures.

Before Fisher began the *Testament,* he depicted Indians in *The Mothers* with a more rounded perspective than in the later frontier novels. Valuations of the minor Indian characters partake of the prejudices of the time. When Paiutes raid the Donner camp, they are identified only as "Diggers," and protagonist Bill Eddy goes after them because "he wanted to shoot an Indian before this trip was done."[21] The two Indians who come back with Charley Stanton to rescue the party are described as "lazy shirkers" (123) because they refuse to waste energy on work they consider futile. When Will Foster suggests that the starving party called the "Forlorn Hope" kill and eat the two Indians, he says, "They're only Indians" and Bill Eddy retorts, "[T]hey're men—and brave men" (184–85). Later, after Foster murders them, they are referred to as "brave Indians" (194). Finally, the Indians who meet Bill when the "Forlorn Hope" emerges from the Sierra are charitable and generous, no different from any human community of the time (196–97).

It is after a decade of research into "primitive man" that Fisher's Indians become stereotypes, marionettes dancing to a polemical tune familiar to the reader of the *Testament.* In *Pemmican,* the character of the part-white, part-Indian girl Sunday makes clear Fisher's adherence to the nurture rather than the nature theory of cultural identity. In two key scenes, David wonders at the degree to which the presumedly innate white character is submerged in Sunday's red upbringing. In the first (102–3), she is butchering buffalo, up to her armpits in gore. In the second (177), she performs a native dance with passion and conviction David thinks a white woman incapable of expressing. David subscribes to the James Fenimore Cooper school of genetic theory: There are red gifts and white, and that's how it should be. Sunday is Fisher's proof that David is wrong. A primary action of *Pemmican* is David's discovery that the citizens of a Stone Age culture, regardless of their genetic makeup, will behave in a certain way. He learns, as a character in *Tale of Valor* would suggest later, that "The Indian under his copper skin was about like the white under his milk" (84).

David's own perspective is judgmental but not explicitly racist. He sympathizes with the Indians cheated and degraded by the trading companies (52), and he recognizes that the whites at the trading posts are in some ways as degraded as the Indians they despise. His concern about Sunday's race relates to a practical issue: How will an Indian wife be accepted when he returns to Scotland? Love ultimately renders the question moot, and David eventually comes to understand that "you had to take the red man's indolence if you liked what abiding kinship with mountain, river, and sky had done for him; his haughtiness if you admired his courage; perhaps even what white men called his treacheries and cruelties if you were to love your own children" (301).

In *Mountain Man,* Fisher's vision evolves into something less doctrinaire than the polemic of the two preceding frontier works. One sign of this is the change in his depiction of the wolf. In *Tale of Valor,* Fisher adopts the vocabulary of the nineteenth-century Euro-American wolf-hater to describe the "craven things" that hunt in packs. His wolves prefer to kill pregnant does but are such cowards that they hunt even these innocent creatures by driving them into water and drowning them. In *Mountain Man,* however, Sam Minard admires the wolf: "He thought it the most intelligent of all the wild beasts."[22] Instead of the cowardly skulking murderers of Bambi's mother, the wolves of *Mountain Man* are brilliant tacticians willing to take on a grizzly bear when the need arises (218 ff.) and capable of driving it off. Fisher clearly had updated his knowledge of wolves, as he explicitly challenges the nineteenth-century canard that wolves preyed on men (262).

Similarly, the continuing theme of the Indian as child is mitigated by a more complete understanding of the Plains Indian cultures. Notably, there is a return to the rounding of Indian characters into a complete range of human beings, as in *The Mothers,* and more emphasis on mutual failure to appreciate racial character. As Sam reflects on his "contempt for red people and some of their ways," the authorial voice adds that "the contempt, on both sides, had its beginning in the earliest association of redmen and white," and that each race "thought the other fantastically stupid" (30).

Like *Pemmican* and *Tale of Valor, Mountain Man* draws on Fisher's *Testament* research for its portrayal of the Indian. Like the earlier books, it is full of descriptions of Indian life too one-sided to take seriously, such as

Sam's observation that he could ride through a thunderstorm unconcerned for his safety because "no brave ever skulked around in such a deluge, but cowered in his miserable leaking tent while the sky raining dogs and cats scared him out of his wits" (93). Descriptions such as the horrific picture of Indian hunters devouring game practically before it died are repeated from previous books (compare *Pemmican*, 102–4, *Tale of Valor*, 249, and *Mountain Man*, 96). There is little question that these views are Fisher's, not merely an authorial adoption of the protagonist's point of view. Fisher remarks on the same page: "[Sam] did not know that Lotus felt there must be some fatal lack in her, or he would have ordered her to do the cooking and the chores. Among her people the husband was lord and king; he hunted and made war and beat his wife and that was about all he did." Sam's description of how the Indian father "itched all over with avarice the moment he sensed that a paleface coveted one of his females" (44) is almost a paraphrase of the greedy daydreams of Alzina's father in *The Divine Passion* (113). In *Adam and the Serpent*, the matriarch Rainmaker regards her beautiful granddaughter as the potential source of a small fortune.[23]

Similarly, the descriptions of Indian superstition in *Mountain Man* owe more to *The Divine Passion* than to Robert H. Lowie, Clark Wissler, and Charles Eastman. "The redman was the servile creature of ritual and ceremonial" (130), Fisher observes. "The Indian's world was so overrun by evil spirits and wicked powers that there were times when he was immobilized" (137). Sam spends a winter at "Colter's hell" (Yellowstone National Park) because "no Indian would dare follow him, for they thought that evil spirits were working their magic there" (177). The paralyzing effect of "evil spirits" echoes Fisher's descriptions of prehistoric heroes in such books as *Adam and the Serpent*, where three different people are, in separate incidents, paralyzed with horror when they lose their genital amulets (see 68, 136, and 251–52), where Dove nearly dies of a curse (54–55), and where the death of Dove's wife Lotus is attributed not to the abscess on her cheek but to an evil spirit that got in through the wound (277).

On the other hand, the mellowing of Fisher's perspective is evidenced in his depiction of the two Crow boys who try to kill Sam Minard. The youth and obvious inexperience of the first both touches and horrifies Sam (171). The second boy's death moves Sam to understand that there is more to the Crow hatred of him than mere savagery and bloodlust. When the boy attacks Sam, it is by jumping into the river to catch him, carrying nothing but a knife in his teeth. It is, Sam allows, "the most spectacular act of courage he had ever seen" (315). "He sensed that this young one had been so outraged in his tribal and personal pride that he was resolved to prove that a Crow warrior could be a braver man than The Terror." As he fights the boy, he is reminded of the appalling tenacity of the badger that attacked a grizzly in the first scene of the novel.

Sam must learn the Hobbesian lesson that all mankind are little more than savages. Meditating on the boy's courage, he begins to recognize this. He observes that civilized people kill "for a handful of coins or for the simple ghoulish pleasure of it." The specter of the Mexican War rises briefly as he compares the bullying thievery of the United States to the Indian tribes who "seemed pretty well matched." He allows that no mountain man would "torture for the hellish pleasure of it" (318) and learns differently twenty pages later. Having seen the superhuman devotion of Kate Bowden, he is moved equally by the unnamed Indian woman who chooses to die with her husband (the Blackfoot chief Elk Horn who had captured, tortured, and nearly killed Minard). Sam finds their bodies in an isolated tepee, and he thinks, observing them, "The chief had been his deadly enemy but he must have had remarkable virtues to have won from a woman such love as this" (362). A few pages later he learns that Kate has died, frozen to death in her cabin, and has been buried by the Crows: "[A]n act of such gracious mercy and pity—or, if not that, of atonement—that he sat humbled before it" (366).

Fisher follows his customary authorial technique in *Mountain Man,* half-identifying with the protagonist, leaving us to sort out the difference between his point of view and the limited viewpoint of his nineteenth-century hero. As a result, the reader cannot be sure that Fisher appreciates ironies that Sam misses. For instance, Sam believes that Indians are cowards and white men brave. Yet he recalls stories of incredible courage on the part of Indian braves, and having repeatedly characterized the Indians as children, he illogically calls the West "a man's country, and not for tall boys called men" (176). For all his insistence that white people are reasonable and Indians petulant children, he tells the story of a flyting match between a band of trappers and an Indian war party to show that "redmen had a child's fondness for insulting words" (142). Sam fails to note that it takes two childish insult-lovers to make a flyting match.

Unwittingly, Sam's accounting for the white man's "courage" while reflecting on the difference between red attitudes and white toward probability belittles both. White "courage," it turns out, is, like Indian "cowardice," based on a statistical fallacy:

> If sixty redmen faced an enemy every single one of them would figure that if one and only one of his party was killed he would be the dead man. If two were killed, or three or five, he

> would be one of them. It was for this reason that the warriors of most tribes would turn and run after one or two or three had been killed. The whiteman, on the other hand, figured that if only one of sixty were to die the odds were fifty-nine to one in his favor. He was likely to think the odds greater than that, for the reason that he did not look on himself as an average fighter. (131–32)

Fisher's Indians present a serious problem to the student of Western American literature. Ultimately, Fisher's presentation of the Indian is dishonest in that he presents the worst of Indian cultures while mitigating the white culture they are in conflict with. Consider, for example, that Sam Minard does not, like his real-life counterpart John Johnston, eat his victims' livers. The historical Johnston bragged of escaping from the Blackfeet and taking with him the leg of his captor to tide him over till he could hunt. In contrast, Sam "had wondered if he ought to take one of the guard's thighs, but he was a sentimental man and he thought he would rather starve than eat human flesh" (254). As a little "practical joke," Johnston spiked a pan of biscuits with wolf poison and left it for a Blackfoot war party to discover in his cabin. Sam and his mountain man friends attack a Blackfoot war party that outnumbers them more than two to one.[24]

Fisher was a child of his culture, first of all, and his culture taught him a stereotype of the Indian that he saw confirmed by the degraded poor vagrants who visited the family cabin. Leona McMurtrey's complex character mix—half passionate "Indian," half devout Mormon—did nothing to improve his personal experience of Indian people. More than this, however, he was the child of his reading, and his reading, so often cited as a positive value of his work,[25] may have been more ambiguous a resource than has generally been observed. Most of his research was done by mail through a sort of improvised interlibrary loan. If the list in *God or Caesar?* is any indication, his reading was voluminous but less broadly based than it might have been if he had been working directly with scholarly libraries and a community of scholars. What is more, the list suggests that his book choices tended to be conservative, shading toward the out of date.

Fisher's picture of prehistoric man owes more to Victorians James G. Frazer and Edward B. Tylor than to the cutting edge of anthropology in the thirties and forties when he was researching and writing. Tylor's thesis that culture evolves as a result of reasoned choices would have been much more appealing to Fisher's rationalist point of view than the "anti-intellectualism" of the Boas school, which held that culture is an agglomeration of habit and that individual cultures are unique entities rather than instances of some generalized superculture.[26] Tylor's primitive man aspires to be a Victorian gentleman; Fisher's aspires to be a modern, technological Western man. Fisher's view of prehistoric humankind as a whole is limited by a fallacy popular but discredited professionally long before he began the series, the notion that "primitive" and "prehistoric" were synonyms. (Cultural anthropologists have always recognized that the study of primitive cultures cannot be assumed to tell us about prehistoric cultures.)[27] Fisher clearly ignores this problem; he is, in the jargon of anthropological theory, a "unilateral evolutionist," committed to the idea that all cultures pass through roughly the same stages and that all humankind has essentially the same mind and evolutionary "goal."

Applied to fictions about prehistoric Western man, this idea is harmless and heuristic. It allows Fisher to combine his own emotional and intellectual character with the speculations of anthropologists and create a fascinating, persuasive picture of modern man as a primitive. By combining his own (i.e., Vridar Hunter's) neurotic fear of God with the documented primitive belief in the supernatural, he is able to present a terrifying picture of the strength of superstition. We should not lose track of the fact that the neurotic reaction of a prehistoric man to losing a talisman may be no more characteristic of general primitive belief than Vridar Hunter's religious pathology is typical of the twentieth-century Christian. And neither explains the other.

Applied to historic and even contemporary human cultures rather than prehistory, the idea of cultural evolution, with its intellectual baggage asserting that all "primitive" cultures are incipient "modern" cultures, is inherently and implicitly racist, however. Unless the human "races" have different beginning dates (as some turn-of-the-century Nordicists held, with no supporting evidence), then all cultures are equally "mature," having had the same life span. The Cro-Magnon philosopher of the Neander Valley who invented holy wars may be the childish ancestor of warmongering Western man, but the nineteenth-century "Stone Age" Indian is not. That Indian is a human who chose a different growth path, one posited on different religious and philosophical values and shaped by a different geographical and climatic environment. He is John Stuart Mill's brother, not his great-uncle; she is Ellen Glasgow's sister, not her grandmother. It is a tribute to Fisher's intellectual character that he was able, in *Mountain Man,* to see past the self-imposed blinders of his scholarly research to the essential common humanity of us all. It is an embarrassment to those who love his work despite its faults and limitations that he wrote for so long and, sometimes, so persuasively, wearing those blinders.

Notes

Full citations for references in these notes are listed in the bibliography.

1. Vardis Fisher, *Pemmican: A Novel of the Hudson's Bay Company* (Garden City, NY: Doubleday, 1956), 38. Subsequent references are cited parenthetically.
2. Vardis Fisher, *Tale of Valor: A Novel of the Lewis and Clark Expedition* (Garden City, NY: Doubleday, 1958), 448. Subsequent references are cited parenthetically.
3. The negative picture of the Indians in *Tale of Valor* has its foundation in the paternalism and ethnocentricity of philosopher and rationalist Meriwether Lewis, whose view of the Plains tribes is so embarrassingly racist that Stephen Ambrose feels compelled to apologize for it throughout his recent history of the expedition, *Undaunted Courage*.
4. Critics have faulted *Mountain Man* for romanticizing the fur trade, usually citing Sam Minard's fixation on classical music. But surely the most "romantic" element in the novel is Sam's idyll with his "perfect" wife, Lotus. In both *Mountain Man* and *Pemmican,* Fisher posits as an element of the beloved's attraction that she appears to be part white. There is no space here for a full discussion of the effect that Leona had on Fisher's thinking, but it takes no great investment of amateur psychology to see in both Lotus and Princess Sunday attempts to build in the ruins of Fisher's relationship with his first wife. Vridar Hunter accounts for Neloa's mysterious, contradictory character by attributing it to her "Indian blood." Like many Southern families, Leona's was supposed to be part Indian (Woodward, *Tiger on the Road,* 48).
5. *In Tragic Life* describes the passage through Swan Valley of a family of gypsies/Indians who are morally and economically degraded. They and Neloa's family are the only clues to the nature of Fisher's direct contact with Indian people as a child. If we assume that such people as these constituted Fisher's own childhood images of the Indian, then this experience, however anachronistic to the nature of frontier Indian life, accounts for some of his negative assessments of western Americana.
6. The degradation of the Cree in fact was a consciously pursued agenda of the fur companies, as Peter C. Newman's *Company of Adventurers* and *Caesars of the Wilderness* (his two-volume history of the Hudson's Bay Company) make clear (see *Caesars,* 113–15). Fisher's views anticipate Newman (*Pemmican,* 51, 194). The most degraded Indians in *Pemmican* are described in terms lifted directly from journals of the fur trade, notably those of Duncan MacGillivray.
7. The seventh novel, *The Island of the Innocent,* appeared in 1952, and Fisher worked on *Tale of Valor* and his writer's handbook, *God or Caesar?* (1953) while attempting to find a publisher for the eighth novel, *Jesus Came Again* (1956). Three years later, in 1956, Alan Swallow revived the series by publishing this and the ninth novel (*A Goat for Azazel*), then completed publication of the *Testament* over the next four years.
8. Unfortunately, the partial destruction of Fisher's library and records as a result of twenty-two years of neglect has left little direct evidence of the course of study that preceded the first five novels. Beginning with *The Valley of Vision* (1951), Fisher began concluding each book with a bibliographical essay invaluable as an indicator of what he was reading. I have not found similar editions of the earlier novels. Fisher concluded *God or Caesar?* with a reading list that offers some hints. (See *God or Caesar?* for citations of the listed titles.) Presented as an admittedly subjective selection, the titles are "calculated to give a young person a broad knowledge of the past" (265). Clearly the titles are books Fisher was currently or recently interested in; they include volumes like Lea's *History of the Inquisition,* Coulton's *The Medieval Scene and Life in the Middle Ages,* Cumont's *Oriental Religions in Roman Paganism,* Taylor's *The Medieval Mind,* and Montague Summers's *History of Witchcraft and Demonology*—books with most direct bearing on the latter volumes of the *Testament*. Oddly enough, there is not a single anthropologist specializing in Ameri-

can Indian cultures on this list of one hundred volumes. Freudian theory is well represented by two Havelock Ellis titles and Freud's own *Totem and Taboo*. The only titles obviously pertinent to prehistoric culture are Jane Harrison's *Prolegomena to the Study of Greek Religion,* three James G. Frazer volumes, Malinowski's *The Sexual Life of Savages,* Yerkes's *The Great Apes,* and a handful of generalized titles in cultural anthropology.

Two books on the list, *Civilization and Climate* and *The Character of Races,* are by Ellsworth Huntington of Yale University. In 1928, in an essay entitled "Race and Civilization" (which appeared in Charles A. Beard's anthology *Whither Mankind?*), George A. Dorsey offered this assessment of Huntington: "a confirmed Nordic propagandist" (quoted in Montagu, *Frontiers of Anthropology*, 443). Dorsey goes on to quote and paraphrase Huntington's "evidence" for innate mental differences between one race and another. Then he concludes by quoting Huntington's dismissal of such dissenting voices as Dorsey's colleagues Boas, Kroeber, Lowie, and Goldenweisser: "a relatively small group of scientific men, especially those who belong to races that are not dominant."

Perusing Fisher's list, one is left to surmise whether Edward B. Tylor, Herbert Spencer, Durkheim, Boas (*The Mind of Primitive Man,* 1911), and such reigning stars of American anthropology as Leslie White (*The Study of Culture,* 1949), Paul Radin (*Primitive Man as Philosopher*, 1927), Robert H. Lowie (*Primitive Society*, 1920), and Ruth Benedict (*Patterns of Culture,* 1934) are absent by oversight, exclusion, or ignorance. Certainly their absence suggests that Fisher's own reading was less eclectic than his readers have often assumed.

Some absences are inexplicable: Otto Rank is quoted pervasively throughout *God or Caesar?,* but neither he nor Theodore Reik is cited on the list. Mircea Eliade failed to make the list, as did the James brothers, Jung, Bertrand Russell, and Arthur Koestler. Toynbee made it, but not Van Loon or Will Durant. One cannot conclude that Fisher had not read the excluded writers, nor can one conclude that exclusion was an implicit judgment on the writer's value. Fisher obviously admired Rank, and he would have found Koestler in many ways a kindred spirit. Nor is it the case that writers of obvious merit were left off because reading them "goes without saying." At the time of Fisher's list-making, Lewis Mumford, Margaret Mead, Havelock Ellis, and Bertrand Russell were all hot intellectual properties. But if reading them "goes without saying," why did Ellis make the list, and not the other three?

The most persuasive argument is that the list, despite its pretense of universality, represents little more than those volumes most on Fisher's mind in the early fifties, when he had finished novels on Solomon and the Maccabees, the historical, pre-Christian era of Jewish history, and was engrossed in the novel set in the time of Jesus and the next, set fifty years later in Rome. Of the hundred titles listed, twenty are specifically on the Middle Ages (subject of *My Holy Satan*, 1958), two are on the period of the Desert Fathers (for *Peace Like a River*, 1957), and nineteen are on the birth of Christianity. Given that Fisher spent five of the twelve *Testament* novels on prehistoric "primitive" life and that the one novel on the Middle Ages served to take us from 1190 to 1890 in a single historic leap, the universality of a list that devotes twenty percent of its titles to medieval Europe is suspect at best.

Twelve of the titles on the list are related to the Solomon and Maccabees books, which also seem rather odd focal points for a general course of literacy. Another twenty-four are on the history of such things as art, medicine, sex, and costume. With the exception of Toynbee, none covers any aspect of history since the Renaissance. Oriental cultures warrant two titles, and a third covers India. It is, as Fisher admitted, perhaps with tongue in cheek, a "subjective" list.

9. As an instance of this, take his assertion in a newspaper column in 1945: "What but an exaggerated opinion of himself [an anonymous letter-writer that Fisher is rebutting] and

his country can lead him to the notion that we Americans can feed European minds? The people of Denmark, Holland, Belgium, and France—to name only four—are more cultured than we are" ("Our Brother's Keeper," *The Idaho Statesman,* October 7, 1945). In our present-day view, of course, culture, like environment, is not something one has more or less of. (The semantics of the word wriggle like a snake to serve our purposes.) It may be difficult to recall that Fisher is writing in a period when languages of low-technology cultures were regarded as "simple" and a culture was judged by the size of its statues, libraries, or tanks.

10. "The whiteman was far more adult than the redman, who, in fact, was only a child in his emotions" (131). After rattling off some nonsense that he claims is a literal translation of "Crow talk," trapper Dutch Charley opines that "they talk like children talk" (141). "The Indian braves, [Sam] was thinking, were only boys at heart" (215). Sam believes that Indians loved to torture "because they were children" (236).
11. For a full-scale discussion of the idea of race, its history and its scientific value, read Ashley Montagu's slim summary, *The Idea of Race,* or Thomas F. Gossett's *Race: The History of an Idea in America*. Stephen Jay Gould has discussed the subject of races in the context of biology and intelligence testing in his *The Mismeasure of Man*.
12. Gould has outlined the ways that these adaptations have been used as evidence of racial superiority rather than difference.
13. A fascinating anthropological document offers evidence that sickle cell anemia is in fact a positive adaptation that turned negative when the carrier of the gene was removed from the environment that fostered it. The series of factors is convoluted, but what it amounts to is that hunting cultures are generally not exposed to malaria; the sickle cell gene was related to the protective adaptations to malaria that occurred when those cultures turned to agriculture; and the appearance of sickle cell anemia as an illness today is the result of the control of a greater evil, malaria. For the full discussion of this subject, see Frank B. Livingstone's "Anthropological Implications of Sickle Cell Distribution in West Africa," collected in Montagu, *Frontiers of Anthropology* (566–92).
14. Vardis Fisher, *The Divine Passion* (New York: Vanguard Press, 1948), 113–14, 291–93. Subsequent references are cited parenthetically.
15. In the October 7, 1945, article cited above, Fisher goes on to condemn the "racial prejudice and persecution of minority groups," which, in his view, characterize the culture Americans would "feed" to Europe.
16. And the last in spite of the fact that two respected fellow trappers are Hispanics.
17. Fisher took the issue on directly in a newspaper column in 1946: "We can hope that human beings some day will be born with equal opportunities, and in this matter the world does make steady progress; but people can never be born with equal endowments. Not even plants are." He continues: "[I]t is the fashion at present to pretend that races are equal in their mental endowments. The Germans made such stupid outcry over Nordic superiority that as a corrective it seems to be generally assumed that one race is in any respect as good as another.... But it isn't. Differences apply to races as to individuals of a race" ("The Myth of Equality," *The Idaho Statesman,* February 24, 1946).
18. I would argue that the white "race" is a negative set. White people are those who do not belong to any of the races they presume to identify. In their own genetic character, they are by history and nearly by definition mongrels, from the blond-obsessed Hitler to the Oklahoma Aryan simultaneously contemptuous of Indians and proud of his Cherokee great-grandmother. Fisher made a similar point in a newspaper column in 1945, this one on the Jewish racial minority: "I have no race, and feel no need of any. I am Dutch, German, Irish, Scotch, English, with possibly still other admixtures; and I am glad of it. Most of you who read this have no 'race' to be proud of, or to be persecuted for" ("The Racial

Minority," in *The Idaho Statesman,* October 21, 1945).

19. Consider the fallacies in the sequence of logic that begins with the observation that a white soldier's heart was cut out and eaten by the Indian who killed him in hand-to-hand combat and leaps to the conclusion that Indians are less "decent" than white folks. This is an instance of the premise that Plains Indians mutilated the dead, which leads to the conclusion that they are therefore cruel by nature and inferior in humanity to white people. The initial observation is a misunderstanding of the event: eating the heart of an adversary was not mutilation but a way of honoring him. Assuming that other instances would support the premise (Plains Indians did mutilate dead adversaries, of course, for a complex of reasons that included the universal savagery of men at war), a series of hidden minor premises bridge the gulf separating it from the conclusion, notably that white people did not mutilate dead adversaries (and, of course, they did), that mutilating a dead body is cruel and inhuman (not "decent"), and that what we were really talking about is not mutilation of the dead but torture of the living, of which the eucharistic consumption of the soldier's heart is not an instance at all.
20. Ironically, the notion of progressive development of species is actually another example of the same tacit assumption. Stephen Jay Gould and other biologists have begun to popularize the understanding that "higher animals" is a statement of opinion, not observation. Evolution is not necessarily progressive; change is not necessarily improvement, nor is lack of change a sign of viability. The idea that the beaver represents progress from the perspective of a platypus, or that a human is "more evolved" than a cockroach is worthy of debate.
21. Vardis Fisher, *The Mothers: An American Saga of Courage* (New York: Vanguard, 1943), 63. Subsequent references are cited parenthetically in the text.
22. Vardis Fisher, *Mountain Man: A Novel of Male and Female in the Early American West,* (New York: William Morrow, 1965), 221. Subsequent references are cited parenthetically in the text.
23. Vardis Fisher, *Adam and the Serpent* (New York: Vanguard Press, 1947), 74. Subsequent references are cited parenthetically in the text.
24. Johnston's exploits are recounted as an amazingly unabashed hymn to Indian-hating in Raymond W. Thorp and Robert Bunker's *Crow Killer.* It is a measure of how political correctness evolves that this unpleasant stew of frontier racism was published by Indiana University Press. Thorp and Bunker did not even record the man's name correctly, preferring the more "popular" spelling. It is not unusual to hear the historical Johnston referred to as "Jeremiah Johnson." Johnston's name is spelled with a 'T' in legal records and in a surviving letter, a biography excerpted from the Carbon County, Montana, history of Red Lodge, Johnston's home (the text of the letter is available at http://www.ida.net/users/cstmzd/Johnston.html/).
25. Joseph Flora says the reader "must respect the vast amount of scholarship that guided [the *Testament*]" (*Vardis Fisher,* 97). "The research behind his books is tremendous, but Fisher has realized with considerable success what the researches show life to have been" (75).
26. See Elvin Hatch's *Theories of Man and Culture* for a full discussion of Tylor's thought. Briefly, Tylor held that culture is the result of reasoned human choices. He believed that human beings always choose the logical course, and he accounted for both human error and cultural divergence by asserting that they were the results of ignorant implementation of reason. Hatch contrasts Tylor with Franz Boas, the father of American anthropology and opponent of Tylor's views. According to Hatch, Tylor's theory of cultural evolution as a reasoned process languished until Leslie White revived the theory, with the twist that he assumed that the "organism" that evolved was culture itself rather than the individual member of the culture colony. By an odd coincidence, White received his Ph.D. in anthropology at the University of Chicago in 1927, two years after Fisher received his, in English

literature, from the same school.

27. In his *Totemism and Exogamy* (quoted in Kardiner and Preble, *They Studied Man*) James G. Frazer wrote: "The chasm which divides the modern from the ancient savage may very well be much deeper and wider than that which divides the lowest modern savage from a Shakespeare or a Newton."

Bibliography

Ambrose, Stephen. *Undaunted Courage: Meriwether Lewis, Thomas Jefferson, and the Opening of the American West*. New York: Simon and Schuster, 1996.

Fisher, Vardis. *Adam and the Serpent*. New York: Vanguard Press, 1947.

———. *Darkness and the Deep*. New York: Vanguard Press, 1943.

———. *The Divine Passion*. New York: Vanguard Press, 1948.

———. *God or Caesar? The Writing of Fiction for Beginners*. Caldwell, ID: Caxton Printers, 1953.

———. *The Golden Rooms*. New York: Vanguard Press, 1944.

———. *In Tragic Life*. Caldwell, ID: Caxton Printers, 1932.

———. *Intimations of Eve*. New York: Vanguard Press, 1946.

———. *The Island of the Innocent: A Novel of Greek and Jew in the Time of the Maccabees*. New York: Abelard Press, 1952.

———. *The Mothers: An American Saga of Courage*. New York: Vanguard Press, 1943.

———. *Mountain Man: A Novel of Male and Female in the Early American West*. New York: William Morrow, 1965.

———. "The Myth of Equality." *The Idaho Statesman,* February 24, 1946.

———. "Our Brother's Keeper." *The Idaho Statesman,* October 7, 1945.

———. *Pemmican: A Novel of the Hudson's Bay Company*. Garden City, NY: Doubleday, 1956.

———. "The Racial Minority." *The Idaho Statesman,* October 21, 1945.

———. *Tale of Valor: A Novel of the Lewis and Clark Expedition*. Garden City, NY: Doubleday, 1958.

Fisher, Vardis, with Opal Laurel Holmes. *Gold Rushes and Mining Camps of the Early American West*. Caldwell, ID: Caxton Printers, 1968.

Flora, Joseph M. *Vardis Fisher*. New York: Twayne Publishers, 1965.

Gossett, Thomas F. *Race: The History of an Idea in America*. Dallas: Southern Methodist University Press, 1963.

Gould, Stephen Jay. *The Mismeasure of Man*. New York: W. W. Norton, 1981.

Hatch, Elvin. *Theories of Man and Culture*. New York: Columbia University Press, 1973.

Kardiner, Abram, and Edward Preble. *They Studied Man*. Cleveland: World Publishing, 1961.

Livingstone, Frank B. "Anthropological Implications of Sickle Cell Distribution in West Africa." In *Frontiers of Anthropology*, ed. Ashley Montagu, 566–92. New York: G. P. Putnam's Sons, 1974.

Lowie, Robert H. *The Crow Indians*. New York: Farrar and Rinehart, 1935.

Montagu, Ashley. *The Idea of Race*. Lincoln: University of Nebraska Press, 1965.

———, ed. *Frontiers of Anthropology*. New York: G. P. Putnam's Sons, 1974.

Newman, Peter C. *Caesars of the Wilderness*. New York: Viking, 1987.

———. *Company of Adventurers*. New York: Viking, 1986.

Thorp, Raymond W., and Robert Bunker. *Crow Killer: The Saga of Liver-Eating Johnson*. Bloomington: Indiana University Press, 1958.

Woodward, Tim. *Tiger on the Road: The Life of Vardis Fisher*. Caldwell, ID: Caxton Printers, 1989.

8 Music, Violence, and Nature in Vardis Fisher's *Mountain Man*

Barbara Howard Meldrum

I have taught Fisher's last novel, *Mountain Man* (1965), a number of times and have also led adult discussion groups on this novel. Most readers like it because of the vivid sense of nature Fisher creates in his text, the exultant joy in living that Sam exemplifies, and the appeal of living a life free from the worst aspects of civilization. But readers are also disturbed by the terribly violent scenes Fisher portrays. I, too, find the violence distasteful at times, though Fisher always seems within the bounds of realistic portrayal of his chosen subject. I have also been puzzled by Fisher's frequent allusions to classical music—his mountain man knows repertoire of Mozart, Beethoven, Corelli, and others, singing arias at the top of his lungs or playing favorite themes on his mouth organ. Though teasing our credulity, Fisher does have historical precedent for such a character in the biographical accounts of some of the trappers of Sam's era. It is not simply a question of realism, however.[1] I am somewhat disturbed by a hero who repeatedly denounces "civilized" life yet cherishes music that is a product of that culture, and who loves music yet can kill Indians with no compunction. Are these elements truly in uneasy conflict in Fisher's novel, or are they held together in an artistic and philosophical whole?

Tim Woodward, in his biography of Fisher, relegates *Mountain Man* to a low position in Fisher's canon. As evidence that the book "was written almost as if he were exhausted...or in a hurry to finish," he cites instances where "the text contradicts itself" and observes, "In a novel about a man who lives in the wilds, eats dripping hunks of freshly killed meat and devotes much of his time to killing Indians, long passages are devoted to descriptions of classical music."[2] Woodward obviously sees an inherent inconsistency in the juxtaposition of classical music and violence.

Yet we know that although music is more readily associated with moods of peace and affirmation of beauty, it can in some contexts be linked with violence. There are the rousing marches that give impetus to warfare, or the bugle call to battle, or the drums and chants of Indians on the warpath. There is the irony of a seeming complicity with genocide in the chamber music of the death camps where millions of Jews were exterminated by the Nazis (though in this instance the Jewish musicians used their music in their own struggle for survival). John Dryden's *Alexander's Feast, or the Power of Musick* (1697) attributes the burning of the Persian palace to the power of music; the intertwining of revenge, love, and music anticipates Fisher's complex interweaving of these themes.[3] Some of the most chilling examples I can cite of an apparent alliance of music with violence are in Anthony Burgess's *A Clockwork Orange* (1962), when Alex commits rape to the strains of Beethoven's "Ode to Joy" in his Ninth Symphony and commits murder in an attempt to seize a stone bust of Beethoven. Music, Alex says, makes him feel powerful, like God. It is no accident that Fisher's Sam Minard obviously loves Beethoven's music and refers more than once to his Ninth Symphony. Sam loves, and knows, a variety of music, some of it peaceful and orderly; but Beethoven's power as well as his keen sense of nature and imitation of natural sounds in his music correlate with Sam Minard's—and Fisher's—musical bent and philosophical perspective.

Fisher interweaves music and violence in his text, linking both to nature. We can see this in key scenes throughout the novel. The first chapter begins with this interweaving:

> He had paused to listen to the exquisite madrigal of a Western meadow lark, and had offered to sing with it, choosing as his own, "Give Me the Sweet Delights of Love"; but he had found no bird that would sing with him, though now and then one, like the chat, would try to entice him into mimicry. On his packhorse in a piece of cheverel, the fine soft leather made of kidskin, he had a mouth organ; and a mile and ten minutes later he took it out and looked round him for sign of enemies. He had learned that playing Bach or Mozart arias when in enemy country was not only good for his loneliness; the music filled skulking Indians with awe. At this hour, back home and far away, his father might be playing the pianoforte.[4]

We immediately see Sam (not yet named) linked to the world of classical music through his father's influence, participating in the "natural" music of birds through his singing, and using Bach or Mozart arias to protect himself from the possible violence of hostile Indians. This opening paragraph leads us into a dramatic scene of violence in nature as Sam watches a badger bravely fighting a grizzly, wounding his attacker severely before being ripped apart by his much larger and stronger opponent. Again, music, nature, and violence are juxtaposed when Sam "heard a lark singing, and for a moment he thought how strange it was that in the same scene a bird's throat was pure music and two beasts had turned as black as night with murderous fury" (5).

Fisher moves his story from this prelude to introduction of a main narrative theme in chapter 2: the massacre of Kate Bowden's family by Blackfeet warriors and Sam's response to Kate who, like the badger, has struck out at the enemy, killing four Blackfeet before the others flee her murderous axe. That night, after burying the dead, Sam plays softly on his mouth organ, expressing his homesickness and the compassion he feels toward a mother deranged by grief and the terrors of human violence. Beethoven's music enters this scene through association. First, Beethoven's imitation of birds' songs through the music he wrote for various instruments is paralleled by Sam's efforts to imitate birds' songs with his mouth organ. Then, the philosophy implicit in Beethoven's symphonic music is identified with Sam's mood:

> He wanted to stand up and shake a clenched fist at that malevolent fate that knocked on the door in the opening bars of Beethoven's C-minor symphony and proclaimed to the world its power over Beethoven's hearing. It was the same unpitying ruthless fate, knocking there in the grand arrogant manner, that had brought savages to this spot, to hack three children to death and take a father away to torture. What was it there, he wondered, looking up at the home of the stars, a divine benevolence or a mindless malevolence? (21–22)

No answer is given to Sam's question, one he continues to ponder throughout the novel.

During Sam's wedding journey south with his bride Lotus, Fisher emphasizes the inspirational role of music as it provides consolation and enjoyment. Sam plays the role of Don Giovanni as he serenades Lotus with a baritone aria on their first day alone together (56), then plays French chansons on his mouth harp (58). Later, when a tremendous thunderstorm breaks, Sam is carried away with ecstasy as he matches his voice with the raging elements, "trying to become a part of it," and Lotus sings too (90–91). Sam exults in the violence of nature—"no thunderstorm could be too violent for him" (92)—and his gestures are "like those of a man using a pine tree for a baton" (91). The storm seems to embody the life force of nature, and Sam seeks to identify himself with that force, carrying Lotus with him on emotional waves of sensory stimulation.

In this section of the novel Fisher clearly establishes the link between nature and music, drawing directly from a source he quotes in his forward to the novel: Lawrence Gilman's 1914 study, *Nature in Music*. In his "To the Reader" Fisher quotes from Gilman's book to substantiate his portrayal of a nature lover who is a music maker and, in temperament, is emotional and unconventional. In describing Sam's southward journey with Lotus, Fisher draws (without acknowledgment) from Gilman when he describes how Sam's father told Sam "that Knecht's 'Musical Portrait of Nature' had fertilized the soil for Beethoven's Pastoral Symphony" (59–60; Gilman had used the word *anticipated* rather than *fertilized*).[5] Sam recalls how "his father had striven to paint tones—to evoke mental images with auditory impressions"; Gilman quotes William Wallace, an English theorist, who describes tone painting as "that order of music 'which attempts to excite a mental image by means of an auditory impression.'" In contrast to many music theorists, Gilman gives an eloquent defense of programmatic music, claiming that it is more complex than "absolute" music, which embodies "an idea of beautiful utterance in the mind of the composer." Like the music-drama or song, programmatic music depends "for its full realisation upon an element external to itself." It seeks to "excite" by "direct tonal imitation" (seeking to reproduce the sounds of birds or thunder), or to suggest more subtly (suggesting "flowing water, dawn, moonlight, cloud forms, by imaginative analogies of colour and design"), or to "communicate a particular mood, a definite state of feeling."[6] We can recognize these concepts in Sam's efforts to imitate the sounds of nature and to match the mood of a storm or a sunset in the music he plays or sings.

Sam, however, goes beyond Gilman's linkage of music and nature when he opts for primitive nature over the accoutrements of civilization. During the gigantic thunderstorm of chapter 9, Sam and Lotus remove their leather clothes (for the practical need to avoid shrinkage), thus removing anything that would separate them from nature's elements. As the rain brings out the fragrances of the earth, "all the harmonies of rain music were infused with fragrance." The intensity of this experience prompts Sam to reflect "that an opera house ought to be drenched with sweet essences, instead of with the bad breath and body odors of a thousand overdressed creatures" (91). In yet another way Sam goes beyond Gilman's observations. Gilman points out that the last fifty years (prior to

1914) have seen the introduction of "harmonic effects" that were not available to earlier composers such as Beethoven or Mozart—innovations that "Beethoven would have bartered his soul to be able to achieve."7 Sam also observes that Beethoven's music cannot match that of the "thunder-symphonies" he so enjoys—in comparison, "Beethoven had hardly done more than whisper among the aspens" (90). What Sam is looking for is not, however, harmonic innovations but some human way to match or become one with the symphony of nature itself: "He strove to improvise his mood, pouring forth wild baritone harmonies that dissolved into the winds" (90). For Sam, nature *is* music.

In his wedding journey south, Sam's happiness contributes to his perception that nature, music, and even violence—the violence of the thunderstorm, at any rate—are good. His frame of reference is the world of classical music: he speaks of a "Mozart moon" that looks "like a round golden note from a French horn" (59–61). The familiar landmarks they pass—mountain peaks, rivers, valleys—are "like the call of the French horn in a Mozart concerto" (103). But when he returns to Lotus after a winter of solitary trapping and finds her bones strewn around her winter quarters and evidence of her murder by Crow warriors, his vision darkens and there is no music. He climbs to the snow line and speaks his vow of vengeance (129). During his slow journey north toward Laramie he can sing but one song: "Sorrow, Sorrow, Stay" (133). The "arias" of birds serve only to remind him of his lost Lotus; he takes "his mind off song and [puts] it on vengeance" (138, 145). His grief intensifies his sense of disharmony between human life and nature. To him, the birds and animals and "the whole diapason of music" seem "so much more in tune with land and water and sky." His own music must wait for the "war" of vengeance he has sworn (166).

Sam meets and kills Crow warriors who are hunting him, and the bloody violence matched by exhibitions of valor prompt ruminations about the interweaving of violence with the beauties of nature and the admirable traits of valor and courage to be seen in both human and animal life. He ponders the violent lovemaking of both man and beast and concludes, "It was terribly beautiful country covered with violent life" (176). This section of the novel is titled "Kate," and it is the influence of Kate on Sam that shapes these chapters. Sam's first visit to Kate after Lotus's death is intended to help her, but instead it is Sam whose music is reborn by listening to the "strange music in her words" as she reads from the Bible and speaks to her dead children. He is moved to play his mouth organ, and Kate begins to sing; hymns, "Corelli phrases," and the sounds of nature intermingle to form healing harmonies (185–87). He then goes to the Yellowstone to winter away from the Crows, and his love of nature and music fills him with a love of life that confirms his awareness that "men who loved life were not men who liked to kill" (197).

As in the opening chapter of the novel, we again see Sam's admiration for the courage of one who fights well. The violence of the fight seems secondary to the commitment of the fighter, whether human or animal. Sam associates these displays of courage with great works of classical music, especially those of Beethoven, specifically his Ninth Symphony and the F Minor Sonata. Four wolves fighting a grizzly bring Beethoven's Ninth to mind, as does the devotion of Kate in caring for her children and her courage in fighting their attackers (219–20, 222, 276). His respect for fighters leads him to make a nearly fatal mistake when he tries to free the interlocked antlers of two bull elk and is surprised by Blackfoot braves who easily capture him (232). But his use of music aids his escape when he sings and shouts challenges to his captors, inspired by Beethoven's sonatas and putting on a performance that builds a crescendo to become "his thunderous overture to the infinite" (247). During his arduous journey to freedom through winter snow and ice he is inspired by music he remembers (Mozart, Beethoven, the Ave Maria, and songs of birds and animals) and by focusing on his goal: to reach Kate's cabin. Throughout this section of the novel the violence of worthy fighters is recognized as a part of nature—of God's plan as Sam sees it. His philosophy blends music, violence, and nature into a coherent belief:

> Part of the force that sent Sam trudging across the white prairies was love of life, a gladness for health and youth that filled him as Mozart's gayest music filled him; and part of it was his belief that the earth on which he walked had been designed by the greatest of the artists, and that if a man had the courage and fortitude not to fail it, it would not fail him. (267)

The interweaving of music, violence, and nature reaches a resolution in the final movement of the novel, headed "Sam," as this central-consciousness figure resolves his need for vengeance and experiences atonement. Having reached Kate's cabin where he slowly recovers from his ordeal, he finds it "natural and right" to play hymns and softly sing with her (296). This peaceful, healing interlude is followed by a southward journey that pits Sam in a deadly struggle with a Crow youth whose courage and hate nearly defeat Sam. The boy dies, but the look in his eyes haunts Sam and, combined with later echoing events, leads to his renunciation of vengeance. Sam ponders his situation and Kate's, the dualities of male vengeance and female devotion, the "ugly level" of killing practiced by so-called civilized people, and the order of nature where "nothing killed except for food, or for mates, or in defense of itself or its kind." The Indians make of war "a philosophy and a way of life"; seen in that light, Sam concludes that the Crow youth had died a glorious death in a momentary consummation of courage and power. Sam, however, does not share that philosophy; he would prefer to sing rather than kill—to "shout into the heavens the concluding bars of Beethoven's C minor than [to] follow the bugles and Zachary Taylor to Resaca de la Palma and Buena Vista."[8] Fisher then writes, "In his moralizing Sam felt the outlines of a symphony" (318–19). It is as though philosophical reflection is an act of musical composition. In a way, it is just that, in Fisher's novel. Symphonic form in particular is a way of giving shape and meaning to what is otherwise morally chaotic in human experience. And in Fisher's novel, nature is a symphony. Living in tune with nature brings form and meaning as well as beauty into one's life.

But before Sam can experience the full meaning of nature's symphony, he must resolve his vengeance, which is now twofold: vengeance against the Crow nation for the death of Lotus, and vengeance against the Blackfeet for their treatment of him in captivity. This need is something the other mountain men understand without discussion: they simply know that retribution is necessary, and they set a time and place to meet for that vengeful raid against the band that had captured Sam. Fisher narrates this scene externally, individualizing the participation of the twenty-three mountain men. When Sam's thoughts are rendered, it is Beethoven's music superimposed on nature that captures his impulse: "How wonderful it would be, Sam thought...if at the moment of attack the Creator would fill the world with a thunderous theme of vengeance, with chords like those that opened the Fifth!" (332). But after wreaking his vengeance against the chief who had spit in his face and brutally slapped him, he is haunted by the hate and humiliation he sees in the chief's eyes after he has injured and scalped him. The "look in the eyes" is one Sam has seen before and is "weary of seeing," for "in the eyes of all wounded or helpless things there was something that laid a hand on his heart" (338). Sam seems ready to turn away from violence, but for the time being he can turn away only by avoiding it, which he does by visiting Kate or retreating to the safety and seclusion of the Yellowstone, where music of nature and of his own making provide comfort.

René Girard's writings on violence may provide some help in understanding the interweaving of music, violence, and nature. In his *Violence and the Sacred* (1977), Girard claimed that violence and the sacred are one and the same. There is "bad violence" that leads to endless reprisal and "good violence" that, through some form of sacrifice, provides an outlet for violence and stops the chain of reprisal. In "civilized" societies a system of justice utilizes public vengeance whereby retribution is "forged into a principle of abstract justice that all men are obliged to uphold and respect," whereas in "primitive" societies the chain of reprisal is broken or prevented by sacrificial rites or by compensatory measures, such as trial by combat.[9] The death of a surrogate victim can restore harmony to the community and initiate the rebirth of a "new or renewed cultural order."[10] Although Fisher's novel is neither directly influenced by Girard's work nor fits precisely into Girard's theoretical framework, there are some striking parallels. Nature, violence, and the sacred seem to be one and the same: to use Girard's words, "The sacred consists of all those forces whose dominance over man increases or seems to increase in proportion to man's effort to master them."[11] Sam certainly recognizes that his quest for vengeance has trapped him within an endless chain of reprisal. And the death of Kate functions as a kind of surrogate sacrifice, generating a new cultural order that draws Sam within the Crow community.

Kate freezes to death during an exceptionally frigid winter. She is not a sacrificial victim in the usual sense, for she is not chosen by the community; her selection is, however, "arbitrary," which Girard states is essential[12]—but it is nature itself that is arbitrary, or perhaps "indifferent to her human fate" would be a more precise phrasing. The mode of Fisher's narration shapes her demise into a symphony of power and beauty. Sam is hundreds of miles away from her, but Fisher uses Sam's perspective by stating what he "would have said" had he been present. Thus the construction of the scene as the unfolding of a symphony is an extension of Sam's perception of nature as music. The symphony is preceded by overtures of winds that have "Beethoven's patience, and his skill in devising variations on main themes and in building crescendo on crescendo" (355). Then begins the first movement—"a vast playful statement of themes, as the winds rearranged the snowface of the earth" (356). This interweaving of nature and music continues as Fisher brings Sam into the experience:

> Everything in their path the winds played upon; and when they found an object...the voices would change in both intensity and pitch, and sometimes leap up and down an octave or two, as they modeled the themes to fit the curves and contours of the world.... Sam would have loved it; shouting with all his being to make himself heard, he would have played one of the themes over and over in different keys, as in the third overture to [Beethoven's]

> Leonore, and imagined that his melodies were small vocal pockets riding in the winds. He would have gone singing and dancing over the earth, and returned, when weary, to eat four elk steaks and sit by the fire with his pipe and praise the Lord. (357)

All this beauty, this music of nature, is lost on Kate. She struggles to survive, but her feet and one hand are frozen "[b]efore the divine orchestra brought in its third movement" (358). Finally, the winds seem to prepare for the coda as

> all the instruments built steadily to the first fortissimo, and in deafening apotheosis came roaring past Kate's door in such cyclones of sound that the sky literally was filled; and on top of it all, in frenzied explications, came the first crescendo, and on top of it the second, in such thunderous frozen magnificence that Kate was lost within the soul of it.
>
> The next morning there was utter silence. Kate Bowden was dead. (359)

The snowfall intensifies, "gently and softly" burying Kate and spreading "the purest winter white" over the scene (359).

What Fisher accomplishes in this elaborate scene is transformation of the death of Kate into a divine act of grace, purification, and beauty—a work of art. In Fisher's hands Kate's death becomes what Emerson called "tuneful tragedy, solemn and soft with music, and garnished with rich dark pictures."[13] On the simplest, literal level, we see a woman aged by grief and malnutrition and crazed by trauma slowly freezing to death as her already circumscribed world closes in on her. She hears no music, sees no beauty in what is happening to her. It is Fisher's words that transform her death into an artistic whole. Before narrating her death, Fisher tells how she has become increasingly "other-worldly in her moods" so that she is "ready to enter [heaven] and be with her angels [her dead children]" (353). Then he describes the winter storms as a symphony and interposes the hypothetical perspective of Sam, whose own response to nature's thunderous symphony has already been given in a more joyful scene with his young bride Lotus. Nature has an objective reality but is experienced subjectively. Gilman, in a headnote to his discussion of music cited by Fisher, quoted the following lines from Walt Whitman:

> Nature consists not only in itself objectively, but at least just as much in its subjective reflection from the person, spirit, age,

> looking at it, in the midst of it, and absorbing it: faithfully sends back the characteristic beliefs of the time or individual...falls like a flat elastic veil on a face or like the moulding plaster on a statue.[14]

Fisher would seem to agree.[15] I have said before that in this novel nature is music. It is, but in an Emersonian sense: it is music to those who can hear it.

As Sam makes his way north toward Kate's cabin in the spring following her death, he comes across a tepee that houses the bodies of the Blackfoot chief he had scalped and humiliated and the chief's wife. He concludes that the chief "had killed himself because his people had cast him out," and his wife had knelt beside him, covering his dishonored head with her own hair and freezing to death. Sam's thoughts are these: "What beautiful devotion in a wife! What a poem, what a symphony this picture before him was!" (362). Fisher here uses two art forms—poetry and music—to convey the meaning of this scene. If nature is music, so too can human behavior be music.

During his northward journey Sam had wondered why no Crow warriors had tried to kill him, as they had during the seemingly endless chain of reprisals since the death of Lotus. He discovers why when he reaches Kate's cabin. The Crows have placed her bones in a cairn of stones near the one he had built for the bones of Lotus and his unborn child. He sees this as "an act of such gracious mercy and pity—or, if not that, of atonement—that he sat humbled before it." He tries to pray, in the only way he can, by thinking of the "opening of light in the last movement of the Fifth [symphony by Beethoven]" (366). He immediately goes to the Crow village and makes peace with the chief. "I figger mebbe there's too much killing in the world," Sam tells the chief (368). Sam is integrated within the Crow community when the chief offers him his daughter as a bride, and Sam responds with gifts and swears that he "would fight for his red brothers before he would see them robbed of their ancient lands" (370). Kate's death has become a sacrifice of atonement that brings about reconciliation and integration. A novel filled with violence and the casual killing of Indians who are regarded by the mountain men as inferior beings concludes with this moment of interracial harmony. The potential of violence is still there—Sam knows that the younger Crow warriors may yet try to kill him. But Sam identifies himself with nature and the people who live by nature at the same time that he consciously rejects the encroaching tide of white settlers he sees filling the dusty Oregon Trail. There is no ultimate solution—even the Indians despoil nature as their human wastes poison the earth (345). Sam's most tenable solution is to live in "the free wide world of valleys and rivers and mountains, of natural odors and natural music" (371).

In what must be an intentional revision of the stock ending of Hollywood Westerns, Fisher describes Sam's departure from the Crow village: "Turning on a hilltop, he looked back at the thousand Sparrowhawks watching him, and made a sign which said that he would come again someday; and then he galloped off into the southwest and a brilliant Rubens sunset" (371). The Western cliché shows the solitary hero rejecting a potential lover and, after "saving" the community in some way, riding off into the sunset. Sam also avoids immediate marriage and any possible "settling down" to community life, but he has "saved" the community by ending the chain of reprisals and renouncing vengeance. That community, however, is an Indian one; he rejects the white communities of his birth. But he retains the music of the civilization he renounces, and Fisher uses Rubens, and later Breughel—artists of the civilization Sam renounces—to describe his hero's alliance with nature.

Fisher has portrayed a primitivist hero in a pastoral novel. Sam, in renouncing most aspects of his inherited civilization, chooses a way of life he recognizes will not endure. Unlike Boone Caudill, A.B. Guthrie's *Big Sky* hero who lacks the historical perspective to recognize the ways he is betraying his own natural paradise, Sam recognizes that his free western life will not endure. What comes to his mind is a musician's response to Mozart's *Don Giovanni* overture: "[H]e had been seized by terror as there unrolled the ascending and descending scales, as answerless as fate and as inexorable as death" (372). These expressions from a civilization that Sam renounces become Fisher's means of affirming "primitive" values to a "civilized" audience from which he cannot extricate himself. Fisher attributes to Sam and even to Jim Bridger a degree of foreknowledge and emotional response that surely comes from the agonized perceptions of Fisher himself:

> During the hour that he watched the slow dust-saturated serpentine crawl of a wagon train four miles long there filled him the realization that his way of life would someday be no more. For a little while there would be patches of it left up in Canada but here it would all be what Jim Bridger said it would be, swarming human masses, with the effluvium of their body smells and city smells and machine smells rising to fill the heavens and wash away the blue. Sam didn't know if the Creator had planned it this way or if it was only the blind way of the blind.[16] (372)

Fisher was revolted by the violence he found in nature and in human beings from his earliest childhood days. In what may well be his best novel, *Dark Bridwell* (1931), he portrayed a complex protagonist who enjoyed his primitive life in the paradise of nature. But Charley Bridwell is violent, even sadistic, and destroys his paradise through ruined family relationships. In Fisher's last novel he creates in Sam Minard an alter ego who loves life and nature, who is bigger and stronger than the puny Fisher boy could ever have dreamed of becoming, who can mete out the violence necessary to survive but prefers good food, the love of a woman, the sensuous pleasures of nature—and good music. Fisher became more and more caustic in his criticism of contemporary civilization in his last years, believing that overpopulation, technology, and pollution were destroying any hope for the future.[17] We can see this pessimism in Sam's rejection of civilization and in Fisher's choice of words, as in the passage cited above. Indeed, the greatest violence he portrays in this novel may well be the violent effects of human activity on nature. Fisher experiences as a writer and captures in his novel a pastoral interlude through his creation of the story of Sam Minard. But his expression is rooted in the culture of modern civilization, and his best hope for the future lies in the ability of human beings to use their reason as well as their emotions to face the reality of violence and to channel it in constructive ways. That is Fisher's best hope, and it is captured in Sam's musical ordering of his world. But Sam can turn his back on civilization while carrying its music with him in ways that Fisher could not.

Fisher is not alone in his perception of conflicting values and his condemnation of contemporary civilization. In an interview following the publication of his *Errata: An Examined Life,* George Steiner says: "After 50 years of teaching, the question remains, 'How to explain those who sing Schubert in the evening and torture in the morning?'...I'm going to the end of my life haunted more and more by the question 'Why did the humanities not humanize?' I don't have an answer."[18] Girard theorizes from a classical, essentially pagan perspective in *Violence and the Sacred.* More recently, he has moved from a secular to a Christian perspective.[19] Fisher portrays a religious quest in Sam's meditations, but stops short of a Christian resolution. In his last days Fisher sought solace increasingly in alcohol and classical music, turning away from the human debacle surrounding him. He does not answer the question he and George Steiner ponder, each in his own way. His last novel is as close as he came to an answer. His novel may also be as close as we will come to answering our own questions about his death: suicide or reckless accident.[20]

Notes

1. For an excellent analysis of realism and depictions of violence in fiction, see Michael Kowalewski, *Deadly Musings: Violence and Verbal Form in American Fiction* (Princeton: Princeton University Press, 1993). My own approach to Fisher's novel would probably be

called "translative" by Kowalewski, but I seek throughout to pay close attention to "how an author says a thing" (see Kowalewski, *Deadly Musings,* 19–20).

2. Tim Woodward, *Tiger on the Road: The Life of Vardis Fisher* (Caldwell, ID: Caxton Printers, 1989), 262. Joseph M. Flora also sees a problem: "The tension between Sam's love for opera and other music (tastes dependent on civilization and in constant need of refurbishment) and his love for an untainted wilderness works against a convincing narrative, making readers too aware of the author's unresolved conflicts" ("Vardis Fisher [1895–1968]," in *Fifty Western Writers: A Bio-Bibliographical Sourcebook,* ed. Fred Erisman and Richard Etulain [Westport, CT: Greenwood Press, 1982], 117). I shared a draft of this essay with Naida West, author of *River of Red Gold* (1996), who spent much of her childhood with her grandparents in the southern Idaho region where Vardis Fisher grew up. Her grandfather went to school with Fisher, and her grandmother most likely knew him. West wrote in response to my essay, "The link between Idaho wilderness and magnificent symphonic music runs so deep in me that I tend to think, 'Of course, what literary person of Fisher's generation wouldn't use classical music to evoke the power of nature?' The critics you mention who felt his use of music was contrived don't know what was happening in Fisher's area when he was young." She describes her musical grandmother, who rode a circuit giving piano lessons and whose absorption in classical music "struck me as no different than that of the Mountain Man on his horse in a storm. A woman of the West with a love of the great outdoors, she saw life as drama accompanied by Music" (e-mail correspondence, Naida West to Barbara Meldrum, May 3, 1999).
3. In Dryden's poem, the music of Timotheus arouses Alexander's desire for his Athenian mistress Thais, who in turn urges Alexander to revenge the earlier burning of Athens by the Persians. Music is portrayed not as a force for harmony and order, but as a power that moves the passions. Handel, in setting the poem to music (1736), implicitly heralds the power of music.
4. Vardis Fisher, *Mountain Man: A Novel of Male and Female in the Early American West* (New York: William Morrow, 1965), 3. All future page references to *Mountain Man* are cited parenthetically in the text.
5. Lawrence Gilman, *Nature in Music and Other Studies in the Tone-Poetry of Today* (1914; reprint, Freeport, NY: Books for Libraries Press, 1966), 18.
6. Ibid., 19–20.
7. Ibid., 30.
8. Fisher's Sam Minard is partly modeled on the legendary John Johnston, whose career is reconstructed from interviews and research by Raymond W. Thorp and Robert Bunker in *Crow Killer: The Saga of Liver-Eating Johnson* (Bloomington: Indiana University Press, 1958). [For an explanation of the name *Johnston* see chapter 7, n. 24.] Fisher's Sam Minard differs from Thorp and Bunker's character in many ways. Sam's attitude toward war, cited above, is contradicted by John Johnston's enlistment in the Union army. According to Thorp and Bunker, "He enlisted when the War seemed to him the best fight going" (89–90). Fisher develops Sam's relationship to Kate in ways not entirely supported by the Thorp and Bunker account and portrays Kate as more helpless and dependent on the mountain men than was the historical model, Jane Morgan, who lived twenty years beyond the massacre of her children.
9. René Girard, *Violence and the Sacred* (1972), trans. Patrick Gregory (Baltimore: Johns Hopkins University Press, 1977), 20–21.
10. Ibid., 255.
11. Ibid., 31.
12. Ibid., 257.

13. See Kowalewski's discussion of Emerson's "The Tragic" in *Deadly Musings*, 248–49.
14. Gilman, *Nature in Music,* 11.
15. Fisher gives a gendered slant to differing subjective perceptions when he writes, "The fiercer harmonies and wilder movements, even the major themes, were not for the female, whose nest-budded instincts compelled her to seek the tranquil" (357). Discussion of Fisher's views on gender differences is beyond the scope of this paper. Suffice it to say that I disagree with Fisher on this point.
16. Fisher acknowledged that what one writes reveals oneself—it is autobiographical even if the physical facts of one's life are "disguised" (John R. Milton, *Three West: Conversations with Vardis Fisher, Max Evans, Michael Straight* [Vermillion, SD: Dakota Press, 1970], 30).
17. Fisher wrote a weekly newspaper column for many years, in which he goaded his readers on many subjects. For an overview of these columns, see Woodward, *Tiger on the Road,* 229–43. Louie W. Attebery excerpted one of these columns, published the same year as *Mountain Man,* in which Fisher predicted proliferating freeways, sprawling cities, and suffocating smog. He bemoaned a future population living "in the noise and stinks and crowding of huge cities, who will never know the smell of the clean beautiful land before it was swarmed over...and the marvelous beauty of the thousands of unpolluted lakes and streams" ("Vardis Fisher," in *A Literary History of the American West,* ed. J. Golden Taylor et al. [Fort Worth: Texas Christian University Press, 1987], 880).
18. Peter Applebome, "A Humanist and Elitist? Perhaps," *New York Times,* April 18, 1998, A15.
19. For a discussion of Girard's spiritual journey see Leo D. Lefebure, "Victims, Violence and the Sacred: The Thought of René Girard," *Christian Century* 113 (December 11, 1996): 1226–29.
20. Fisher died of an overdose of sleeping pills following an evening of drinking. Biographer Tim Woodward interviewed Fisher's friends and relatives and concluded that if it was suicide, it was an impulsive act; more likely, it was accidental (*Tiger on the Road,* 245–54). Literary critics who knew Fisher are not unanimous. Louie W. Attebery, for instance, believes Fisher's death was probably suicide ("Vardis Fisher as I Knew Him: The Legend and the Legacy," lecture and discussion, Lewiston, Idaho, June 21, 1995).

Bibliography

Attebery, Louie W. "Vardis Fisher." In *A Literary History of the American West,* ed. J. Golden Taylor et al., 862–96. Fort Worth: Texas Christian University Press, 1987.

Applebome, Peter. "A Humanist and Elitist? Perhaps." *New York Times,* April 18, 1998, A13, 15.

Fisher, Vardis. *Mountain Man: A Novel of Male and Female in the Early American West.* New York: William Morrow, 1965.

Flora, Joseph M. "Vardis Fisher (1895–1968)." In *Fifty Western Writers: A Bio-Bibliographical Sourcebook,* ed. Fred Erisman and Richard Etulain, 110–20. Westport, CT: Greenwood Press, 1982.

Gilman, Lawrence. *Nature in Music and Other Studies in the Tone-Poetry of Today.* New York: John Lane, 1914. Reprint. Freeport, NY: Books for Libraries Press, 1966.

Girard, René. *Violence and the Sacred* (1972). Trans. Patrick Gregory. Baltimore: Johns Hopkins University Press, 1977.

Kowalewski, Michael. *Deadly Musings: Violence and Verbal Form in American Fiction.* Princeton: Princeton University Press, 1993.

Lefebure, Leo D. "Victims, Violence and the Sacred: The Thought of René Girard." *Christian Century* 113 (December 11, 1996): 1226–29.

Milton, John R. *Three West: Conversations with Vardis Fisher, Max Evans, Michael Straight.* Vermillion, SD: Dakota Press, 1970.

Thorp, Raymond W., and Robert Bunker. *Crow Killer: The Saga of Liver-Eating Johnson.* Bloomington: Indiana University Press, 1958.

Woodward, Tim. *Tiger on the Road: The Life of Vardis Fisher.* Caldwell, ID: Caxton Printers, 1989.

9 Fisher and Meriwether Lewis

John D.W. Guice

In his dedication of *Suicide or Murder? The Strange Death of Governor Meriwether Lewis* (1962), Vardis Fisher described Meriwether Lewis as "the greatest American of his breed and the most neglected." While the recent attention to Lewis would delight Fisher, the declaration by best-selling author Stephen E. Ambrose in *Undaunted Courage* (1996) that Lewis killed himself would deeply trouble him. Because of the power of the medium and because Ken Burns echoes Ambrose's dictum of suicide, Fisher would find Burns's 1997 television special equally disturbing. On the other hand, Fisher would enthusiastically applaud efforts of forensic scientist James E. Starrs to answer the question of suicide or murder through an examination of Lewis's remains.[1]

Fisher's obsession with the mysteries surrounding the death of Lewis grew out of his research for *Tale of Valor*, his 1958 novel about the expedition to the Pacific led by captains Meriwether Lewis and William Clark. Based on a meticulous study of the Reuben G. Twaites edition of *The Journals of Lewis and Clark* and a mastery of scholarship relating to the expedition, Fisher's *Tale of Valor* is a factually accurate reconstruction of the experiences of the Corps of Discovery.[2] Because Fisher did not frame this book around a contrived plot, his is the first successful novelization of the Lewis and Clark expedition.[3]

Though other authors wrote books on Lewis and Clark, Emerson Hough in *The Magnificent Adventure* (1916) attempted the first novel. Rather than focusing on the actual adventure, Hough developed his story around a fictional—and distracting—love affair between Meriwether Lewis and Aaron Burr's married daughter, Theodosia Burr Alston. Novelist Donald Culross Peattie, in *Forward the Nation* (1942), also proved incapable of coping with the massive data provided by the Lewis and Clark journals. Instead of concentrating on the accomplishments of Lewis and Clark, Peattie celebrates and exaggerates the role of Sacajawea and he exaggerates foreign implications of the exploration. Ethel Hueston, though she lacked Fisher's mastery of the sources and his insight into the characters, in *Star of the West* (1935) approached her topic in a manner similar to that of Fisher. Rather than create a plot, she allowed the incredible experiences of the Corps of Discovery to carry the story. Fisher perfected Hueston's formula.[4]

Tale of Valor is both good history and good literature. Scholars during the four decades since its publication have gained new insights into the expedition as well as into Lewis, Clark, and their corps. Fisher's description of one of the world's most epic explorations is as accurate as it is detailed. He wisely recognized that the journals describe so much drama, suspense, excitement, and pathos that he need not tamper with the truth. Even the best historian would be hard-pressed to use the available sources more critically.

Though Vardis Fisher penetrates the character of many members of the Corps of Discovery, he best reveals his talent as a novelist through his depiction of the personalities and minds of Meriwether Lewis and William Clark. Both were natural leaders who extracted from the diverse and often crude enlisted men more strength, courage, and allegiance than the soldiers themselves realized they possessed. The red-headed Clark, four years older than his co-captain, was the quieter and more realistic of the pair. Lewis, while philosophic, introspective, and at times introverted, was an impulsive risk-taker with a clever sense of humor. Though sentimental, the fearless Lewis was also a stern disciplinarian. Clearly, Fisher favors Lewis. Even so, the author leaves no doubt about the deep mutual respect and affection they shared. And he also makes it abundantly clear that the co-captains provided a rare example of authentic teamwork in the exercise of leadership roles.

Not only did Lewis and Clark understand their men, they also understood a good deal about the Native Americans. Indeed, of the countless obstacles facing the corps, none concerned them more than the avoidance of conflict with the natives of the vast continent that they crossed. Lewis, formerly Thomas Jefferson's private secretary, constantly kept in mind the president's abiding interest in the Indians. Nor did he forget that the establishment of peaceful relations with them was a primary goal of the expedition.

Few novelists have thought more about the nature and behavior of Native Americans than Vardis Fisher. Consequently, in *Tale of Valor* he writes about them with ease and authority. Even had his previous works not dealt considerably with that topic, his study of the journals of the expedition provided him with considerable insight into the culture of the Native Americans of the Plains, Rocky Mountains, and Pacific Northwest. Whether or not one agrees with their attitudes toward the natives, Lewis and Clark ventured from St. Louis to the Pacific and back without a single fatality from Indian hostilities. This is prima facie evidence of their ability to deal with the native culture of that time.[5]

The captains, particularly Clark, in *Tale of Valor* continually view the Indians as possessing the minds of children. The child image appears virtually from their first encounter with the natives. "The red children," they explained to some chiefs, "must now surrender French and Spanish flags and medals and receive American flags and medals."[6] And in their conversations throughout the book, Lewis and Clark repeatedly attribute to Indians childlike dispositions and an absence of real courage. In their view, the Indians display a pretended courage such as a child would display. At every opportunity Fisher accurately presents the captains as agents of pacification and paternalism, an American policy derived from British colonialism.

Fisher causes readers to ponder his treatment of the Pacific Coast Indians, whom white men had already contaminated:

> One evening a dozen squaws came to the white man's camp, and soon a dozen of the men were laughing their heads off. Stripping almost naked, the squaws were proudly showing them what whiteman sailors had tattooed on their arms, legs, and bellies. On a brave who had come with them, a young fellow with bright red hair and a freckled face, was the name Jack Ramsay. Whereupon, one of the corps quipped: "Here's one guy who knows his father!" Another added: "Who at the moment is probably in a Liverpool whorehouse."[7]

En route back to St. Louis, Fisher has the white men and Clark's black slave, York, laughing at themselves. At first they whooped and howled at the sight of a mother who proudly displayed her new baby, "an infant with [N]egroid features and kinky hair."[8] More of York's babies appeared. But he was not the only proud father. "They began to search among the new infants for one that looked like them, and almost got into a fight over the matter, they were so ridiculous.... A number of the men went round staring at the squaws and feeling frightfully silly because unable to tell whether this squaw or another, had been their woman."[9] Fisher raises interesting questions. Were the Americans much different from the hated

British? Why did the native women seem prouder of their half African-American babies than of their other babies?

Though he wrote *Tale of Valor* in 1958, Fisher made no effort to skirt the question of miscegenation. Sexual promiscuity troubled Lewis and Clark for reasons of health, morale, and morality. Among some tribes, it was the custom of the men to offer the sexual favors of their wives to important visitors, and some of the Indians on the West Coast had learned to barter their bodies for trade goods. The captains frequently expressed concern about the debilitating effects of syphilis, which was endemic among some tribes. They realized, however, that some of the young men would not resist temptation. Because neither Lewis nor Clark recorded their personal sexual thoughts or activities, Fisher is silent on that subject.[10] On the other hand, he writes frequently of Clark's affection for Sacajawea—presumably never consummated sexually.

Fisher makes it abundantly clear in his foreword to the book that in the absence of documentary evidence, he does not subscribe to various legends regarding Sacajawea's sexual involvement with members of the corps other than her husband, Charbonneau.[11] In *Tale of Valor* he depicts her as a Shoshoni child who was "any man's girl" while among her Blackfeet captors, but who bore a child by Charbonneau when she became nubile after he acquired her. Fisher does not, however, diminish her contributions as a guide, interpreter, trade negotiator, pacificator, gatherer of food and medicinal herbs, and servant. Sacajawea quietly submits to the abuses of her brutal, lazy husband. She admires Clark and showers him with affectionate glances; he delights in them and reciprocates. Lewis recognizes and values her vital role, and though he is clearly aware of the mutual admiration shared by Clark and the Shoshoni girl, he is more amused than critical or jealous.

In addition to analyzing the characters of the men who made up the Corps of Discovery, Vardis Fisher excels in his representation of the international implications of its mission. No man understood better than Lewis the importance Thomas Jefferson placed on the expedition to the Pacific. The establishment of friendly relations with the Native Americans was a prime goal of the exploration, as was the collection of geographical and scientific data. The existence of an all-water route to the Pacific, for instance, was a matter of tremendous interest to Jefferson. As significant as were these publicly stated objectives, however, Jefferson's desire to establish American claims to the Oregon country after the Louisiana Purchase was of paramount importance. Although the term "Manifest Destiny" was not coined until the 1840s, American design on the trans-Mississippi West was very much on Jefferson's mind during his presidency. While only a few Americans concerned themselves with Oregon then, untold settlers of the lower Mississippi Valley already had their eyes on a trans-Mississippi empire. Fisher's Meriwether Lewis clearly reflects Thomas Jefferson's anti-British sentiments and obsession with the urgency of countering British claims to Oregon by the presence of the Corps of Discovery in the Pacific Northwest.

On Sunday, August 18, 1805, his thirty-first birthday, Lewis pondered his lifetime achievements in one of the passages most often cited as evidence of his introspection and moodiness. During his musings that day, his thoughts also turned toward the importance of the Pacific empire to the United States: "It was what the United States needed—all this, all of it—to become the greatest of the nations, to fill the dream that Tom Jefferson had for it."[12] Sprinkled throughout *Tale of Valor* are other comments and thoughts, the origins of which are clearly in conversations between Lewis and Jefferson. For instance, when Lewis realized the trade potential of the untold millions of salmon, he wondered aloud: "If the United States got control of the salmon, instead of the damned British—. But at that point he broke off, feeling that he had said too much."[13]

While Vardis Fisher viewed the facts of the event as the essential ingredient for historical fiction, he also recognized that authors must "try to get inside the minds, souls, habits, superstitions, fears, and ignorance of his people." Furthermore, in order to achieve accuracy, Fisher continued, he "will have to put aside practically all his views, beliefs, values, and nearly all his knowledge. He will have to strip off...strip down and go back, culturally naked, to a primitive time of life."[14]

Was Fisher able to apply his own philosophy of total objectivity in *Tale of Valor*? Not completely. Try as they might, writers cannot "strip down" so that they are "culturally naked." To Fisher's credit, however, he remained amazingly faithful to the journals of the expedition. Nevertheless, the essence of the romantic myth of Sacajawea inevitably seeps into the novel. The Shoshoni girl, undeniably, was a heroine. If not labeled as such in the journals, she is a heroine in Fisher's novel. Although finding no evidence of a sexual relationship between Sacajawea and Clark, Fisher has them exchanging affectionate looks and words. Evidently these dalliances with myth did not offend Fisher's readers. The reviewer for the *New York Times,* for instance, gave his approval of Fisher's formula for *Tale of Valor:* "The book is brimming over with the fruits of scholarship. Yet the author's trips back and forth across the line dividing fact from fiction do not spoil the dramatic impact."[15]

Because Fisher focuses so often on the relationship between Thomas Jefferson and Meriwether Lewis, one is tempted to compare Stephen

Ambrose's *Undaunted Courage* with *Tale of Valor*. Indeed, Ambrose's subtitle, *Meriwether Lewis, Thomas Jefferson, and the Opening of the American West,* applies to *Tale of Valor* as well. Although *Undaunted Courage* is classified as biography on the copyright page and generally viewed as nonfiction, it has some of the qualities of historical fiction. Since both authors based their research heavily on *The Journals of Lewis and Clark,* there are many similarities between their works. A particularly striking example is their treatment of Private Cruzatte's accidental shooting of Lewis. The nearsighted Cruzatte mistook Lewis for an elk and shot him through the thigh and buttocks.[16] Indeed, it would be interesting to compare their entire texts carefully, keeping in mind that Ambrose had the advantage of an additional four decades of Lewis and Clark scholarship. Ambrose, for instance, used the most recent edition of the journals so skillfully edited by Gary Moulton, whereas Fisher relied on an edition published in 1904 and 1905.

Ambrose and Fisher share many interpretations, particularly those relating to Jefferson's motivations and aspirations, but the two authors are poles apart with regard to the manner in which Meriwether Lewis died at Grinder's Stand on the Natchez Trace on October 11, 1809. Ambrose states unequivocally, emphatically that Lewis shot himself. Fisher doubted that the death was suicide, but he could not prove that it was murder. So strong were his doubts that he devoted two years of intensive research to his 1962 publication, *Suicide or Murder? The Strange Death of Governor Meriwether Lewis.*

Wayne Chatterton was not dealing in hyperbole when in 1972 he described *Suicide or Murder?* as "a textbook upon the methods of thorough and scrupulous evaluation of historical evidence."[17] After carefully studying this work on several occasions and reading some of Vardis Fisher's correspondence pertaining to his research for it, I am convinced that his research was the most thorough ever done on the topic and that he was, indeed, scrupulous in every sense of that word.

In his opening chapter, Fisher summarizes Lewis's personality and his close association with President Thomas Jefferson during his two-year residence as his personal secretary. Here Fisher also introduces Jefferson's acceptance without challenge of the news of Lewis's suicide and his later reference to Lewis's "hypoc[h]ondriac affections" and his inherited disposition to "depression." Before moving on, Fisher emphasizes that Jefferson's selection of Lewis to lead a mission of "supremest importance to him and the nation" belied his words published in 1814.[18]

In chapter 2, Fisher analyzes Lewis's record as governor of Upper Louisiana Territory and searches for verification of Jefferson's contention that Lewis was unable to bear up under pressures of administering his office. Fisher concludes that "Jefferson simply didn't know what he was talking about."[19] Indeed, the problems and frustrations faced by Lewis were typical of those endured by all territorial officials. Lewis was certainly not an ineffective governor; to the contrary, his success in Indian affairs was admirable.

The relationship between Territorial Secretary Frederick Bates and Governor Meriwether Lewis is the subject of chapter 3. Bates apparently harbored a resentment toward Lewis that dated back to Jefferson's selection of Lewis rather than Bates as his secretary. Though he was inept at dealing with Indian affairs, Bates rather capably administered the territory during the year between Lewis's appointment and his arrival. Once Lewis was on the scene, however, Bates constantly disagreed with him and interfered. Maybe it was ambition; maybe it was simply a personality clash. Richard Dillon, author of an excellent biography of Lewis, used another figure of speech: "Whereas Bates faced east, Lewis faced the West, and always would." Consequently, Bates became an "implacable enemy."[20] Even so, Fisher emphasizes, Bates, in his numerous letters in 1809, never mentioned that Lewis was deranged.[21] Surely Bates would have, given the slightest chance.

Those who argue that Lewis committed suicide make much over the status of his finances in St. Louis. The refusal of the War Department to honor a $500 voucher to cover the expenditures of returning Chief Big White to his people, as promised, precipitated Lewis's decision to travel to Washington. Should he have to pay the $500 personally, he would face a serious financial crunch. Hence, Fisher's brief chapter 4 on Lewis's financial difficulties. Though many more records of Lewis's financial transactions in St. Louis are now available, what Fisher did not discover is significant: Lewis was not alone in finding himself in a momentary cash-flow problem. Since an opportunity to speculate in land, minerals, and trade ventures was the primary attraction of low-paying territorial jobs amid often miserable conditions, more than a few of his counterparts throughout the West found themselves in a bind. Actually, Lewis was more of an investor in real estate than a speculator.

In order to dispel myths that Lewis had shown signs of mental instability while in the governor's chair, Fisher in chapter 5 examines records of his business, official, and medical transactions without uncovering evidence of emotional problems. As stated above, Fisher traces myths of mental problems to Jefferson's 1814 statement. He concludes: "Unless evidence turns up which until now nobody seems to have found it must be regarded as probable that before he left St. Louis there was nothing in Lewis's behavior to justify Jefferson's extreme statements."[22]

Because historians who argue in favor of suicide place considerable weight on reports of Lewis's "derangement" when he arrived at Fort Pickering at Chickasaw Bluffs (present-day Memphis) and on a letter that he wrote to President Madison while there, Fisher in chapter 6 discusses evidence of Lewis's condition on arrival at Fort Pickering. En route from St. Louis to Fort Pickering, Lewis wrote a will at New Madrid. Rather than viewing this as a prudent act of an unmarried man wishing to bequeath his property to his mother, some historians interpret it as evidence of impending suicide. According to Captain Gilbert C. Russell, commander of the fort, Lewis arrived after the eleven-day trip in a state of "mental derangement." But after six days, he was "completely in his senses."[23] Some historians suggest that the unsteady hand and numerous corrections in the letter to Madison the day after his arrival indicate mental instability. However, the same critics fail to see the complete rationality in his letter written from the fort to former army comrade Major Amos Stoddard and in his notation in his account book.

Fisher next devotes a chapter to the trek from Fort Pickering to Grinder's Stand, where Lewis died. Because Russell was unable to obtain a furlough so that he also could go to Washington regarding his own disputed payments, Chickasaw Indian Agent Major James Neelly agreed to escort Lewis as far as Nashville. So on September 28 the governor—armed with a rifle, two pistols, a dirk, and a tomahawk—left the fort accompanied by his free mulatto servant John Pernier, Neelly, and his black slave. Obviously Lewis did not view the route as safe. A pack horse carried two trunks and a portfolio containing sixteen journals, documentation of the disputed claims, and personal effects.

For a hundred miles they followed Indian trails that connected with the Natchez Trace at the Chickasaw agency near present-day Houston, Mississippi. The exhausted Lewis rested there two days. Later Neelly wrote that at the agency he "appeared at times deranged."[24] There is evidence, however, that he was clearly in control of his faculties. No historian doubts that Lewis was ill on arrival at Chickasaw Bluffs or at the agency. Travelers up the Trace often experienced serious illnesses as did many on the Mississippi. Lewis suffered from malaria, which causes intermittent chills, fever, sweating, and at times delirium. From the agency the party rode up the Trace to the Tennessee River supposedly at a rate of fifty miles per day—an unlikely pace over rocky hills and across ravine. Fisher's treatment of the journey includes a history of violent crime on the Trace and introduces a seldom-cited myth that some Indian chiefs left the fort with Lewis. If true, this adds to the intrigue.

While Lewis, Neelly, and the servants slept a day's ride north of the river on October 9, two horses escaped. The next morning Lewis and the two servants rode on while Neelly searched for the horses. On the evening of the tenth when the governor reined into Grinder's Stand some seventy miles southwest of Nashville, he was alone with the servants not far behind. Fisher devotes a chapter to the genealogy and history of the Robert Grinder family (actually "Griner," but spelled "Grinder" in most instances) to show the inaccuracy of the generally accepted accounts of who most likely was present that fateful night.

"James Neelly: Chief Witness," chapter 9, is one of the strongest, if not the strongest, of the book. The opening lines are: "Let it be said at once that James Neelly was not the chief witness, for he was not even on the scene when Lewis died and knew nothing about it except what he was told—unless it is to be assumed that he examined the pistols, the wounds, and the premises. It is not known that he did or that he did not; he never mentioned these matters. But Neelly is the chief witness for those who have argued for suicide."[25] This is because Neelly, who arrived "sometime after" Lewis died, wrote the oft-quoted letter informing Jefferson of the two self-inflicted pistol wounds—a letter based on a report of Mrs. Grinder, who did not actually witness the firing of the shots. Based on a subsequent letter from Captain Russell at Fort Pickering to Jefferson and on other evidence, Fisher concludes that Neelly was a shady character who evidently gained the title of major from militia service and who ended up with Lewis's valuable pistols. Fisher points out that a report of murder would have made Neelly appear incompetent as a guardian. Russell, who clearly had doubts about Neelly's character, implies that he ended up with Lewis's cash, for which no one has accounted, and about which, Fisher says, historians seem to care little. This powerful chapter contains far more data and analysis than can be capsuled here.

After a brief chapter raising questions regarding letters by Captain John Brahman, an infantry officer stationed near Nashville and an acquaintance of Neelly, Fisher devotes a chapter to the noted ornithologist Alexander Wilson. Wilson, who visited the grave of his dear friend Lewis in 1811, interviewed Mrs. Grinder regarding the events surrounding Lewis's death. Then he proceeded down the Trace to Natchez from whence he recorded for a friend a second account by Mrs. Grinder that varied considerably from that of Neelly. "Of all the stories of Lewis's death," concludes Fisher, "Wilson's is the one we have to take most seriously, for the reason that he talked to her and made notes and then wrote it all down."[26] Fisher lists a host of questions regarding the discrepancies between Mrs. Grinder's two stories, questions that raise doubts about her credibility. She told Wilson that as she peered through the cracks in the kitchen cabin, she watched Lewis stagger around the yard after she heard two shots, and she refused to give him water when he begged for a drink. Fisher, the son of an Idaho pioneer woman, finds such behavior unlikely. I agree. Her self-described behavior is totally out of character for one reared on the Tennessee–Carolina border, one of the toughest, bloodiest frontiers in America.

In order to create more doubt on the conclusion of suicide, Fisher reviews another version by Mrs. Grinder, one by a former Grinder slave (Malinda), assorted newspaper accounts, and a collection of local oral traditions. Fisher contends that one can uncover some facts "hidden in the legends and lore, the inventions and embellishments." Neelly and a neighbor named Runion or Runions emerge as suspects out of "the tantalizing realm of wraiths and specters."[27] Fisher's organization of the middle portion of *Suicide or Murder?* is a bit curious. The chapter on Thomas Jefferson is of such significance that one wonders why he tucked it in the middle of his discussion of various versions of the death scene. Many readers may not approve of the manner in which Fisher took Jefferson "off his pedestal and looked at a few of his frailties." (Fisher charges that Jefferson "has been placed by a host of image-makers on a plane above suspicion and criticism.") He humanizes Jefferson by discussing his romantic attentions to married women and some of the errors in fact included in his statements regarding circumstances surrounding the last days of Lewis's life. Jefferson's ready acceptance of the suicide report and his 1814 references to Lewis's inherited "hypoc[h]ondriac affections" carry great weight with proponents of suicide. Jefferson's reactions form the cornerstone of their arguments. Fisher is absolutely correct: "Judged by such standards of evidence, both Neelly's statement and Jefferson's need confirmation from strong sources before they can be accepted as facts."[28] As admirable and marvelous a man as Jefferson was, he was a politician as well as a statesman, and a declaration of suicide is a neater, cleaner process, especially considering the place of Lewis's death. Besides, as a former president, Jefferson had no authority to order an investigation.

Vardis Fisher has fun with his introductory paragraph in chapter 18, "Was There a Coroner's Jury?" He answers in his first sentence: "It is easy to believe that there was not." Fisher refers of course to the primitive, isolated spot where Lewis died. Then, citing a host of oral traditions, he concludes that there probably was such a jury, but its members were afraid to render a verdict for murder. Biographer Richard Dillon was also unable to find hard evidence of a coroner's jury, but in conversations with me, Dillon stated that he suspects one had met.

Chapter 19 relates to the decade of research by Tennessee attorney James D. Park before his death in 1897. Park, relying heavily on oral tradition, argued passionately for murder as the cause of Lewis's death. Neelly and Grinder were the most likely suspects. Jefferson's strong statement also troubled him, not that he viewed Jefferson as implicated. Chapters on writers Vernon S. Pease and William J. Webster follow; they favor the argument for murder.

In the penultimate chapter, Fisher studiously analyzes an oft-cited 1956 article by Natchez Trace Parkway historian Dr. Dawson A. Phelps, who views Lewis's suicide with as much certainty as one does the law of gravity.[29] I have followed Phelps's steps in numerous archives and have great respect for most of his work on the Trace. Unfortunately, he allowed his emotions to taint this article. Like so many who argue for suicide, he begins with that premise and searches for supportive evidence. In particular, he makes many unfounded statements about Lewis's career in St. Louis, and he accepts as gospel the words of Neelly and Russell. From my view, Phelps had not one, but two axes to grind. The first was his obsession with the safety of the Trace by 1809; the second was his anti-Turnerian bias. The latter attitude was grounded in his close professional relationship with native Mississippian William B. Hamilton, longtime professor at Duke University and preeminent historian of the Mississippi Territory, whose work is laced with negative comments about Frederick Jackson Turner's "Frontier Thesis."

"Suicide or Murder?" is the final chapter. After reviewing the dozens of questions that he raises, Fisher admits that "it must be said in all fairness to the evidence that we still don't know how he died."[30] Almost as an afterthought, Fisher adds in a footnote that "Mrs. Grace Lewis Miller...may know of evidence that has not been presented here."[31] She did. No relation to Lewis, Mrs. Miller devoted forty years to quietly amassing an impressive collection of Lewis documents, particularly those dealing with his career in St. Louis. It is unfortunate that historians advocating suicide as the cause of Lewis's death did not use her collection, which is now in the Jefferson National Expansion Memorial Archives administered by the National Park Service in St. Louis.

Despite the depth of Fisher's research and the intriguing nature of the book, many historians continue to view Dawson Phelps's piece as the authoritative statement. Indeed, he did not equivocate. His concluding sentence reads: "In the absence of direct and pertinent contemporary evidence to the contrary, of which not a scintilla exists, the verdict of suicide must stand."[32]

One wonders why *Suicide or Murder?* has not been taken more seriously by historians of the American West. Anyone who studies the book carefully and who delves into the Vardis Fisher Papers at Yale University must admit that he was a meticulous, diligent researcher—a man of great integrity and insatiable curiosity. So why is his stock no higher? First of all, he made his mark as a novelist, not as a historian; his doctorate from the University of Chicago was in literature. Perhaps a better explanation relates to his alienation of Julian P. Boyd and Donald D. Jackson—giants in the historical profession. It is easy to understand how he offended Boyd more than he did Jackson.

The staid and proper Boyd, a Princeton historian who for years edited the *Papers of Thomas Jefferson,* took offense at the manner in which Fisher quoted him. Although he did not state so in his correspondence, Boyd probably was antagonized by Fisher's criticism of Jefferson. Even before publication of the book, their exchange of correspondence pertaining to Fisher's efforts to uncover Jefferson memoranda regarding Lewis's servant, Pernier, was not exactly cordial. It became quite heated after Boyd fired off a blistering letter on April 26, 1963, in which he questioned Fisher's integrity: "Now, looking at the note appended to your Chapter 5 in which I am unwarrantably associated with your extraordinary analysis of evidence, I begin to wonder about something even more important than civility—about honor."[33]

Fisher immediately requested that James T. Babb, librarian in charge of special collections at Yale, return to Fisher the correspondence with Boyd. After satisfying himself that he had not misrepresented Boyd, Fisher defended his statements. Then he unloaded: "What I suspect, my dear Sir, is that you have an idolatrous attitude toward Jefferson, that my book disturbed; or that you liked to feel that Jefferson had settled the matter and that nobody less than a Jefferson scholar had a right to raise it; or that you feel you have right of preemption in the Jefferson domain and resent intrusions."[34]

More difficult to understand are the comments of Donald D. Jackson published long after Fisher's death in 1968. Their exchange of numerous letters regarding research for *Suicide or Murder?* and the completed manuscript had a warm, friendly—even chummy—tone. On August 3, 1960, after reading Fisher's manuscript twice, Jackson wrote him a critique in excess of seven single-spaced pages. "First," Jackson assured Fisher, "I am fascinated by the thoroughness of your research and the expertness with which you have ferreted out material where I have supposed none existed." Toward the end he wrote: "You have convinced me that Neelly probably was a dishonest man and that Mrs. Grinder was a real nut." Then he added that "I am positive that you've got a good book here." His last sentence read: "But I think you owe it to our mutual friend, Meriwether Lewis, to see this thing through."[35]

To be sure, Jackson had a host of criticisms and suggestions, which stand as a tribute to his scholarly perception. At the top of his list was a lecture on mental illness and suicide. He wrote in part, "Certainly nobody condones suicide, but it is possible to believe that an admirable, courageous man can commit it under certain conditions.... For if Lewis did kill himself, how are you and your readers going to salvage any respect for the man?"[36] But his published criticism was harsh.

Jackson, in his 1978 edition of *The Letters of the Lewis and Clark Expedition,* describes Fisher's book as "verbose and inexact" and accuses him of approaching "the subject not in the manner of a historian but like a detective following a very cold trail."[37] Again in his 1987 anthology, *Among the Sleeping Giants,* Jackson takes Fisher to task for writing as a "storyteller" rather than as a historian. His lists of criticisms include Fisher's "manipulation of evidence," "reliance on oral tradition," and "emphasis on negative evidence." Jackson repeats his "Holmesian detective" imagery.[38] One can imagine the tone of his informal, private comments.

No historian of Jackson's generation even approached his prominence in the eyes of scholars of Lewis and Clark—thus his denigration of Fisher's work and praise of the Phelps article undoubtedly explain why so many historians of the American West place little credibility in Fisher's book. Indeed, a surprising number of historians will not even consider the possibility of murder, but numerous colleagues who are not specialists in Lewis and Clark find the topic intriguing. As a scholar who has studied the Natchez Trace for a decade, I find murder not only a possibility, but a probability. Lewis's most notable biographer, Richard Dillon, agrees.[39]

James E. Starrs, professor of law and professor of forensic sciences at George Washington University, is convinced that a forensic examination of the remains of Meriwether Lewis can answer the question posed in the title of Fisher's book, *Suicide or Murder?* As a first step toward realization of his goal, Starrs petitioned authorities in Lewis County, Tennessee, where Lewis is buried, to empanel a coroner's jury and hold a formal coroner's inquest to determine whether Lewis was murdered or killed himself. A jury was empaneled and an inquest was held on June 3 and 4, 1996, in Hohenwald, Tennessee. Fourteen witnesses testified over a two-day period. In addition to the testimony of expert witnesses, descendants of Meriwether Lewis testified that they favored the forensic examination of the remains.[40]

The team assembled by Starrs included experts in the fields of history, geology, document examination, forensic psychology, forensic pathology, forensic anthropology, firearms, and wound ballistics. It is unfortunate that the inquest could not have been dedicated to Vardis Fisher. He would have reveled in the testimony of many of the witnesses and, with his curiosity, he would have listened intently to and enjoyed all of it. He would have been most excited, however, over the testimony of the documents experts and the psychologist.

Two nationally known documents examiners independently analyzed identical samples of documents attributed to Lewis and Gilbert C. Russell, the commander at Fort Pickering. Both experts found the handwriting of Lewis in the famous letter to Madison written at Fort Pickering consistent with earlier samples. Both viewed it as a rough draft full of corrections, cross outs, additions, and deletions that should not be interpreted as anything but what they are. Documents examiner Gerald B. Richards testified regarding the Lewis letter: "As far as the writing goes, the style of the writing, the relative size, the speed, the quality of what we call the rhythm of the writing, it's all totally consistent with the other two samples."[41] In sum, it was not degraded or deteriorated. Fisher had suspected this. The two witnesses added, however, that document examiners cannot, as a rule, detect mental disease from handwriting.

This testimony would have certainly pleased Fisher, but he would have become absolutely ecstatic over that pertaining to the much-discussed statement of November 26, 1811, by Gilbert Russell. When Fisher received from Donald Jackson a transcription of this document, it fell upon him like a "bombshell." He immediately wrote Jackson: "I read half the first page and was so astonished that I went back and reread, knowing that if this is authentic it overthrows my thesis that Lewis did not kill himself. Somewhere early in the second page I was strongly feeling that Gilbert Russell never wrote this, and by the time I reached the end of it, I was convinced that he did not."[42] In a 1987 essay Jackson made fun of Fisher's reaction: "Instead of accepting the Russell document, Fisher fought it.... He was behaving not so much as a historian but as a special investigator who had put himself on a case and was going after the perpetrator."[43]

Perhaps—just perhaps. One day Fisher may be vindicated. Both experts are reasonably certain that a third party wrote that document; neither Russell nor Jonathan Williams wrote or signed it. Of course, there is a possibility that the extant copy was made by a clerk, and that the opinions therein are those of Russell. The testimony at Hohenwald, nevertheless, casts doubt upon the authenticity of the Russell statement on which Jackson and others place so much weight.

After listening carefully to two days of testimony, the jury, made up of educated business and professional men and women, recommended that the Tennessee courts order the exhumation of the Lewis remains for forensic examination. But Lewis is buried on ground administered by the National Park Service, which is not obligated to honor the court order. On June 18, 1997, Professor Starrs filed an application for a federal permit under the archaeological resources protection act to excavate/exhume the remains of Meriwether Lewis. One hundred and fifty-one of his descendants have signed statements of support for the exhumation. Maybe a Park Service decision will have been announced by the time this anthology is published. If it is negative, Starrs most likely will pursue the request through the courts. If he prevails and if skeletal remains exist as predicted, Fisher's question may well be answered. If the evidence precludes suicide, interest in the oral traditions will intensify. And then, Vardis Fisher will have had the last laugh.

Notes

1. Vardis Fisher, *Suicide or Murder? The Strange Death of Governor Meriwether Lewis* (1962; reprint, Athens: Ohio University Press, 1993); Stephen E. Ambrose, *Undaunted Courage: Meriwether Lewis, Thomas Jefferson, and the Opening of the American West* (New York: Simon and Schuster, 1996); Ken Burns, *Lewis & Clark: The Journey of the Corps of Discovery* (Alexandria, VA: Public Broadcasting Service, 1997).
2. Vardis Fisher, *Tale of Valor: A Novel of the Lewis and Clark Expedition* (Garden City, NY: Doubleday, 1958).
3. The author gratefully acknowledges the assistance of Angelic Rodgers-Webb, doctoral candidate at the University of Southern Mississippi Department of English, in the compilation of bibliography pertaining to *Tale of Valor.*
4. Joseph M. Flora, *Vardis Fisher* (New York: Twayne Publishers, 1965), 122–23; Ronald W. Taber, "Vardis Fisher: New Directions for the Historical Novel," *Western American Literature* 1 (Winter 1967), 291–92.
5. The most comprehensive analysis of the expedition's relationship with the American Indians is in James P. Ronda, *Lewis and Clark among the Indians* (Lincoln: University of Nebraska Press, 1984).
6. Fisher, *Tale of Valor,* 40.
7. Ibid., 370.
8. Ibid., 410.
9. Ibid., 410–11.
10. For a discussion of claims that William Clark fathered a son by a Nez Perce woman, see Ronda, *Lewis and Clark among the Indians,* 233. Fisher undoubtedly was aware of this widely known claim, but he chose not to deal with it in the novel.
11. Taber, "Vardis Fisher," 294–95. For a full discussion of this topic, see Donna J. Kessler, *The Making of Sacagawea: A Euro-American Legend* (Tuscaloosa: University of Alabama Press, 1996).
12. Fisher, *Tale of Valor,* 266.
13. Ibid., 332.
14. Taber, "Vardis Fisher," 290. Here Taber quotes Vardis Fisher, *Thomas Wolfe As I Knew Him, and Other Essays* (Denver: Alan Swallow, 1963), 96.
15. Lewis Nordyke, "Pioneers of American Empire," review of *Tale of Valor,* by Vardis Fisher, *New York Times Book Review,* June 29, 1958, 20–21.

16. Ambrose, *Undaunted Courage*, 385–86; Fisher, *Tale of Valor*, 434–37.
17. Wayne Chatterton, *Vardis Fisher: The Frontier and Regional Works* (Boise: Boise State College, 1972), 42.
18. Fisher, *Suicide or Murder?*, 28; for the complete text of Jefferson's biographical memoir of Lewis, see Jefferson to Paul Allen, in Donald D. Jackson, ed., *Letters of the Lewis and Clark Expedition with Related Documents, 1784–1854*, 2d ed., with additional documents and notes (Urbana: University of Illinois Press, 1978) 2: 586–93.
19. Fisher, *Suicide or Murder?*, 47.
20. Richard Dillon, *Meriwether Lewis: A Biography* (New York: Coward-McCann, 1965), 300, 307.
21. Fisher, *Suicide or Murder?*, 56.
22. Ibid., 76.
23. Statement of Gilbert C. Russell, November 26, 1811, in Jackson, *Letters*, 2: 573.
24. Neelly to Jefferson, Nashville, October 18, 1809, in Jackson, *Letters*, 2: 467–68.
25. Fisher, *Suicide or Murder?*, 127.
26. Ibid., 151.
27. Ibid., 188, 195.
28. Ibid., 178, 171, 182.
29. Dawson A. Phelps, "The Tragic Death of Meriwether Lewis," *The William and Mary Quarterly* 13 (July 1956): 305–18.
30. Fisher, *Suicide or Murder?*, 249.
31. Ibid., 249n.
32. Phelps, "The Tragic Death," 317.
33. Julian P. Boyd to Fisher, Princeton, April 26, 1963, Vardis Fisher Papers, Beinecke Library, Yale University.
34. Fisher to James T. Babb, Hagerman, Idaho, May 1, 1963; Fisher to Boyd, Hagerman, Idaho, May 14, 1963. Vardis Fisher Papers, Beinecke Library, Yale University.
35. Donald D. Jackson to Fisher, Urbana, Illinois, August 3, 1960. Vardis Fisher Papers, Beinecke Library, Yale University.
36. Ibid.
37. Jackson, *Letters*, 2: 748.
38. Donald D. Jackson, *Among the Sleeping Giants: Occasional Pieces on Lewis and Clark* (Urbana: University of Illinois Press, 1987), 70.
39. Dillon, *Meriwether Lewis*, 344. See also John D. W. Guice, "A Fatal Rendezvous: The Mysterious Death of Meriwether Lewis," *The Journal of Mississippi History* 57 (Summer 1995): 121–38.
40. Coroner's Inquest: Death of Meriwether Lewis (transcript of the proceedings taken on June 3 and 4, 1996, before the coroner and jury of Lewis County at Hohenwald, Tennessee).
41. Testimony of Gerald B. Richards, Coroner's Inquest, 216.
42. Fisher to Jackson, Hagerman, Idaho, July 9, 1960.
43. Jackson, *Among the Sleeping Giants*, 69.

Bibliography

Ambrose, Stephen E. *Undaunted Courage: Meriwether Lewis, Thomas Jefferson, and the Opening of the American West*. New York: Simon and Schuster, 1996.

Burns, Ken. *Lewis & Clark: The Journey of the Corps of Discovery*. Alexandria, VA: Public Broadcasting Service, 1997.

Chatterton, Wayne. *Vardis Fisher: The Frontier and Regional Works*. Boise: Boise State College, 1972.

Coroner's Inquest: Death of Meriwether Lewis. Transcript of the proceedings taken on June 3 and 4, 1996, before the coroner and jury of Lewis County at Hohenwald, Tennessee.

Dillon, Richard. *Meriwether Lewis: A Biography*. New York: Coward-McCann, 1965.

Fisher, Vardis. *Suicide or Murder? The Strange Death of Governor Meriwether Lewis*. 1962. Reprint. Athens: Ohio University Press, 1993.

———. *Tale of Valor: A Novel of the Lewis and Clark Expedition*. Garden City, NY: Doubleday, 1958.

———. Papers. Beinecke Library, Yale University.

———. *Thomas Wolfe As I Knew Him, and Other Essays*. Denver: Alan Swallow, 1963.

Flora, Joseph M. *Vardis Fisher*. New York: Twayne Publishers, 1965.

Guice, John D.W. "A Fatal Rendezvous: The Mysterious Death of Meriwether Lewis." *The Journal of Mississippi History* 57 (Summer 1995): 121–38.

Jackson, Donald D. *Among the Sleeping Giants: Occasional Pieces on Lewis and Clark*. Urbana: University of Illinois Press, 1987.

———. ed. *Letters of the Lewis and Clark Expedition with Related Documents, 1784–1854*. Vol. 2. 2d. ed., with additional documents and notes. Urbana: University of Illinois Press, 1978.

Kessler, Donna J. *The Making of Sacagawea: A Euro-American Legend*. Tuscaloosa: University of Alabama Press, 1996.

Nordyke, Lewis. "Pioneers of American Empire." Review of *Tale of Valor*, by Vardis Fisher. *New York Times Book Review*, June 29, 1958: 20–21.

Phelps, Dawson A. "The Tragic Death of Meriwether Lewis." *The William and Mary Quarterly* 13 (July 1956): 305–18.

Ronda, James P. *Lewis and Clark among the Indians*. Lincoln: University of Nebraska Press, 1984.

Taber, Ronald W. "Vardis Fisher: New Directions for the Historical Novel." *Western American Literature* 1 (Winter 1967): 285–96.

10 An Anthropological View of the *Testament of Man*

Marilyn Trent Grunkemeyer

On cards he took tens of thousands of notes, that eventually would add to hundreds of thousands of words. The note-taking was an irksome chore that he did not like, especially when, as so often happened, he had to fill two or three hundred cards from just one book. He knew that he was taking down a great deal more than he would ever use, but the books had to be returned to libraries, far away; and to save time and postage he copied everything he thought it likely he might need.

—Vardis Fisher, *Orphans in Gethsemane*

Vardis Fisher's *Testament of Man* is a massive exposition of one of the greatest perduring male fantasies of all time, a fantasy that the past was a universal matriarchy that was overcome by universal patriarchy. It can be discerned in the Pentateuch and is woven all through our literary heritage. A staple in fairy tales, it also runs through the Tarzan stories of Edgar Rice Burroughs, the whole "tough-guy detective" collection, "spy" novels, and much contemporary science fiction. Eventually, the fantasy was racially parodied in John Landis's 1987 film *Amazon Women on the Moon*. In Fisher's *Testament,* the aesthetic interpretation of a deep male longing reaches mythic proportions.

Why has Fisher's epic exposition of this mythic fantasy in the *Testament* not achieved commercial success? Why have the books in this series not remained perennially on the best-seller lists? Why have his *Testament* novels not been made into films, plays, musicals of the plays, films of those musicals, and, ultimately, popular television series? I think there are at least two answers. They go hand in hand, and they both emerge from the personality of Vardis Fisher himself.

The vast majority of rational men know in their heart of hearts that the whole fantasy is just that. No matter how delicious it is, it is neither factual, historical, nor in any other sense true. If it were, they would not derive so much pleasure from fantasizing about it. Vardis Fisher, however, really believed it. This caused him to make a paradigm shift that rendered his incarnation of the fantasy and its consequences less than perfectly successful.

It may be that the millennial, rather than the centennial, celebration of Fisher and his work puts him before the public again. This is not because he was ahead of his time. On the contrary, he was exquisitely of his time—and our time. We have not yet achieved sufficient temporal detachment from Fisher or from ourselves to have an objective view of his work. I visualize future cultural anthropologists studying his work as an authoritative source for understanding us and our times. It is this possibility that has made my task of reading his *Testament* so fascinating.

I have placed some parameters on my conclusions. It would be both uninteresting and unfair to focus exclusively on the specifics of Fisher's science. Much has been learned since he finished this work in 1960. Much of what was believed in Fisher's day about early hominids has since been overturned and will, no doubt, be overturned again and again as more data become available. Except for a few examples that seem to me preposterous by any standards, his specifics are not the most salient elements of his argument in any case. It is his fundamental axioms that are relevant and provocative.

In this essay, I analyze the *Testament* from the generalities of the anthropological discipline rather than from the perspective of any particular scholar or group of scholars. I prepared for this writing by reading all twelve of the books in the *Testament*. There is really no way to eliminate any of them and have a full view of the opus. None by itself is sufficiently illustrative of Fisher's vision; and, since the work as a whole makes frequent temporal shifts, there is no valid way to take core samples by reading a little of this or a little of that.

I found *Orphans in Gethsemane* (1960), the last of the series, one of the most difficult reading experiences of my life. It is not intellectually difficult, but it is spiritually exhausting and emotionally toxic. It is an incessant drumbeat of unmitigated suffering. For me, it was the literary equivalent of being beaten steadily with a stick. It took weeks rather than days to complete. I had to rest from it frequently to avoid a serious depression. My problem could have been avoided by not taking the work as seriously as I did; but it is a serious book, to be taken seriously. A serious reading of *Orphans* can be a valuable experience—one I would heartily recommend—with the warning that one should take one's time.

As I was making my way through *Orphans,* I was berating myself for not having read it first. It explains so well why Fisher took the philosophical and literary approaches that he did in the previous eleven volumes. However, I have now concluded that reading it last is best. Following sequential order allows one to read the *Testament* series with a more open mind, and, I hope, an open heart.

A review of the sequence of the works may be useful here. Fisher begins with a volume about ape-humans in *Darkness and the Deep* (1943). In *The Golden Rooms* (1944), he presents his view of the mastery of fire and a clash between what is probably Neanderthal and Cro-Magnon. *Intima-*

tions of Eve (1946), about a supposed matriarchy, is followed by *Adam and the Serpent* (1947), in which the beginnings of patriarchy are sketched. Then there is a shift of setting and emphasis in *The Divine Passion* (1948), which seems to take place in the context of henotheistic pre-Judaism. *The Valley of Vision* (1951) casts Solomon as a religiously syncretic hero; *The Island of the Innocent* (1952) takes place during the Maccabean revolt; *Jesus Came Again* (1956) explains Fisher's view of the origins of Christianity. *A Goat for Azazel* (1956) studies the experience of a religious seeker in his examination of the history of religions during the Jewish-Christian controversies. In *Peace Like a River* (1957), the characters are surrounded by the Christian desert ascetics; *My Holy Satan* (1958) is set during the Inquisition. The finale is *Orphans in Gethsemane,* a vast autobiographical work that tells how Fisher came to write all the other books and proclaims his arguments explicitly.

Prime Directives of Anthropology

Although Fisher wanted to write an evolutionary epic, he is specifically not an evolutionist. He is instead a believer in and an advocate for progress—the notion that a species improves and becomes "better." This places him in a theoretical position diametrically opposed to anthropology. To discuss this opposition, I will be using a model of what I have designated as the "prime directives" of anthropology. They are: evolution, as opposed to progress; holism, as opposed to dualism; and cultural relativism, as opposed to ethnocentricity.[1]

Evolution as Opposed to Progress

For anthropology, evolution means change—just change, morally neutral change, nonteleological change. In other words, for us, things change continually but apparently are not headed toward any definite goal; and that may, or may not, be ultimately beneficial. Fisher, on the contrary, personifies nature as a goal-directed female power: "Nature perceived at last that neither security for life nor perfection of machine-like form was the goal she sought."[2] Similarly, he portrays whole species as striving to become other than what they are: "They had no minds, no power of thought, but in them, nevertheless, as part of their heritage, as a part of their inscrutable will to seek and grow, was an urge to leave the ocean.... From the deep these sluggards, both great and small, moved toward a home on land, and their efforts wrote one of the mightiest chapters in the history of persistence and courage" (*Darkness* 33).

Fisher is clearly a Lamarckian rather than a Darwinian. Jean Baptiste Lamarck (1744–1829) believed that acquired characteristics could be biologically inherited. Fisher proclaimed, "This is the law of life: to feel the need of an organ or a faculty is to evolve it if the urge is constant and prolonged" (*Darkness* 20). Lamarckianism was rejected by the scientific collective very early. It is anathema to anthropology and to all contemporary evolutionary theory.

Fisher is not altogether consistent on the means by which progress occurs. He suggests in the early novels that progress comes about through Larmarckian striving and is blocked by contentment and security:

> As long as he was driven to seek speed and size and courage, his [the shark-killer's] evolution was steady and exciting; but when he became king of all the beasts, he was content to feed his hunger and to accept the world as his special province. Having no need of faculties, which he did not possess, he felt no urge to acquire them, and so spent his time in idleness and gluttony. At the height of his glory, his own unparalleled and invincible position sentenced him to death. (*Darkness* 29)

He also suggests that security is the enemy of progress: "The past of this planet is, in considerable part, an enormous graveyard of those creatures that chose physical safety instead of intelligence" (*Darkness* 41); "to urge intelligence to rapid growth, every creature in the sea and upon land and in the air was given its enemies, and in every living heart fear became the vigilant and vivid lighthouse of the mind" (*Darkness* 45). In other passages, Fisher suggests that progress emerges from frustration: "It was restless and frustrated men like Wuh and women like Who-ah who added a little, generation by generation, to the heritage of their race" (*Darkness* 70).

In still different statements, Fisher seems to propose more positive bases for progress: "In the centuries preceding this time, it had been chiefly mother love that had impelled one of the beasts to become a man" (*Darkness* 102). In later works, it is specifically security, not the lack of it, that allows the possibility of progress: "The security which fire had given them had been a powerful stimulus to the development of their minds and interests."[3] Indeed, Fisher sometimes sees stability itself as preventing progress. In *The Valley of Vision*, one of Solomon's women argues with the prophet who proclaims that Yah's commandments never change. She says, "But without change there can be no progress, can there?"[4] Fisher explains in the appendix to *The Island of the Innocent*:

> Readers of this novel who would understand its implications may wish to dwell on Frazer's statement that the "publication of

> the Deuteronomic Code in written form (3rd cen. B.C.) marked an era in the history not only of the Jewish people but of humanity. It was the first step toward the canonization of Scripture and thereby to the substitution of the written for the spoken word as the supreme and infallible rule of conduct. The accomplishment of the process...laid thought under shackles from which in the Western world it has never since wholly succeeded in emancipating itself."[5]

Fisher portrays a biological progress beginning with ape-creatures having grasping feet (*Darkness* 84) and acute senses (*Golden* 101). They have little intellect: "Harg was gazing at a grove of trees. He was not thinking of the trees. For him they were little more than things that stood upright and tried to walk away when the wind was on them and changed color in time of cold" (*Golden* 3). Even more significant to his general notions of progress, the characters of *Darkness and the Deep* are given no morals: "[T]hey had no notions of right and wrong. Selfish, greedy, sly, covetous, and vain, their chief task was to survive, to outwit their enemies, to find an abundance of good things to eat, and to spend their sexual hunger in lustful mating" (58).

In *The Golden Rooms,* Fisher's Cro-Magnon characters have achieved hands and a handsome appearance: "In their faces as well as their bodies they were extraordinarily handsome" and "they had experimented a little with agriculture" (169).

In *Intimations of Eve,* his characters are capable of individuality: "[H]e tried to explain to them that when the Moon woman became angry it was not because of the doing of all people but only of one of them. This notion was so revolutionary that the women were unable to grasp it."[6] The males engage in artistic expression. The women suffer no "male interference," but the men strive "to enrich the leaner destiny of hunting by turning to simple forms of art" (25).

Fisher proposes that the people of this era had little capacity for thought: "Harg had thought about fire. Perhaps it would be more exact to say that he felt about fire rather than thought about it, inasmuch as his attitude toward it was chiefly emotional, and he had so few concepts with which to think" (*Golden* 40). In *Intimations of Eve* Fisher explains: "The phenomenon of physical death had forced their ancestors to think; but after a few generations the mind became the abject and impotent vassal of the emotions. The only function of the mind now was to formulate in concepts...the conclusions which fear drove the emotions to accept" (24).

Fisher is critically concerned with emotional progress. In *Darkness* he proposes: "There was the need to be and to grow, and this need would devour or destroy the weak and the ill-adapted; for in this time of coming to more complex birth, there was no pity, no mercy, no charity, all these being, upon their appearance later, either a distortion of the cosmic harmonies or a higher manifestation of their inscrutable will" (12). He concludes: "They were all of them vain, selfish, and strutting egoists whose greatest delight was in being cock of the walk" (108).

In *The Golden Rooms,* Fisher proposes the near absence of affection: "Except for the affection between mothers and their smallest children, their family life was little more than a loose association of persons who lived together for their own protection" (36). "His [Gode's] emotion was not of affectionate interest, because in men of this time there was no love" (182). Gode does display affection and pity toward a pet wolf (215, 236).

In Fisher's epic of progress, there is a puzzling pause for an expression of nostalgia: "Long ago...they had been afraid only of things they could see.... There was no superstition in them, no dependence on magic, no notions of good and evil...and no fixed and harrowing anxiety in regard to the present or the future. In their own simple way they had all been scientists in a world where all things could be explained by one with enough knowledge. In that time, and only in that time, have human beings been free" (*Eve* 22). His sudden nostalgia is puzzling because in his earlier books that describe this period, there is nothing free or positive about it. Kindliness, such as Fisher describes it, appears with early Judaism: "Kindliness in these persons developed only as their ruthless struggle abated, relaxing the will to survive and its accretions of fear."[7] In *A Goat for Azazel,* after the establishment of Christianity, Damon, the seeker, ponders: "The Christians did some of these things better than the other cults did them! Did they have something that the worshipers of Dionysus and Mithra did not have? Yes, there was something: he thought the word for it was tenderness."[8]

The ultimate key to emotional progress is the achieving of emotional adulthood—as Fisher defines it through his autobiographical protagonist, Vridar Hunter: "But mankind, I think, has enough courage and brains to build a better order, once it becomes adult."[9] At the end of the novel, Vridar concludes: "He would never have a father or Father, or even a father-image any more, or be childish enough to apply the masculine pronouns to the universe or any aspect of it. He would be an adult, or if not an adult, he would struggle to free himself from the abominable suffocating strangling unclean association of parents, as long as he lived" (968).

Emotional progress is critical to Fisher's scheme because, for Fisher, morality and ethics consist of having correct emotions and not of the engagement in, or avoidance of, any particular actions. He prizes, along with tenderness, compassion and tolerance. Vridar "began to understand, deep in him, that the capacity to view objectively was the greatest of the human virtues. Next to that and inseparable from it was compassion" (738). Much earlier in his life a colleague had told him:

> "Vridar, you've got a bad medieval odor about you. Before you accept Christian dogmas, why don't you read the great scholars and find out where the dogmas came from?...Now what is sin? Another name for prejudice. Is murder a sin? Millions in Europe are murdering one another right now—and they're all Christians. Is masturbation a sin? Only for those who think that all pleasure must be evil. Is copulation a sin? Only for those who want more of it and don't know how to get it. Prejudice, damn it, prejudice!" (220–21)

All of these virtues are passive emotional states that do not necessarily lead to any actions. As to sin, Fisher sees it as residing not in wrongdoing leading to guilt but in guilt itself. With respect to Betty, a prostitute, Vridar ruminates to himself: "But always he went into her room and sat for a while and talked; and he thought it very strange that he should like this girl, that he should respect her even, for she was a whore after all. He liked her because there was no shame in her, no sense of guilt, no pious pretense: in so many ways she was what he was not and despaired of ever being" (427).

Much of Fisher's picture of progress is focused on religion. For Fisher, religious progress means beginning with no religion and ending the same way by overcoming religion with science and adulthood: "They had no religion, but were awed by many things, and toward some things, like their home fire or the warmth-giving sun, their attitude was touched by reverence (*Golden* 175). For Fisher, religion, as such, begins with male reverence (*Golden* 200) and male dread: "Gode was weeping.... He was making the dry terrible sound of a man choked by terrors, of a man driven by unutterable dread to abase himself in the strangled and heartbroken humility of what in its own way was the first human prayer" (*Golden* 324).

Fisher's thoroughly negative view of religion is expressed often in his books. There religion is characterized by misogyny, fanaticism, persecution, doctrinal squabbles, and murder. In *Peace Like a River,* his male character Hareb berates the women around him: "'Where in all the desert' he said, 'is there more wickedness than here?'...'The gateway to hell,'... 'You women should all be filled with shame.'"[10] Hareb's views lead to ascetical extremism, which Fisher makes vivid through his character Agios, who "had shaved his head. He then had dug a deep hole in the sand, so deep that when he stood in it only his head was above the surface.... Agios descended into the pit and put his arms down at his side and said to Mark: 'Bury me'" (*Peace* 320). In *The Golden Rooms,* in a poignant prelude to later burnings of heretics in order to save their souls, Gode kills Agger in order to save her from the indwelling ghost: "Before the woman could realize where she was or what he intended, he was raining boulders and earth upon her. She screamed and fought, but he was only dimly aware of her cries or her struggle. Using his powerful hands as shovels he poured the earth down.... He did not pause until the grave was level with the surrounding surface" (320). Fisher describes the violence of the Inquisition itself: "In this form of torture an iron screw was turned in upon the thumb. The men were turning the screws.... At the next partial turn of the screws agony convulsed the whole upper part of his [Richard's] body and was like an imprisoned violence in his skull trying to burst the bone asunder."[11]

Although he knows he hates it, Fisher is not consistent in his opinion of various aspects of religion. He is critical of religion when there is a lack of it and when there is an abundance of it. For instance, in a description of his youth, he notes: "In Sunday School he [Vridar] found that the service was almost barren, with little ritual and no mysticism" (*Orphans* 214). Later in the same work, he describes rituals as empty:

> Vridar wondered why human vanity indulged in what seemed to him to be silly rigmaroles of conduct—of the solemn and outlandish dignity of apes, some as grand goblins and kleagles, or as gaudy regents of Church and State as professor, deans, and a president, robed in medieval black and looking as grave and unimportant as owls. It was, he knew, the heritage of primitive customs, all darkly related to prayer wheels and euchologies, exorcisms and cabals and golden calves. (566)

For Fisher, religion itself, as an anthropologist would describe it, is a violation of progress—a backward move. It is childish (*Orphans* 792), ignorant (852), bitter (966), and altogether a nightmare (848). In his personal notion of utopia, dogmas of any kind would not exist. In spite of his negative view, Fisher writes eloquently about faith; but it is not clear that he is aware that he has done so. It is as if his meaning is greater than the sum of his words. The passages concern a female character named Basket:

> She never presumed on prophecy, and she left all curatives and magic to those who professed to understand them. With a

> disposition as unwrinkled as her face, she was content to sit back from the violence of egoistic striving, doing the humble things which she had learned to do well and leaving other matters to those who emptied their hearts while spurning the uses of their hands.
>
> ...she was not constantly the prey of anxieties and fears.... Basket had the kind of homely intelligence that refused to burden supernatural beings with all the shortcomings of her people.[12]

Although an anthropologist would argue that progress does not reflect the data accurately, the notion of progress is one of the grand unexamined presuppositions of our culture. Almost any political campaign assumes the existence and necessity of progress and argues that the particular individual candidate under discussion is the best qualified to bring it about.

Furthermore, Fisher's progressivism brings a poignancy to his novels that would not be there were they to have been written from an evolutionary perspective. A great sadness pervades his narratives—a sadness resulting from his dualistic worldview, rather than from the holism espoused by anthropology.

Holism as Opposed to Dualism

Anthropology assumes that all elements in an ecological setting are interrelated and insists that any subject be studied in its entire context.[13] Fisher, as a dualist, sets up oppositions throughout his entire *Testament of Man* and articulates them insistently.

Fisher sets in opposition mind and body (*Orphans* 660), soul and body (*Adam* 14), flesh and spirit (*Eve* 19), rage and fear (*Passion* 235), allegory and literalism (*Eve* 215), meat-eating and vegetarianism (*Passion* 281), words and actions (*Adam* 126; *Passion* 290), real prayer and empty prayer (*Passion* 43), ritual bread and flesh (*Passion* 296), men and women (*Golden* 194; *Eve* 24, 88), right and left (*Passion* 128, 135–36), and Satan and God (*Peace* 255). Many of his dualisms reflect his progressivism: words over actions (*Adam* 194), religion over rules (*Island* 173, 192), science over religion (*Satan* 260, 268; *Orphans* 915), reason over faith (*Island* 257), evolution over God (*Orphans* 661), and, in general, the present over the past and the future over the present (*Island* 257).

A conspicuous dualism also occurs when Fisher writes about language. Repeatedly, he describes his heroes as having thoughts without language: "There were things Gode wanted to say for which he had no words" (*Golden* 182).[14] For the priestess Rainmaker "there was no word for murder in her language" (*Adam* 142). In *Intimations of Eve* Raven tries to explain to the grandmother that "some persons were singled out for special punishment, but he had no words to express a notion of sin" (276). In *Adam and the Serpent,* Dove has the same problem talking with Owl: "[H]e was moved by the hunger in him close to the concept of a god. There was no such word in his language, nor any such recognition among his people, but he felt an overwhelming need of it" (15). Fisher places the mind of concepts over, above, and before the physical action of language. We have no reason for assuming such a dualism reflects reality. It is not so much that Fisher is mistaken (although he probably is) but that he operates from an unexamined assumption.

Because anthropologists are not permitted to indulge in dualisms or notions of progress, they do not disparage any other animal. Fisher does. While reading about Nazi atrocities at Belsen, Vridar reflects: "It was there in the faces.... These were not human beings, not one of them; they were degenerate ape-men and ape-women. The story was in all their brutal stupid faces; and in all the other hideous incredible photographs of the dying and the dead" (*Orphans* 971). Fisher has used a common and effective literary device: he has labeled particularly heinous human actions as brutal, nonhuman. From an anthropological view, however, the perpetrators of the Holocaust were only too human. The brutes do not behave so badly.

Dualisms are to be discerned in every culture; they are an especially prominent feature of our own. Our thoroughly ingrained mind/body dualism enables us to practice (and certainly to legalize) divorce, secret adoption, separation of siblings, or surrogate parenting. And these examples do not begin to describe our obsession with achievement through mental effort—"mind over matter."

DATA GATHERING

For anthropologists, holism also contrasts with a common form of data gathering. Forms of observation, such as those associated with double-blind medical studies, attempt to isolate variables under scrutiny by controlling for any possible influences in their ecologies. Fisher's propensity toward isolation is both evident in, and formative for, his epistemology. Because holism is lacking, Fisher's epistemologies are shallow. His methods for collecting biological data reflect this and are a source for many of his mistakes.

Although we have only skeletal remains and material artifacts of past humans available for study, anthropologists are careful to choose contexts that are most closely related to those of our subjects from the past. For instance, even though primates are not analogous to earlier hominids, they are vastly more closely related to us genetically than are domestic animals and inhabit an environment much closer to that of our remote past. Fisher/Hunter, however, concludes much about his characters from the observation of domestic animals on the farm:

> His discoveries (all of them to be found, he supposed, in books but he liked to make them himself) delighted him: he had imagined that beasts recognized people with their sense of sight: this, he found, was not true of barnyard animals and he wondered if it was true of beasts anywhere: that recognition came through their sense of smell he proved again and again.... Farmers with whom he talked added to his knowledge of these things. He had known that an orphan lamb could be put on a ewe that was not its mother, if the skin of her own dead baby covered it; or if, a sheepman told him, he rubbed the smell of the dead lamb's anus on the other lamb's anus.... [H]is thought went back to his father's crude earthy sisters, changing diapers, slapping their babies' rumps, shrieking. (*Orphans* 828)

All of this explains why he ascribes a keen sense of smell to hominids well after anthropologists currently believe it would have been so.

Vridar also observes rodents and wild birds:

> It had been a law of life with his parents that if an article was hung at the end of three or four feet of wire, mice could not get it.... Hiding, he waited to see what they did: from the rafter the cunning little fellows slid down the wire to the pail; and after filling their stomachs, they balanced a moment on the edge of the pail and then dropped lightly to the floor. (828)

> One autumn day he saw a number of pheasant hens feeding under a black locust tree, and a male pheasant in the tree. It seemed to him that the cock was shaking the seedpods loose for the hens below.... There could be no doubt of it—with wings and feet and beak the male was actually dislodging seedpods, which fell to the hens, scurrying around under him. (828–29)

Fisher here shows us his mind at work. His accounts go far toward explaining how he came to some of the conclusions he wrote into his *Testament*.

Even when Fisher chooses to study primates, he studies them in zoos rather than by going to their native habitats to observe them there: "There were the zoos: he had spent many hours in them, studying the great apes, seeing in them himself and friends, and them in his friends and himself" (*Orphans* 812).

Fisher/Hunter has his own methods of analysis. He studies nonhuman animals by imitation: "He so completely fell in the habit of imitating the bow-legged bent-legged posture of walking, with head sunk down in shoulders and prognathous jaw thrust out, that he had one embarrassing experience after another, when people happened to be watching him" (813). Vridar "struggled time and again to put himself in the primitive man's emotions, standing above his prey. But the act of killing actually filled him with horror: kinship of animals had gone too deep in him, in childhood" (829). "He spent hours in different postures...while thinking, no, while feeling (that was more the way of it) into the various symbols and meanings that had come out of fear and ignorance" (853–54).

Projection is Fisher's most commonly used method of interpreting data. He reports that Vridar "got so that he chronically felt the wide abdominal hip-spreading heaviness of one who had given birth after birth" (942). "...[H]e wanted to project himself into the primitive man, standing above his prey. He wanted to learn why the only animal making claims to compassion was the worst killer of them all" (829). Primates, certainly, are credited with compassion; and we could probably make the case that other animals engage in it also.

Vridar's efforts at projection provide some surprising moments for his wife Angele. Once "she found him stretched out on his belly, his shoulders propped on his elbows, his face fairly alive with contortions and grimaces...for he was in the preliminaries of a scene in which he was striving (he had rehearsed this a number of times) to project himself, with a positively uncontrollable carnal frenzy, into the soul and lecherous bloodlusting of a depraved priest about to rape a helpless child" (977).

Fisher's efforts here produce an Inquisition scene in *My Holy Satan* paralleling this experience:

> "Now you seduced this girl and ran away and when you returned you told around Patres that Father Luce had seduced her. Did you?"
>
> Richard glanced again at Father Luce and said: "She was pregnant when she died."
>
> "Did you say that Satan doesn't copulate with women?"
>
> "I don't know.
>
> "Do you think he does?"
>
> "No."

> "Then if you didn't and Satan didn't you think Father Luce did?"
>
> Richard turned and looked full into Father Luce's eyes.
>
> "Answer the question."
>
> Still looking into the eyes Richard said, "Yes," and inside him he said, It is all over with me. (255)

Fisher also collects data by immersing himself in a study of himself: "Adam and his serpent! Vridar had read everything he could find about the serpent, and had come to nothing. Concluding that the analogy was based on more than the obvious similarity in shape and appearance, he went off to conceal himself and to study his penis.... The penis as the serpent" (853).

One of the tenets of holism is the assumption that no individual is utterly transcendent to his culture. Fisher's heroes are all such transcendent beings: "This new perspective was to become his [Wuh's] great advantage over less intelligent competitors" (*Darkness* 60). "Harg was the most intelligent member of his family and had by far the greatest knowledge of things" (*Golden* 16). "Among the people of his time Raven was a genius" (*Eve* 201). "He [Rabi] was the most infallible oracle in his clan" (*Passion* 6). "He was a lonely man" (*Passion* 5).

Fisher's epistemology is rampantly transcendent. As noted above, he prefers his own experiences, even with respect to domestic animals, to information from books on the subject. Fisher/Hunter consistently reasons from his own premises: "War then had been a sacred matter, and the gods had fought side by side with their people (as parents would with their children, wouldn't they?), sometimes dropping stones from the sky or hurling thunderbolts. It had been necessary to flatter and praise the gods (with such subterfuges children still sought to win advantages over their parents), and the people had quaked with fear lest their gods be offended (and what child had not?)" (856).

Fisher assumes rather surprisingly often that he, and only he, has a monopoly on truth: "[A]fter a lot of reading in the right things nothing becomes more obvious than this, that Christians won't face the historical facts of Christian and Judaic relationships; and the Jews won't either" (863).

He takes this transcendence even further when he writes of Solomon: "After reading a great many scholars, and then looking at the whole broad picture of the thing, Vridar decided that for the purpose of limning certain major truths against the sky he would have to make Solomon a greater king than the scholars thought he had been" (879). He writes from a feeling of superiority to practically everyone: "I'd not mind if I could have the few thousand readers who belong to me, but those are precisely the ones who have never heard of me. My books are at the mercy of numskulls who know what the Bible says!" (887). "Truly men hate the truth, they'd liefer meet a tiger on the road" (921). He even feels superior to Solomon: "The real Solomon, I suppose, wouldn't have had a gnat's notion of what I'm talking about" (879).

Most saliently for this discussion, Fisher dismisses the anthropologists out of hand:

> In Ruth Benedict, he [Vridar] read, "[H]istory is by no means a set of facts that can be discovered by introspection. Therefore these explanations of custom which derive our economic scheme from human competitiveness, modern war from human combativeness, and all the rest of the ready explanations that we meet in every magazine and modern volume, have for the anthropologist a hollow ring." Vridar closed the book and said..."She says the matter is one of honest-dishonest situation, not of honest-dishonest persons. She's as wrong as hell there." (852)

Fisher doubted that professional anthropologists would find his work valid and feared that if he followed their various theories, his books would never be successful (852). But he soon finds himself in strong agreement with Margaret Mead. Vridar describes Simone de Beauvoir's *The Second Sex* as "so penetrating that it brought from Margaret Mead, an anthropologist, a statement that exactly summed up one of Vridar's beliefs—that the virtues found in greater strength in women than in men had not been employed in the development of the Western world's institutions and values" (894).

Fisher's shallow epistemology is most conspicuous in his presentation of Christianity. Fisher had studied "higher criticism" of the Bible. Through these writings, he understood that Christianity is a synthesis of many elements from Judaism and from paganism—especially Mithraism. One of his heroes describes Christianity as a "patchwork" (*Goat* 161). Although Christianity is indeed a synthesis, Fisher comes to an illogical conclusion because he is insufficiently holistic. He decides that because Christianity is a synthesis, it is untrue. Because many people believe in Christianity, he concludes that it is false. But the fact that many people from many times and places believe a proposition is no guarantee of either its truth or its falsehood. Once a text is analyzed, it remains to be decided whether or not it is useful, beautiful, good, or true. Criticism (such as Fisher understood) is only a beginning; Fisher disengages after this step.

An anthropologist, as anthropologist, must remain agnostic on the subject of the contents of any particular religion. The methods of spiritual discernment are equally rigorous to those of anthropology but are outside the scope of the anthropological discipline. Fisher, however, becomes atheistic. It is that stance that renders his novels about Christianity not so much incorrect as tactless.

Fisher would not consider my criticism unkind. Rather, he would see it as a compliment because he sees tactlessness as a virtue. Hunter is a teacher, and his "honest portrayal of life" so inflames a parent that a student is removed from his school. The president takes him aside: "'Hunter, your trouble is lack of prudence. You can teach anything if you know how.' ...But Vridar was not and would never be a prudent man" (*Orphans* 572).

For Fisher, truth itself does not matter because it is relative. He proposes, for instance, that it does not matter that there probably never was a Matthew (*Goat* 221) and that there is no evidence for God (*Orphans* 821).

Similarly, Fisher argues that the gospel presentation of Joshua/Jesus is the result of a catastrophic misunderstanding. In Fisher's *Jesus Came Again*[15] Joshua does not heal, does not raise another from the dead, and does not experience a resurrection. For Fisher, Christianity is not about a historic individual but about an ever-generating mythic reality that is forever renewed (*Satan* 279). Fisher concludes, via Hunter, that the historical facts do not matter:

> There wasn't an iota of trustworthy evidence that the Jesus of the Gospels had lived in human flesh: this, he had come to see, did not matter at all. There was not a scrap of evidence that a Jesus in Palestine ever uttered a single word of all the words attributed to him by the gospel stories: this did not matter either: indeed, the great thing about the story was that the early leaders had sense enough to have him say the things he ought to have said just as, earlier, Jewish writers had had sense enough to make Solomon say what he should have said, if he was to be a great king. (*Orphans* 913)

Having concluded that neither Judaism nor Christianity is what it seems to be, Fisher is at pains to account for a host of customs previous to the contexts in which they appear to reside. This results in a plethora of explanations, which may or may not be historical. He attempts to explain sneezing, clothing, the Trinity as being in the moon, the use of rabbits' feet and horseshoes as amulets, Easter, a link between the virgin and the Dog Star, resurrection on a third day, death on trees, blood rituals, carrying brides over the threshold, kissing brides, the Samson stories, bells, glossolalia, and wheel day; and this is far from a complete list. A few samples will demonstrate his argument. For instance, Fisher moves the baptismal controversy backward into matriarchic prehistoric times: "Her grandmother and mother, and Rainmaker herself, had used the magic of water only to sprinkle. The use of it for immersion had for Rainmaker the quality of blasphemy. She had no time for innovators who thought that sprinkling was not enough" (*Adam* 118). He also projects crossing oneself into prehistoric times: "[T]o protect herself while changing from one apron to the other, Myrtle made a magical sign. With a finger she made a line downward across her belly and then crossed it with another line. This symbol, indicating the creative principle, momentarily strengthened a woman and made her impervious to evil" (*Adam* 89). With reference to worship of the Sun-god, Fisher proposes, "The twelve constellations, through which he moved each year, were his apostles, of whom one was also his betrayer who doomed him at the winter solstice and forced him to descend to the abode of his enemies, there to fight for his own life and for the lives of his people" (*Passion* 25).

Although any one of these explanations is interesting, there are so many that the overall effect is one of degeneration into silliness—like the child who comes home from Sunday school talking about a "cross-eyed bear." Similarly, he offers explanations for a host of inventions that are virtually without documentation of any kind and arise from the transcendence of a single individual over culture.[16]

One can imagine the effects of Fisher's practice on his reading audience. In fact, we are beginning to approach what I think cost Fisher his place in contemporary, but not future, popularity. It is in his tactlessness and his disregard for the opinions of others, specifically his editors, that makes the *Testament* less than it might have been.

The *Testament of Man* failed to reach as wide an audience as it might have for multiple reasons—many aesthetic. Certainly the novels suffer from unsatisfactory editing. A good editor could have helped Fisher a great deal. The lack of editing arose, however, from Fisher's extreme individualism.

Orphans reveals a bit about Fisher's relationship with his publishers, and a few paragraphs are very telling. It is clear that Fisher/Hunter is listening to nothing other than his own feelings and reflections. One publisher counsels him to continue to write "American historical novels" and forget the *Testament,* saying that "Nobody cares about father and mother symbols, and Adam and Eve" (788–89). Hunter rejects the notion, thinking "If you weren't afraid to look at the Adam in you, you wouldn't have that tic in your eye." He contacts Rhode, a publisher friend, who reacts enthusiastically but notes: "Go right ahead, old man, go right ahead. It's a magnificent project.... I don't publish books to make money. We take fantastic losses, simply fantastic. On your books which we published our losses were simply incredible" (789).

Friends begin to argue with him, but Vridar persists. Although Fisher, through Hunter, admits that he embellished Solomon, he responds angrily when this is discerned by Rhode, who says: "You're a great scholar, old man, and I'm just a small country publisher. I haven't read all the books you have, but I just don't believe you've told the truth. As I read the Bible...." Vridar explodes: "Christ O God, as he and other ignoramuses read the Bible! I tell them what the greatest scholars in that field have concluded, and they say, yes, but as we read the Bible! ...Not even with shock therapy could you make them understand that the only persons who can read the Bible are the Higher Critics!" (886–87). His position is not only tactless but flies in the face of the entire thrust of the Reformation.

Even Rhode has to surrender in the end when Hunter refuses to allow his manuscripts to be read by scholars of Rhode's choosing: "'I, fighting all these years to be free of tyranny!' Trying to control his voice he said, 'A Catholic scholar? There is no such thing in matters relating to his Church.... Do you actually mean to tell me that I must submit the findings and conclusions of a hundred or two hundred of the greatest scholars to the judgment of a small closed mind—'" (919). Given the circumstances, it is understandable that a publisher who knows in advance that he will be losing money on books would not want to go to even more expense to have them well edited.

Cultural Relativism as Opposed to Ethnocentricity

Fisher's *Testament* should also be viewed in light of cultural relativism—as opposed to ethnocentricity. While all the directives are easier to explain than obey, ethnocentricity slips its way in very easily. Fisher's culture-boundedness is formative for all of the *Testament*. It is especially evident in *Peace Like a River*, one of my favorites in the *Testament*. I like both his heroine Helene and her friend Mark. They emerge from the craziness of their desert environment as wholesome and faithful. Helene refuses to accept the misogynous interpretation of herself: "Our holy books say that God created this earth. It is men who have spoilt it. You spoil it with war, with torture, with slavery, with whorehouses—for none of these things come from women. You men have corrupted it, and now, to save your stinking little souls, you try to put off on women the shame and the wickedness" (255–56). Mark refuses to forsake his innate humility: "But I'm the sort of poor devil who can never be very good or very bad. It takes a lot of wickedness to make a saint" (120). Fisher writes disparagingly about the practices of the Christian desert ascetics. As above, he is incorrect in his facts but not in his interpretation of them. All religious practices viewed from a temporal or spatial distance can appear remarkably silly. Fisher, however, seems not to understand anything about the fundamental ascetical perspective that can indeed lead to fanatical extremes if not undertaken with sound advice. In short, asceticism, at its best, is not about sacrifice but about abundance. Ascetics believe in the existence of spiritual "gold," are looking for it, and are eliminating those things that they think will interfere with their finding it. In Fisher's story, there are no healthy ascetics who live with simple joy.

Fisher/Hunter is also class-centric. His epistemology concerning earlier humans is class dependent: "He came closest to the Female and Eve, to Adam and the Male, when he went far out and back and mingled with the peasants: the skeins there were not yet so mixed, the things that belonged primarily to the one or the other were plainer" (849).

Ethnocentricity comes in many forms. The classic definitions focus on an investment in cultural superiority, but such investments can operate quite close to home. Much of racism, for instance, is ethnocentric, as are generational prejudices and misogyny. Misogyny is crucial to Fisher's *Testament*. It is at the heart of his progressivism and the cardinal moment of his revolution. Fisher writes vividly of the evil of misogyny and the suffering it causes. Fisher's heroes were all individuals utterly transcendent to their own settings; however, Fisher was not—none of us is.

I believe Fisher when he says he hates misogyny and when he accuses others of it: "Vridar would go storming to his typewriter. 'I'll let a woman tell these horrors what stinkers they are, these mewling mom-boys vomiting their fear into their generations of vipers!'" (967).

On the other hand, Fisher/Hunter, as himself, is usually thoroughly negative about women. Others reinforce his habit. In college, Vridar's roommate declares: "A girl measured a man by the crease in his trousers and the polish on his shoes. Her interest was not amorous but economic. What they were really after, Forenoon said, was a husband; and a husband meant a man who would buy a nest for babies and furnish it" (331–32). Vridar later declares to a seductress, "Listen, Blanche, the first move you women make is to get a man to lie with you. The second is to get him to marry you. The third is to get children. The fourth is to choose your daughters-in-laws [*sic*]. Your fifth is to be a tyrant in an armchair. Your sixth and the only decent move you ever make, is to die" (472).

Although Fisher writes his misogyny into the mouths of other characters, the most devastating and revealing statements occur in the words of Fisher/Hunter himself. Fisher writes that Hunter "had developed an extraordinary interest in the female breast. He had become almost obsessed with the signs of woman that were not the signs of man" (164). Unfortunately, that fascination was not one of admiration: "He had always felt a little resentful toward human mothers. The foolish things got a babe in their arms and pulled out a large dug, and seemed then to think that the whole world gathered round in reverence" (762).

In *Adam and the Serpent,* Fisher twice refers to something extremely strange: "Rainmaker was a woman who in any land or time would have been an arresting figure. Tall and very lean, with empty breasts hanging so low that sometimes to get them out of her way she tossed them back across her shoulders" (38). "She [Rainmaker] stopped and flung the breasts across her shoulders, and Myrtle hastened forward to clasp and tie them behind her neck" (288). Fisher notes the phenomenon again in *Orphans:* "After months of striving in every possible way to project himself in Eve, Vridar became alarmed.... He got so that he chronically felt...the long empty sagging breasts, with swollen ugly nipples brushing across his belly as he worked, or touching the back of his neck like eels, when, in the way of ancient women, he flung the breast back over his shoulders and tied them together to keep them out of the way" (*Orphans* 842).

I have no idea where Fisher could have read about such a phenomenon. I performed an experiment with a roll of fabric and determined that to accomplish the feat, as he describes, would require approximately ten linear feet of breast tissue. The possibility is extremely unlikely—in fact, preposterous. How revealing that Fisher did not find it so.

We also see his misogyny in his projection of rape fantasies onto the women in his books and in his life: "[T]his stark fact that some women liked to be raped and that some men liked to rape them was like corroding acid upon his ideals" (*Orphans* 449). Fisher includes a rape scene in *Adam and the Serpent:*

> Like a man in whom emotion, sudden and blind, had destroyed all self-control, he moved forward softly but swiftly, approaching the girl from the rear. When close to her he leapt and seized her and bore her down, dragging her at the same time into a thicket.
>
> She made no outcry. Perhaps she thought he was the agent of a benevolent spirit; or possibly she had wandered off alone, hoping to be attacked. When he bore down upon her she surrendered completely and even reached out to assist him. (60)

Even more revealing of misogyny than Fisher's words are his/Hunter's actions. In his youth, Hunter is a voyeur. Seeing his classmate Lottie Ulster: "He hid behind a snow-covered bush and looked at her a few moments; he withdrew to examine his emotions and his courage and returned; and again he spied on her" (237). As an adult he becomes a womanizer: "Athene [his second wife] said, 'How many women did you have?' 'It doesn't matter does it?' ...And she threw at him a taunt that she was to throw again, in the years ahead: 'You old Brigham Young!'" (625).

Fisher/Hunter marries three times, having lost his first wife to suicide, as the aftermath of his plan to leave her for his second wife, and abandoning his second wife for the third. Compared to Hunter's cruelties, his parents' actions do not appear to have been quite so evil. Most of Hunter's cruelty is directed toward women in general and toward his first wife, Neloa, in particular. They begin even before he marries her: "Because he was abnormally proud and lonely of temper and because he gave to chastity a value which it could never possess, he resolved to put her to some kind of test." He lies to Neloa that he had had an affair and an illegitimate child with another woman. "He was looking at her eyes. He saw them darken and then become bright and wet; he saw tears gather to her lashes and fall" (284).

Fisher later analyzes why Hunter wants to hurt Neloa: "He wanted to make her weep, and in later years he was to understand his reasons. For one thing her tears always stirred his erotic longings and gave to them softness and glamor [*sic*]" (345).

When writing of his youth, Fisher emphasizes, via Vridar, the hatred he had for his parents; but he, nevertheless, sends his first wife to live with them (and be another victim of theirs) while he is in the armed forces.

Fisher/Hunter is an abuser in his first marriage: "He seized her arm and drew her up and twisted her arm until her gaze met his. He looked at her a moment and then out of his awful bitterness he said: 'You whore'" (458). Neloa's presuicide letter is haunting: "Dear Vridar, I am sick of it all and I'm going. No matter what I do, no matter how hard I try, you find fault with me. You abuse me and call me names and I won't stand for what you called me today. Please be good to our baby and never tell him what" (135). Neloa does not finish her sentence, which contributes to the haunting effect. If Neloa were to tell her story, how different it would be!

In his last marriage Fisher/Hunter remains an abuser, sometimes forcing his wife Angele to seek legal help: "[H]e had seized her by her hair and shaken her up and down, and blacked an eye. She had run screaming into the night to find a policeman" (938). Sometimes the violence is mutual. Following a description of a fight he writes: "In all the arts hadn't it been that way with a man and his woman?" (790). No, it hadn't.

Fisher's ethnocentricity is also brought to bear against the Jewish people. Fisher/Hunter reflects upon Judaism as a producer of orphans: "They were the world's most pathetic orphans, the poor wailing fatherless sons" (877). "He knew now why the Jews had never had a Mother. Their men had been so female-identified that they couldn't stand the thought of femaleness, and so had enthroned the Male in solitary wifeless childless splendor!" (878). "He now looked to another profound truth. When he taught in Manhattan he had again and again heard non-Jews say that the Jews were the most arrogant people on earth. Vridar had admitted to himself that they seemed to be: so many of them were brash and pushing and full of self-praise. But all this, he understood now, was over-compensation: the Jews were, in fact, by nature the most submissive people on earth" (878).

Fisher's ethnocentric misogyny and anti-Semitism are unfortunately not why his books did not sell well. In this aspect, he is only too congruent with our culture.

Patriarchal Struggle and Conflict

"Because she was the vessel of birth the woman in ancient times dominated the man; later, when he became ascendant, because of his long eclipse the man became even more tyrannical than the woman had been" (*Adam* 183). This, in short, is Fisher's view of the great male fantasy.

It is innate in our biology that females do indeed have powers peculiar to themselves alone. Men know this and must wrestle with that given. The great male fantasy paints a world in which that power is, or was, overcome by some form of even more powerful male superiority.

Fisher sees the patriarchy; we all do. He, nevertheless, still feels powerless. He writes as Vridar:

> He wanted to go—to go to Neloa; to kneel to her as to an altar; to beg her to help him see his way out of the darkness. But he felt that she would destroy rather than free him. In her quiet way, in her undeliberate childlike way, she had conquered him at every turn...until she had become not a woman but a force, not a wife to soothe and heal but an elemental power that engulfed his will. He felt that in her ways was wisdom, in his ways the frenzies that were symptomatic of his time." (415)

Even when Vridar lies to Neloa, he feels that she has power that he does not: Neloa asks Vridar to kiss her. He responds, "'I don't want to.' That was a horrible lie, but it made him feel better. He had so completely revealed his soul to her, and her soul was so completely hidden" (274).

Just as Fisher projects his feelings onto his characters from the remote past, he projects them onto politics. Because he feels powerless against women, he believes that their power must have been universally politically instituted.[17] There is no evidence that this was ever the case.

It is matriarchy, not patriarchy, that is the key to the fantasy—the fond notion that in spite of the male's feeling powerless over the female, something has been/is, and therefore can be overcome.

It is through the great fantasy that men are able to play "let's pretend"—to play that they have already won the battle of the sexes. Men of health and good will know that the battle of the sexes cannot be won by only one side. On the contrary, unless both sides win, both sides lose. Men of courage surrender themselves, not to the fantasy (which they indeed enjoy), but to the reality. These are the men that healthy women adore. And, because they adore them, they accompany them to James Bond movies and enjoy the humor in them. Against this background, Vridar Hunter/Vardis Fisher stands in stark contrast.

Fisher articulates the fantasy through the thoughts and actions of Dove, the transcendent hero of *Adam and the Serpent:*

> There came to him [Dove] a thought which he had had before but on which, out of deference to women, he had never dared seriously to dwell. Now he let the lurking thought come boldly out of the shadows and present its outlines, and the revelation which came to him was this: that women were creatures of evil, and that all evil spirits were those of dead women. (57)

Dove continues to develop his heresy throughout the book: "Dove was a rank heretic. In a later time he would have been scourged and crucified; in his own time he was regarded as foolish...but he also lived under the prodding of a restless mind that would strive in spite of contempt and curses to find a respectable destiny for men. In this he would contribute to the greatest social revolution in the history of the human race" (172–73).

Because of his insistence that the matriarchy is historical rather than mythical, Fisher/Hunter is, in a sense, doomed. In *Orphans,* Fisher paints a horrifying picture of his childhood. Vridar hates his father, and Fisher paints a disgusting portrait of the man. For instance, Vridar and his brother, Marion, live away from home to attend school. Their father brings them food but eats a good bit of it himself before he leaves: "Vridar could only stare resentfully and hope that the man's next mouthful would be his last" (146). Vridar also hates his mother: "After she had punished him, he slunk away, hating her, and with horrible bitterness in his soul" (176).

Vridar turns out to be a much worse father than his own had been. Once, when his baby son continued to cry, "Vridar shook the child, crying,

'Shut up, damn it, you monster of bad heritage!'" (433). About the baby he says, "What an ugly brat" (402). Finally, he abandons his own two sons, as he has their mother, to be reared by the very people who had made his life a misery. As they grow up without him, one of his sons continues the pattern: "Scott not only had deserted his wife and children, but never even sent them a Christmas card, much less a buck" (905). Vridar has had little knowledge of Scott's life or the life of his other son, Larry. He is such a bad father that finally, even he recognizes it: "Orphans too, were Vridar's own sons" (904).

The inadequacies of Vridar's parents bloom into deliberate cruelties in their solipsistic child. Vridar is not merely dismissive of others but often fails to recognize even their existence. Everything Vridar does is motivated by supreme self-absorption. He abandons two wives and three sons—all in homage to his talent and self-development. He says to Neloa: "Neloa, my dear, I'm trying to be honest with you and myself. Isn't loyalty to my talent if I have talent—my first loyalty? Wouldn't I be a coward if I sacrificed it? ...Here's a truth, Neloa, that will go over your head like an eagle: any man who wants to leave his wife, or wife her husband, and does not is a coward" (503–4).

Fisher assumes (along with many members of the official feminist movement) that patriarchy is innately tyrannical. It may be, of course. Having noted that, however, it is obvious that not all patriarchs are tyrants. Tarzan, for instance, is not a tyrant. He is, however, necessary. Because of both his mastery of his environment and his reliability toward Jane, she is faithful, admiring, and loving toward him. She honors him. This is the case in all of the successful fantasy stories. The males are successful detectives, heroic military leaders, cunning spies, and so on. They are all masterful (in the sense of having mastered something) and, above all, necessary. In *Darkness* Fisher accurately depicts this reality: "He [Wuh] did not know that Murah felt secure with him because he had killed a man.... She had a dim and happy notion that she, and her children when they came, would be safe with him; and though she felt no love [because they were not yet capable of love], she did look upon him with an emotion akin to respect and pride" (181).

Fisher/Hunter, however, *is* a tyrant. It is because of what Fisher/Hunter becomes that he and, via projection, all his male protagonists experience profound sexual frustration—a deep soul-twisting loneliness of unfulfilled desperate longing: "Because of this constant and tyrannical hunger in him [Wuh], which an ironic scheme had mated with lusting in women that was only periodic, he was driven to the solitary perspective of the bachelor; and day by day his vagrant fancies became stronger" (*Darkness* 200–01).

Similarly, in *Intimations,* Raven "was motivated by more than resentment of an old woman's tyranny and envy of her powers. He was an erotically hungry man" (220–21).

Prophecy

All of Fisher's heroes are clearly Fisher himself. He describes them as intelligent, misunderstood, and lonely. They are all philosophical and, to the extent of their abilities, artistic: "But Gode had little to do. Periodic idleness in the man has led him into the realms of art and philosophy; it has prompted him to reverie, speculation, and abstract ideas" (*Golden* 254). Finally, his heroes find their gods in themselves: "He [Yescha] who had despised them had learned that greater love has no man than this...finding the god in himself when he found his people" (*Passion* 373).

In *Orphans,* Vridar emerges as thoroughly confident in his own intelligence over others: "The time came when Vridar said to Angele, 'Either all the people but a few are too stupid to learn after the eighth or tenth grades, or our system of public education is a colossal farce'" (860). From early childhood on, Vridar's attempts at asceticism make him bitter and lonely: "He did not know that suffer here meant allow. He thought it meant misery. He thought that if little children must suffer to find Jesus, he would have to suffer much more" (184). He agonizes: "If only he had someone to talk to.... But he had no one—no one but books" (230).

Vridar Hunter is who we are. Hunter is not a tyrant because he is a patriarch, or even because he is a man. He is, full blown, what we in the United States are taught to be. As he has said about himself in relation to Neloa, "He felt that in her ways was wisdom, in his ways the frenzies that were symptomatic of his time" (415). Fisher also says about Hunter: "He did not know that his self-pitying tirade was already one of the voices of the self-pitying lost generation" (420). Indeed, Fisher himself comes to the realization that Hunter represents more than merely himself.

Orphans in Gethsemane portrays a man obsessed with himself but, at the same time (perhaps because of that obsession), thoroughly out of touch with himself. Although excessive drinking is an everyday part of his life—"All night they drank and read notes and talked, as they did so many nights, consuming a quart of whisky between late afternoon and morning" (866)—he sees himself as an ascetic: "'Asceticism is my problem, really.' ...He could understand asceticism, being himself filled with it" (968).

He also sees himself as a giver rather than as the taker he actually is: "Vridar would mutter, 'There is nothing left for me but the shell. I have given. I have been one of the Givers'" (934). Even though his brother has died, he is still resentful: "Only Neloa had gone into him so deep: how strange it was, how stupid, that he should break his heart over two persons who had caused him so much humiliation and pain!" (933).

Although it is not an anthropologically valid account of human development, *Orphans* is as revealing a document of our times as anything I have ever read. It is lengthy—987 pages—but that length is what allows the tale its impact. *Orphans* stands as a cautionary tale for us and a window on our times for the readers of the future. I can imagine future anthropologists considering it a classic—necessary reading for students wishing to understand the twentieth century. It is in that future that Vardis Fisher may find the serious literary reputation he so desperately wanted.

Notes

1. For this model I am indebted to Bruce Winterhalder who, in an aside, during a discussion of another topic entirely, noted these as the theoretical perpectives of anthropology. I have called them "prime directives" because I believe they are characterized by a moral, as well as a theoretical, stance.
2. Vardis Fisher, *Darkness and the Deep* (New York: Vanguard, 1943), 44. Subsequent references are cited parenthetically as *Darkness* unless context makes this unnecessary.
3. Vardis Fisher, *The Golden Rooms* (New York: Vanguard, 1944), 199. Subsequent references are cited parenthetically as *Golden* unless context makes this unnecessary.
4. Vardis Fisher, *The Valley of Vision: A Novel of King Solomon and His Time* (New York: Abelard, 1951), 260.
5. Vardis Fisher, *The Island of the Innocent: A Novel of Greek and Jew in the Time of the Maccabees* (New York: Abelard, 1952), 405. Subsequent references are cited parenthetically as *Island* unless context makes this unnecessary.
6. Vardis Fisher, *Intimations of Eve* (New York: Vanguard, 1946), 65. Subsequent references are cited parenthetically as *Eve* unless context makes this unnecessary.
7. Vardis Fisher, *The Divine Passion* (New York: Vanguard, 1948), 235. Subsequent references are cited parenthetically as *Passion* unless context makes this unnecessary.
8. Vardis Fisher, *A Goat for Azazel* (Denver: Alan Swallow, 1956), 129. Subsequent references are cited parenthetically as *Goat* unless context makes this unnecessary.
9. Vardis Fisher, *Orphans in Gethsemane: A Novel of the Past in the Present* (Denver: Alan Swallow, 1960), 981. Subsequent references are cited parenthetically as *Orphans* unless context makes this unnecessary.
10. Vardis Fisher, *Peace Like a River* (Denver: Alan Swallow, 1957), 170. Subsequent references are cited parenthetically as *Peace* unless context makes this unnecessary.
11. Vardis Fisher, *My Holy Satan* (Denver: Alan Swallow, 1958), 283. Subsequent references are cited parenthetically as *Satan* unless context makes this unnecessary.
12. Vardis Fisher, *Adam and the Serpent* (New York: Vanguard, 1947), 135–136,137. Subsequent references are cited parenthetically as *Adam* unless context makes this unnecessary.
13. For the best exposition of holism, see James L. Peacock, *The Anthropological Lens* (Cambridge: Cambridge University Press, 1986).
14. See also *Golden Rooms*, 241, 302; *Adam and the Serpent*, 51, 142.
15. Vardis Fisher, *Jesus Came Again: A Parable* (Denver: Alan Swallow, 1956), 106.
16. See *Golden Rooms*, 68 for example.
17. Compare *My Holy Satan*, 291.

Bibliography

Fisher, Vardis. *Darkness and the Deep*. New York: Vanguard, 1943.
———. *The Golden Rooms*. New York: Vanguard, 1944.
———. *Intimations of Eve*. New York: Vanguard, 1946.
———. *Adam and the Serpent*. New York: Vanguard, 1947.
———. *The Divine Passion*. New York: Vanguard, 1948.
———. *The Valley of Vision: A Novel of King Solomon and His Time*. New York: Abelard, 1951.
———. *The Island of the Innocent: A Novel of Greek and Jew in the Time of the Maccabees*. New York: Abelard, 1952.
———. *Jesus Came Again: A Parable*. Denver: Alan Swallow, 1956.
———. *A Goat for Azazel*. Denver: Alan Swallow, 1956.
———. *Peace Like a River*. Denver: Alan Swallow, 1957.
———. *My Holy Satan*. Denver: Alan Swallow, 1958.
———. *Orphans in Gethsemane*. Denver: Alan Swallow, 1960.
Peacock, James. *The Anthropological Lens*. Cambridge: Cambridge University Press, 1986.

11

"A World of Jerusalems": The Middle East as Contested Space in Vardis Fisher's *Testament of Man*

Anne R. Zahlan

In his monumental novel sequence, the *Testament of Man,* Vardis Fisher fulfills the criterion for "great historical art" set out by Georg Lukács: he brings "the past to life as the prehistory of the present."[1] Having taken on the task of writing the spiritual and intellectual biography of Judeo-Christian people, Fisher recounts the wrong turnings and missed opportunities that from the Stone Age to the twentieth century have determined the tragic course of human history. Early volumes of the twelve-part series record tool-making, fire-building, and the development of language; they also chronicle human conceptualization of the supernatural. Fisher describes prehistoric people who have come to worship the Mother and to live in social groups organized on principles of matriarchy—until men discover their role in procreation and revolt against female domination. Among the ancient Semites, spiritual ancestors of all People of the Book, the Mother was not just displaced but ultimately denigrated; the idea took hold that evil had come into the world in the shape of woman. This error was, in Fisher's view, followed by successive failures to correct a course that would lead to a world not united by love but divided by hatred.

In four books at the center of the *Testament of Man* series, Fisher takes human beings from the brink of literacy and organized religion to the Messianic moment that led to the establishment of Christianity: *The Divine Passion* (1948), *The Valley of Vision* (1951), *The Island of the Innocent* (1952), and *Jesus Came Again* (1956). In these he traces the developing religious and national consciousness of Semitic people, specifically the Hebrews. The story is one marked by relentless struggle between forces of orthodoxy and impulses of tolerance; its author, a man who, according to his biographer, "saw life as deadly combat"[2] fabricates no reassuring Hegelian dialectic to reconcile faith and reason. True to a tragic vision, Vardis Fisher locates crucial stages in the construction of the human condition in a dystopian space of military and political combat and intellectual and ethical strife.

Unfortunately, the space in which seminal struggles for human consciousness are waged may seem all too familiar to late-twentieth-century readers. In *Culture and Imperialism,* published in 1994, Edward W. Said evokes a wounded and fragmented region that bears a sad resemblance to Vardis Fisher's ancient Middle East: "Today state nationalisms fracture into clan or sectarian ones. Lebanon and Israel are perfect examples of what has happened: the desirability of rigid cantonization in one form or another is present nearly everywhere as a group feeling if not practice, and is subsidized by the state, with its bureaucracies and secret polices. Rulers are clans, families, cliques, closed circles of aging oligarchs, almost mythologically immune, like Garcia Márquez's autumnal patriarch, to new blood or change."[3] Even the widespread literacy that is a genuine benefit of nationalist regimes in the region has, Said observes, been co-opted by authoritarian governments to promote obsession with "Identity, always identity, over and above knowing about others."[4] Although the trappings of nation-statehood and advanced technology adorn and reinforce contemporary divisions, Fisher's successive portrayals show a Palestine equally in the grip of desperation, hatred, and fear.

According to Fisher, preoccupation with identity developed early in the ancient Near East, and played a significant role in shaping Western culture. In the author's textual quest to understand monotheistic humankind and the world it has shaped, *The Divine Passion* occupies a point of transition. This book depicts an early Semitic village in which scornful hatred of a marginally different other is cultivated until it leads to violence and aggression. Late in the novel, fanciful reports brought back from a scouting expedition are transformed into reasons for war:

> Laurel's description of this southern tribe shocked them because it was so inappropriate and unreasonable for people to live anywhere who did not look like themselves. Such people they despised and feared. Their word for them was monster, and they were monstrous in the degree that they were different. Now some of them gazed at one another, glad that their noses were not beaked, that their teeth did not protrude, that their bodies were not short and fat. They were what human beings ought to be, and all people who differed from them in appearance or habits were the children of the dark gods who, for their own evil purpose, created their worshipers in their image. There were many reasons why such monsters should be destroyed.[5]

In the Bronze-Age culture described in *The Divine Passion,* the villagers are "a people of medium height, with straight noses, slightly receding foreheads, coarse dark hair, full oversensual lips, and dark eyes which, in moments of meditation, were soft and liquid with melancholia. They were bright and flashing in moments of triumph or rage"(24). The people's names are in many cases Semitic: Hassan, Haroun, Adom, Hiam, Beth, Rabi, Yescha. Grouped in clan settlements within larger tribal regions, they live complex lives: clothes are ornamented; tools and jewelry are made of cast metal; food is imaginatively flavored; scents and cosmetics are used. Besides the material complexity of everyday life, there is a complicated social structure headed in the temporal domain by a chieftain and in the spiritual by a priest. The villagers are polytheistic but increasingly concentrate their religious energy in worship of the almighty sun. They have invested power to protect or to curse in language: words have great force. Their lives are circumscribed by elaborate prescriptions and taboos, and, despite predilections for sensual enjoyment, they live in perpetual fear that the sun-god will be overwhelmed. Never free from some sense of "impending disaster," they are, in Fisher's terms, "an anxious and neurotic people"(214).

Moved by a desire to acquire more sheep, goods, and concubines, the clan chieftain Adom wishes to make war on the tribes to the south. For such an undertaking, however, he must gain the consent of the gods, particularly the almighty Sun-god, who speaks through Rabi the priest. Rabi, reluctant to endorse such an undertaking, is nonetheless aware that he can hold out only so long against secular power and that there is a rival to his spiritual authority in the person of Yescha the prophet. Opposing the rational Rabi, who is a scientist and physician as well as priest, Yescha is a self-hating desert ascetic whose very "unhappiness had made him an oracle among his people"(154). Although Yescha pronounces the people accursed and points to women as the source of all evil, in the matter of conquest, the prophet makes common cause with the chieftain: "[Adom] hungered to wrest lands and spoils from all the strange tribes, for his own people, Yescha had said, were the ones chosen by the gods to drive the degenerates into the wilderness and occupy the favored parts of the earth. In their imperialistic ambitions, Adom and Yescha saw eye to eye"(175).

The imperial adventure fails miserably, however, when Adom and his warriors are ambushed by the "inferior"people they have hoped to rob and kill. The people's resulting frustration and fear make them even more susceptible to beliefs that they are entitled to an Edenic original homeland from which they have been driven and that they are bound by religion to destroy any enemies who impede the fulfillment of their desires. *The Divine Passion* concludes with Yescha's blood sacrifice on behalf of his people—a people now disposed to believe in doctrines of a chosen people and a promised land.

Fisher's anthropological perspective can be compared to that of Chinua Achebe in his 1958 novel of precolonial Nigeria, *Things Fall Apart.* The text of *The Divine Passion* refers to "these people"and interprets their attitudes and customs for the benefit of readers, as does Achebe's presentation of the life of his Igbo ancestors. Both books are didactic, deliberately informing readers about the complexities of preliterate village life. Both the early Semites of *The Divine Passion* and Achebe's Igbo clan are depicted as living by similarly complex economic and social principles that govern marriage and family life, the division of labor, property rights, and the interactions of human beings and supernatural powers.

Although men dominate women and children in Achebe's polygamous West African culture, attitudes toward sexuality and the body are relaxed. Sexuality is associated neither with divinity nor with sin and guilt, and the relation to the earth as mother is maintained: "Ani, the earth goddess and the source of all fertility...played a greater part in the life of the people than any other deity. She was the ultimate judge of morality and conduct. And what was more, she was in close communion with the departed fathers of the clan whose bodies had been committed to earth."[6] Okonkwo, doomed hero of *Things Fall Apart,* is destroyed not only by the intrusion of alien values in the form of colonialism but also by his own fear of the feminine. Driven to prove his masculinity unnecessarily and at all costs, Okonkwo cannot learn the lesson offered by his maternal uncle that "Mother is Supreme"(94). Fisher's Semitic clan, on the other hand, appears bent on extirpating the female principle from their sense of the divine, and the author clearly condemns cultural attempts to value only the masculine. Indeed, he seems to blame much of what has gone wrong in the world on the rejecting of the female principle in the conceptual systems that led to Judaism, Islam, and Christianity.

Without judging the anthropological accuracy of either Achebe's or Fisher's depiction, we can conclude something about each writer's vision. Achebe attributes to his Igbo no collective restlessness, no desire to invade the lands and appropriate the property of others. He attributes to the wise men of the clan a tolerant worldview: commenting on the customs of another tribe, "Obierika's eldest brother"pronounces them "very bad," but then goes on to say, "But what is good in one place is bad in another place"(51). "The world has no end," declares another clansman, "and what is good among one people is an abomination with others"(99). Cognizant as he is of injustices in the ways of his ancestors, Achebe nonetheless suggests that constructive change could have occurred if Nigerians had been spared the shock of colonial encounter. Fisher, on the other hand, emphasizes the destructive potential in his spiritual forebears. In *The Divine Passion,* he depicts a people of energy and talent in whom are already planted the seeds of intolerance, exclusivity, and fanaticism, and who, very early in their communal development, are set on a course toward ideological conflict and warfare.

The anthropological point of view survives in *The Valley of Vision;* the narrative voice painstakingly describes the profusion of beliefs and practices that flourished in ninth-century B.C. Syria and Palestine—and is not above offering the occasional explanation. Although the text makes clear that many peoples inhabit the Middle East of King Solomon's day, attention focuses primarily on the monarch's Hebrew subjects. The novel chronicles the thirty-nine-year reign of Solomon, from his seizure of the throne and killing of his elder brother to his own death at a time of famine and social unrest. Solomon, as Fisher depicts him, is a ruler more concerned with his nation's place in the world than with the welfare of the people. He focuses on ambitious construction and astute and effective foreign policy. He diffuses external opposition by marrying princesses of different nations and religions and by forging commercial and political alliances.

Fisher's Solomon comes across as a pragmatic politician. Ruthless and self-indulgent, he is neither ideologue nor demagogue, but he does have a vision of what he wants for his nation:

> Solomon wanted lightness and light in his kingdom and people. He wanted ways that were gayer and brighter. He wanted a god of agriculture and soft loveliness in meadow and vale rather than a god of war. He wanted to build a splendid kingdom that would be rich and colorful and noble with great buildings and lordly furnishings, a kingdom with libraries and learning and art, a capital city whose hospitality the elite of the earth would be glad to accept. He would make Israel great and wise and respected among the nations. Toward that end he would learn to speak other languages, he would visit other lands, he would acquaint himself with the culture and wisdom of other peoples.[7]

"That,"the text continues, "was his dream,"(71) but it is a dream that would not be realized. If we read *The Divine Passion* as a *Things Fall Apart* of the ancient Near East, we see that Yescha, the misogynistic and self-mutilating prophet, embodies the destructiveness that Achebe associates with imperialist invasion of Africa. In *The Divine Passion,* the privation-born fanaticism of the desert mounts an initial attack on the comfortable life of the agricultural settlement, foreshadowing the central struggle of *The Valley of Vision.* Solomon belongs to a world of field and vineyard; he does not share the wilderness spirit of his forebears embodied in this novel as does Ahijah, spiritual descendant of Yescha. In Fisher's reading of history, Solomon opposes reasonable secular power to the retrograde forces of prophetic religion, only to lose his battle in the end. *The Valley of Vision* recounts Solomon's abortive attempt to turn Israel away from pursuing a destiny as a divinely singled-out people and toward a future as a nation among the nations. As a result of this failure, not only would "the fight between king and prophet...be the history of Israel"(71), but the fight between fanatical ethnocentrism and pluralist toleration would be the history of the Western world.

In the lengthy notes appended to *The Valley of Vision,* Vardis Fisher pointedly takes issue with what he terms "a curious prepossession in nearly all people which impels them to believe that what happened in the past has been in practically all cases better for progress and humanity than what might have happened if in any crucial period another set of circumstances had won"(426). This objection to collective complacency emphasizes Fisher's subversive approach to intellectual and moral history; he denies himself allegiance and belief in order to identify those decisive moments at which Judeo-Christian civilization took the "wrong"road.

Although Fisher endows Solomon with the ability to conceptualize a better way, he portrays him as closer to the worldly Adom than to *The Divine Passion*'s embodiment of rational religion and thought—Rabi. In *The Valley of Vision,* Rabi's healing powers and capacity for compassion and reason pass, not to King Solomon, reputed for wisdom, but to the Egyptian princess he marries. Khate, daughter of the Pharaoh, brings to Solomon and Jerusalem not only the material sophistication and taste of the more advanced Egyptian civilization but also an enlightened monotheism that stands in marked contrast to the beliefs of most people of the time. Solomon's subjects believe in many divinities—a pantheon of nature and local gods. Most significant, they adhere to the principle of tribal deities: each group worships its own god who contends with other gods on behalf of the tribe. Even the most ardently devout Yahwists do not claim that Yah is the only god; they claim rather that he is their god and that with his help they will prevail over other peoples and their inferior deities. Khate, on the other hand, influenced by the theology of Akhnaton, believes in one god who hates war, loves peace, and is god of all. "I don't think he has a name,"she responds to Solomon's question: "He is simply God.... He is a great force for good.... God is love. He is the spirit of compassion, mercy, forgiveness, tenderness.... Just God—the Father of all people"(139).

Khate's rational and benevolent creed influences Solomon, who is not wholly emancipated from his inherited beliefs. Although he has become only "half Egyptian"(382), Solomon refuses to inflict needless suffering on his subjects and chooses not to enforce strictly the draconian laws of his ancestors. He does not chop off the hand of a woman who has accidentally touched the private parts of a man attacking her husband; he does not have a half-starved and overworked little boy stoned to death at the behest of his abusive father. Having taken on the difficult task of depicting a protagonist about whom most readers have preconceived notions, Fisher does not focus so intensely on the "world historical individual"as to lose sight of the common people. In his tender portrayal of the old couple, Ahban and Mara, for instance, he shows these toilers of the Judean hills as both noble and oppressed.

In Fisher's fictional reconstruction of Solomon's Israel, issues of class struggle and economic injustice are foregrounded. Whatever the author's approval is of some of Solomon's views, he does not neglect to point out that the taxes levied to fund the king's projects are unreasonable and that his subjects are afflicted by "tyranny and oppression":

> Everywhere the people were starved, dispirited and sullen. Of what use to them, they asked, was a kingdom and its prince of peace if children died of hunger and their fathers were robbed of the fruits of their toil? Was this the happier life which Yah had promised? Better to return to the wilderness, for there, though poor, the people had lived in justice as neighbors. (370)

Ahijah the prophet, rather than the wise ruler, sees and weeps for the woes of the people. He acts not just as religious teacher but also as social and political agitator, albeit as one who views the privations that afflict the land as a punishment for corruption and sin. Fisher proves perspicacious in his comprehension of the links between religious fanaticism and the sufferings and frustrations of the poor. From Algeria to Iran to southern Egypt, the late twentieth century provides its own examples of the dynamics that Fisher attests to in Solomon's Israel.

Although Solomon rules for thirty-nine years, his reign is rife with conspiracy and discontent. In a final confrontation with Ahijah, the prophet who taxes him with wickedness, the king challenges his adversary as to what kind of king he would have been. Solomon speaks for progress, arguing that Ahijah would "try to drag our people back into the wilderness, back to the sands and storms and waterholes—back to the goatcurd and locusts." Ahijah claims righteousness, insisting that Yah's "laws are immutable and eternal. They do not change." He predicts that "Yah's holy people, his chosen" will be set above others, but only if they "walk in his holy way." Ahijah believes that Israel "should have nothing to do with other people"; Solomon counters that other nations will not take kindly to being cursed as "wicked sons of the no-gods." In the heat of this debate for the heart and soul of the nation, Solomon utters a prophecy that suggests the ferocity of Fisher's rejection of chauvinist extremism: "This much, Ahijah, I can tell you, that if Israel is ruled by men like you there will be no Israel. Other nations will kill us or sell us as slaves. They will throw our walls down and destroy our cities. We will be a stink in the nostrils of the earth"(395).

Fisher does not conclude *The Valley of Vision* with the fierce argument between king and prophet nor with the impassioned curses that Ahijah subsequently calls down on the ruler he judges to have betrayed his people's trust. Rather, Fisher allows himself the ironic luxury of affirmation. At novel's end, Solomon is dying and the contest for the throne that will split the kingdom is expected. But Queen Khate will not let hope die:

> "You haven't failed," said Khate impatiently. "When Akhnaton died they said he had failed, and so he had, for most of his people. But something remained, and something will remain of what you have tried to do, somewhere, in the heart of someone. Your people will never go back to the desert; that is too incredible to think of. They will mix with other people. The prophets can't hold them forever to this desert god. The prophets will realize some day that there is no god of Israel but only one supreme being."(400)

At this last improbable moment of philosophical optimism in Fisher's tragic version of Western history, Solomon and Khate make clear what a truly enlightened belief system would require and what it could mean for the world. "So let's drink to love," the dying king proposes, "and say that love is both the Father *and* the Mother, who together are God"(401).

In *The Island of the Innocent,* Fisher introduces a new and persistent counterpoint to the Judaic worldview as it evolves through the ages after David and Solomon. Thousands of years later in the history of Western civilization, a northern European intellectual points to "Hebraism and Hellenism"and declares that "between these two points of influence moves our world."[8] The *Island of the Innocent* recounts what Fisher appears to have considered the most fateful of all missteps in the moral history of Western humanity: the failure to synthesize Hebraism and Hellenism. The events of the novel take place at a time when Judaism is fully developed and Christianity is yet to be—the moment of opportunity for a marriage between the best of Jewish ethical and religious thought and Greek humanistic philosophy. In the story of the improbable love between Philemon and Judith, a sophisticated Greek man and a strictly brought-up Jewish woman, Fisher illustrates the disastrous cultural failure to bring about an intellectual synthesis that could have saved the world from many of the horrors of its subsequent history. In *The Island of the Innocent,* Fisher sets out to prove his reluctant conclusion that the synthesis of Hellenism and Judaism has missed its chance: as a result, faith is all too often given over to fanaticism, and reason to cynicism and skepticism. Early in the novel the central question is posed—a question in its generic form still relevant today: "Could Jewish *theocracy* and Greek *democracy* ever find a common ground of fellowship?"[9]

Caught up in a turbulent period in which Jews struggle not only against external military and cultural domination but also among themselves, Philemon and Judith do manage, against all odds, to love one another. Eventually they defy law, custom, and circumstances to go through a private marriage ceremony based on the Book of Job. After years of resistance, Judith at last adopts some of Philemon's Hellenistic views (rather absurdly, she determines that she will eat pork), and Philemon devotes himself to the study and defense of the Jewish faith. But the marriage of true minds this man and this woman achieve is a strictly personal matter; it defies rather than influences society. Theirs is a barren union—they have no progeny and therefore leave no living legacy. The tale of Judith and Philemon is one of a doomed love: failing to bring about a world in which they can live together, they can only die together on an apocalyptic battleground.

The Island of the Innocent reads in large part more like a symposium than a novel, and as such it has not been a favorite even among the neglected texts of the *Testament of Man.*[10]

In this book, "Philemon, a Hellene"engages in long debates not only with Judith, but also with Angela, her rebellious sister; Reuben, the Hellenized apostate allied with foreign power; and Hosah, the scholar devoted to reconciling Scripture with the theological exigencies of Orthodoxy. The Hellenic worldview emerges as one that aspires to beauty and can divorce aesthetic value from moral judgment. Judaism, on the other hand, cares only for virtue: in the words of pious Hosah, "Hellas loves beauty, Israel loves righteousness"(130). But righteousness does not come easily; according to a Greek observer, "[T]hese pious Jews think people are utterly evil and must struggle day and night against sin.... Our philosophers say that people are naturally good, but Jews say they are naturally evil"(119). According to a son of Israel critical of his own faith, "[T]he core of religion for Jews was the impotence of man as an instrument of God to overcome the grossness and evil in nature. Nature's assault on history was persistent and dreadful: to overcome nature and subdue it, God had chosen a special people to assist him, who would become the priests to all nations"(29).

In Seleucid Jerusalem, religious differences routinely find expression in violence. Early in the novel, Philemon attends a Jewish festival and finally realizes his own danger when he witnesses the death by stoning of a non-Jew who has intruded on holy ground. This shocking sight brings the Greek outsider to a keener cognizance of the contrast between Hebraic and Hellenic views of the world. At one point Philemon is thrown into a dungeon after defending Judith from the lust of a corrupt Hellenized high priest. Forgotten by all but one, he is brought just enough bread and water to prolong a lingering death. At last he rouses himself to plead for help and is rescued just in time—reborn into a fallen world but, all the same, reborn. After this emergence from the underground cave that was to have been his grave, Philemon takes refuge in other caves dug into the rocky Jerusalem hillsides: one a tiny niche where one person could shelter, the other a large communal dwelling where he lived among his adopted Hasidic family. Pondering the evil in the mind of human beings and the relief to be found in death, he nevertheless decides to live among those who live by the faith they profess: rescued by a Greek, he takes shelter among Jews.

As bitter as the opposition of Jew to non-Jew, however, are divisions among the Jews themselves. Whereas the Pious or Hasidim cling tenaciously to Mosaic law and tradition, the Hellenized Letzim are spiritual descendants of Solomon. Their version of national aspiration involves not a vision of one people chosen to rule over others but rather a desire to diffuse hatred of the Hebrews and to "assimilate to the nations around them the insignificant spot called Israel"(14).

Although the Letzim may appear to offer the opportunity to synthesize Hellenic and Hebraic thought, the rulers with whom they make common cause become increasingly ruthless in their attempts to wipe out the Jewish religion. Jerusalem is now divided between Temple and Citadel, and the cruelties perpetrated in the struggle between the Hellenized supporters of the persecutors of their fellow Jews and the resisting Orthodox serve to ensure that extremism prevails. Forced ultimately to take sides and unable to ignore the atrocities inflicted upon the Pious, Philemon and Judith are caught up in brutal combat and die together in the doomed last stand of the Maccabees.

Beyond the obsessive and conservative religiosity of Hosah and the Pious stands this novel's avatar of the fanatical prophet, Amiel. Spiritually castrated by willed detachment, he feels no earthly passion or desire. He is possessed of a divinely inspired vision of the triumph of his persecuted people. "The Holy Name,"he assures Hosah, "said the saints of the most High will have power and dominion over all the peoples of the earth. All languages, nations and peoples will bow before him; for his dominion is from everlasting to everlasting and will not pass away or be destroyed. All dominions and kingdoms and principalities will obey and serve him—blessed be he—and his chosen will be the priests to all nations"(44).

In the prefatory note to *The Island of the Innocent,* Vardis Fisher refers to the Maccabean revolt as "that most crucial of all struggles for Western Civilization."A dedication to "the many scholars whose labors have promoted understanding and fellowship between Gentile and Jew"precedes the note that also points out "the pride that modern Jewry takes"in the military exploits of the Maccabees. The preface concludes by referring readers to the appended notes (more copious with each successive volume) for "further illumination of the reasons for this struggle and of the irreconcilable differences between Greek and orthodox Jewish beliefs and ways of life."

The explanations with which Fisher envelops *The Island of the Innocent* suggest an increasingly cautious author anxious that this latest historical and philosophical novel not be misunderstood. Writing this book in the turbulent years after the proclamation of the State of Israel when the people of the Middle East were once again fighting for territory and legitimacy, Fisher depicts a second-century B.C. Jerusalem that foreshadows the Palestine of his time and of ours. City and countryside constitute a contested space in which those who promote the reconciliation of religion and philosophy, of belief in a single god and observance of reason and humanity, continue to lose out to forces of political extremism and orthodox fanaticism.

The Island of the Innocent is a daring book. Perhaps only someone raised among Mormons withdrawn from a world of "Gentiles"could, in the late 1940s and early 1950s, have written such a work. In the years after World War II when the horrors of the Nazi Holocaust were being exposed, Vardis Fisher had the courage and clear-sightedness to maintain an adamant opposition to exclusivist religion and politics. Having been exposed as a boy to theocratic-fortress mentality, he could insist on the need to resist the powerful temptation of a tribalist response to even the most extreme persecution.

Although it can be tiresomely didactic, *The Island of the Innocent* serves as the philosophical center of Fisher's monumental sequence. At novel's end, all hopes for a marriage of the best Judaic and Hellenic principles are buried with Judith and Philemon. The work's repeated debates as to the merits of reason and faith, beauty and righteousness end in violent encounter and the tragic failure of synthesis at the heart of the *Testament of Man*. The final chapter leaves us with this book's incarnation of prophetic fervor, Amiel, who, in difficult times, is writing the Book of Daniel and thus providing nationalist reassurance as to the invincibility of Zion. Amiel's prophecy serves also to expand expectations so as to include intimations of immortality for the righteous and promises of a savior-king to come: "The son of David would come soon, with omens and portents announcing his coming"(402).

The promise of redemption—whether political or spiritual—is made and the stage set for the coming of the prophesied Messiah. Unlike the social, historical, and political novels that precede and follow, *Jesus Came Again* is a romance, an elegiac quest narrative of the ministry and martyrdom of a man very much like the Jesus in whom Christians believe. Fisher's protagonist is "Joshua, a Jew,"and the novel recounts his journey through the largely desolate landscapes of Galilee and Judea to the holy city of Jerusalem. As do many others in the Palestine of the time, he moves toward the city where the Messiah is expected. As Joshua makes his way to the city, he collects a band of marginal and outcast fellow travelers, most of whom are women (and thus automatically despised in Israel and elsewhere); a self-sacrificing runaway slave with a child acquired no one knows how; a comically useless old couple (whose speech bears traces of Idaho idiom); and exhausted and ill-used women with dubious sexual histories. Traveling with this ragtag band, Joshua encounters multitudes of the wretched of the earth.

The Israel of the novel bears more than its share of misery, having been destroyed by centuries of warfare, and a social system of "only two classes, the rich and the poor."As for the people, "they had been so oppressed and beaten down, so leached of their humanity, so despised and humbled that few of them...dared speak out."[11] Rich oppress poor, foreigners oppress natives, neighbors inform on neighbors; Zealots despise both followers of other faiths and the less strictly observant of their coreligionists. Even Joshua's otherwise peaceful vision requires the destruction of the latest imperial oppressor, Rome, to which only the Zealots offer real defiance. In the main, however, Joshua's hopes are not political, but rather concentrate on "no more disease, no cruelty, no punishment and no death." In his version of the kingdom, "Righteousness, peace, justice, love would come down from the heavens"(21).

Prophecies have promised the Messiah but do not agree on the exact time or the exact character of the one who is to come. Joshua, however, "was sure that the time would be soon, because there was so much wretchedness and misery, so much brutality and despair and sickness over the whole earth"(19). In *Jesus Came Again,* the land awaits cataclysmic release; the people are in thrall to eschatological hysteria. Everywhere, huge crowds gather and are swayed and impassioned. They witness miracles, they hang on the words of teachers, and they are baptized in the River Jordan.

Into this maelstrom comes Joshua, humbly and hesitantly, to offer lessons that yet may hold some hope of redemption. Joshua teaches, in the first place, by example: the first stage of his journey is dedicated to increasingly deliberate affirmation of the humanity and value of women. The continuing hostility directed against him because he travels with women prompts his uncomfortable memory of the often-heard "Jewish thanksgiving: Blessed be the Lord our God who did not make us a woman!"(46). Soon he is heard to declare that he loves all people (48); at the baths near Tiberias, he teaches that "the poor will be first in the kingdom"and shows mercy to "the dumb and the blind, the epileptic and the paralytic, the insane, the leprous, the old, the sick"(99). Resisting demands that he speak of "rank and privileges and blessings...in the next life,"Joshua resorts to the Beatitudes: "He told them that the poor would be blessed, the humbled would be exalted, the sorrowing would be comforted, the pure in heart would see God, and the peacemakers above all others would be his children"(121). Engaging John the Baptist in debate, Joshua denies that the kingdom is only for Israel, and insists that salvation is available to "all people who repent and humble themselves and love their neighbors and accept the Father"(197). He is disgusted by his mother's harsh rejection of the idea that non-Jews are anything but an irredeemably "godless people"(239). Appalled by the sign at the synagogue prohibiting the entrance of "any foreigner"(241) and by the ethnocentric lessons taught there, he speaks out and is expelled (259–61). He rejects the doctrine of the "Chosen People," the insistence upon the uncleanness of women, and the practice of blood sacrifice. Driven to despair by the unholy obsessions with rules and rituals that "mar" Jewish religious life, Joshua allows himself to be arrested by the Romans and will offer no defense against charges of treason. Sickened by the blood-slaughters that mark the Passover season, Joshua, nevertheless, allows himself to become another sacrifice.

Jesus Came Again ends not with the acts or utterances of male prophets such as Yescha, Ahijah, or Amiel. Instead, this elegiac narrative of the pilgrimage and death of a messiah ends with the words of women. The most faithful of Joshua's disciples strive to understand the events that they have witnessed: "Sibyl now surrendered to a vast and holy quiet, to the great love that had been the soul of Joshua; she gave herself up to it completely and after a while seemed not to be breathing at all. She knew that she was no longer on the earth, but above it, and slowly ascending; she was among the clouds now; she could hear the flutes passing with soft harmonies into the heavenly choirs"(308). Serena, the exiled Greek woman, and Zillah, the dishonored Jewish woman, make use of Sibyl's mystic vision to find their way to the truth: "Don't you see that [the Messiah] has come?—again?...He has come in the only way he will ever come—as he came a hundred or a thousand years ago; as he will come again next year, or a hundred years from now, or a thousand years hence.... He has come, he will come again, he will keep coming, until there are no more Lucias hunting for their lost children, no more soldiers with lances by dead men in the night"(309).

But women would not be accepted as true apostles by future generations, Jews would continue to wait for a national savior-king, and Christians would focus on the very elements that Joshua wished to purge from the religion of his time: miracles, magic, and blood-sacrifice. Rejecting or misunderstanding teachers such as Joshua, the people of Vardis Fisher's Holy Land continue in the erroneous ways of their ancestors and base three major religions on rejection of the Mother and deification of the Word.

Fisher's Middle East focuses on Jews and centers on Jerusalem. Syrians, Hittites, Canaanites, and Amorites—all the myriad peoples inhabiting the Middle East in the millennia before the founding of Christianity—are peripheral to the Hebrews, with whom Fisher is primarily concerned. His concentrating of theological, ethical, and political struggle on the Jews does not, however, unreasonably privilege Jewish perspectives. In fact, he dwells on dissensions among Jewish believers as, in later volumes of the *Testament*, he emphasizes divisions among Christians: Hasidim contend with Letzim, and Essenes with Pharisees, as do the factions of the early church among themselves. A onetime citizen of the Mormon Zion, Fisher no more endorses ways of thinking such as those that underlie right-wing movements in contemporary Israel than he does any other exclusivist ideology. To the degree that he deals with the historic relationship of the Jews with other peoples, Fisher foregrounds tensions similar to those that plague the Middle East today.

Fisher's depictions of Near Eastern lands and populations are based to some degree on an intensive study of history and anthropology, yet they do not (in my view) partake of assumptions of racial and cultural superiority that undoubtedly inform some of his sources. Among the western authorities on Near Eastern peoples and religions cited in Fisher's notes is (William) Robertson Smith. Smith's summing up of the Jewish mind as "deficient in plastic power and the faculty of sustained and orderly effort"[12] suggests the mentality that leads Edward Said to name him among those western scholars and writers who have stereotyped Semitic people. In *Orientalism,* Said introduces Smith as one whose "work on the Semites covered such areas as theology, literature, and history; it was...intended as an aid to the understanding of the modern Semites. For Smith, I think, was a crucial link in the intellectual chain connecting the White-Man-as-expert to the modern Orient."[13]

Robertson Smith exemplifies those numerous western scholars and writers who tend to see the Semitic peoples of the Middle East as living out a kind of racial destiny. "In no people more than in the Oriental Semites,"according to Said's articulation of the position, "was it possible to see the present and the origin together. The Jews and the Muslims, as subjects of Orientalist study, were readily understandable in view of their primitive origins...no Semite could ever shake loose the pastoral, desert environment of his tent and tribe."[14] Although Vardis Fisher traces what he perceives as successive missteps in the evolution of Judeo-Christian civilization with some reference, admittedly, to tent and tribe, he evades, in my view, the trap of Orientalism.

In the second half of the twentieth century, Said explains, the "myth of the arrested development of the Semites"underwent a curious bifurcation: "[O]ne Semite went the way of Orientalism, the other, the Arab, was forced to go the way of the Oriental."[15] In the aftermath of World War II, anti-Semitic hostility has been redirected to Arabs; Israelis now serve the western imagination as new colonial heroes who stand in for "white men" in a depraved Orient. Some of Fisher's depictions of "the Syrians" and "Antiochus of Corinth" fit an updated Orientalist model of cruel barbarians besieging devout Hebrews, but the author of the *Testament of Man* takes no stand above or distant from the Semitic peoples he describes. Although he does not reject all of the cultural stereotyping that pervades Orientalist scholarship, Fisher insists on standing eye to eye with his characters.

Vardis Fisher, unlike those writers whom Said brands "Orientalist,"is concerned with Semitic culture as the forerunner not of Islam but of Christianity. He writes his *Testament* as an albeit apostate inheritor of the Judeo-Christian tradition—not from without but from within. Characterizing *Orphans in Gethsemane* (1960) as "the story of the man who wrote the *Testament of Man,*"Joseph M. Flora retroactively associates the narrative voice with that of the author's fictional alter ego, the twentieth century's still-tormented Vridar Hunter.[16] Portraying the Middle East as he does, Fisher looks not only back but also "ahead"to Hunter's world and his own. He depicts the birthplace of western civilization as a battleground, painting a picture colored by pained awareness of the failings of his own culture.

Brought up in an impoverished and theocratic society, Fisher eschewed the attitude of domination at the core of Orientalism. He lived on lonely homesteads in rugged landscapes, and, perhaps more easily than other Europeans or North Americans, was able to insert himself into the ancient Middle East, to observe on the level of the observed—and to identify with the alienated prophet. His firsthand knowledge of poverty and privation afforded him insight into peoples who think hard, love and hate intensely, and are consumed with anxieties about their relation to God. The struggle to find and defend faith was for Fisher no quaint exercise of primitive folk—it was a struggle that he saw played out in deadly earnest among his family and friends, and within himself. The writer who as a boy read mainly the Bible and contemplated a prophetic calling did not patronize peoples for whom the relation of man to God is the central fact of life.[17]

In a period of the resurgence of fundamentalist religions in many parts of the world, Vardis Fisher's *Testament of Man* may be a text of some significance. Fisher, raised by a strict Mormon mother on a solitary Idaho homestead, commanded a more sympathetic view of zeal than could most American intellectuals of his time. Possessed of a dual consciousness, Fisher rejected the rule-bound exclusivity of any self-appointed "chosen"people, but was all the same drawn to the passion of the prophet. In *Testament of Man,* he carried out his own arduous quest—to understand the moral development of western humanity. He donned the prophet's mantle to warn against the dangers of fanaticism. Chronicling the spiritual development of his forebears, Fisher created a prophetic work mourning the lost opportunities of Judeo-Christian tradition. He identified those points at which, in his opinion, a wrong turn was taken, a wrong road chosen. In dishonoring the Mother, demonizing the "other,"privileging law over ethics, and failing to synthesize love of wisdom with love of God, humanity set a course that has led to Inquisition and Holocaust. At the beginning of the twenty-first century, that course has yet to be adequately altered. Religion and reason have yet to be reconciled, and Reuben's passionate appeal in *The Island of the Innocent* has yet to be answered: "But there's a job to be done or there'll be no Alexandrias. We'll have a world of Jerusalems"(63).

Notes

1. Georg Lukács, *The Historical Novel*, trans. Hannah and Stanley Mitchell (Lincoln: University of Nebraska Press, 1983), 53.
2. Tim Woodward, *Tiger on the Road: The Life of Vardis Fisher* (Caldwell, ID: Caxton Printers, 1989), 69.
3. Edward W. Said, *Culture and Imperialism* (New York: Vintage Books, 1994), 298.
4. Ibid., 299.
5. Vardis Fisher, *The Divine Passion* (New York: Vanguard, 1948), 297. Subsequent references are cited parenthetically.
6. Chinua Achebe, *Things Fall Apart* (1958; reprint, Oxford, UK: Heinemann, 1996), 26. Subsequent references are cited parenthetically.
7. Vardis Fisher, *The Valley of Vision: A Novel of King Solomon and His Time* (New York: Abelard, 1951), 71. Subsequent references are cited parenthetically.
8. Matthew Arnold, *Poetry and Criticism of Matthew Arnold,* ed. A. Dwight Culler (Boston: Houghton Mifflin, 1961), 465.
9. Vardis Fisher, *The Island of the Innocent: A Novel of Greek and Jew in the Time of the Maccabees* (New York: Abelard, 1952), 6. Subsequent references are cited parenthetically.
10. Joseph M. Flora, *Vardis Fisher* (New York: Twayne Publishers, 1965), 89–90.
11. Vardis Fisher, *Jesus Came Again: A Parable* (Denver: Alan Swallow, 1956), 24. Subsequent references are cited parenthetically.
12. Quoted in Fisher, *Island*, 423.
13. Edward W. Said, *Orientalism* (New York: Vintage Books, 1979), 235.
14. Ibid., 234.
15. Ibid., 307.
16. Flora, *Vardis Fisher,* 50.
17. Woodward, *Tiger on the Road,* 40.

Bibliography

Achebe, Chinua. *Things Fall Apart*. 1958. Reprint. Oxford, UK: Heinemann, 1996.

Arnold, Matthew. *Poetry and Criticism of Matthew Arnold.* Ed. A. Dwight Culler. Boston: Houghton Mifflin, 1961.

Fisher, Vardis. *The Divine Passion.* New York: Vanguard Press, 1948.

———. *The Island of the Innocent: A Novel of Greek and Jew in the Time of the Maccabees.* New York: Abelard Press, 1952.

———. *Jesus Came Again: A Parable.* Denver: Alan Swallow, 1956.

———. *The Valley of Vision: A Novel of King Solomon and His Time.* New York: Abelard Press, 1951.

Flora, Joseph M. *Vardis Fisher.* New York: Twayne Publishers, 1965.

Lukács, Georg. *The Historical Novel.* Trans. Hannah and Stanley Mitchell. Lincoln: University of Nebraska Press, 1983.

Said, Edward W. *Culture and Imperialism.* New York: Vintage Books, 1994.

———. *Orientalism.* New York: Vintage Books, 1979.

Woodward, Tim. *Tiger on the Road: The Life of Vardis Fisher.* Caldwell, ID: Caxton Printers, 1989.

12

Vardis Fisher: An Essay in Bibliography

Mark Canada

Interest in Vardis Fisher peaked in the 1930s, when his novels about Idaho pioneers, autobiographical tetralogy, and his historical novel about the Mormons drew extensive, favorable attention from esteemed reviewers, including Fred T. Marsh of the *New York Times* and fellow novelist Bernard DeVoto. After the Mormon novel, *Children of God,* won the 1939 Harper Prize for Fiction, Fisher went on to write two more historical novels of the American West before turning his attention toward a grander project, the *Testament of Man,* a twelve-volume series tracing human psychological and sociological development from Creation to the present day. With this series—buttressed (some would say encumbered) by extensive research in a number of fields—interest in Fisher declined but did not disappear. For this series, and the additional historical novels of the West he went on to write, he continued to attract interest from reviewers, fellow writers such as Frederick Manfred and Larry McMurtry, and even director Sidney Pollack, who adapted Fisher's last novel, *Mountain Man* (1965), for the 1972 movie *Jeremiah Johnson,* featuring Robert Redford. Today, the future of Fisher's reputation rests in the hands of literary scholars. Since his death in 1968, scholars such as Joseph M. Flora, John R. Milton, Ronald W. Taber, Barbara Meldrum, and Mick McAllister have produced a small but steady stream of critical articles, most of them treating Fisher as a western writer.

Bibliography

The most recent bibliography of primary and secondary works related to Vardis Fisher is also the most comprehensive. This annotated list, which appears in Martin Kich's *Western American Novelists, Volume 1: Walter Van Tilburg Clark, Dan Cushman, H.L. Davis, Vardis Fisher, A.B. Guthrie, Jr., William Humphrey, and Dorothy M. Johnson* (New York: Garland, 1995), covers one hundred and eighty works by Fisher—including novels, stories, essays, articles, and poems—as well as nine books and nearly two hundred critical articles relevant to Fisher scholarship. Among the latter are scores of articles that, because they refer only briefly to Fisher, do not appear in other bibliographies. Somewhat cumbersome in size and generally not evaluative, this bibliography nonetheless is invaluable for its extensive coverage, detailed annotations, and judicious headnote on the future of Fisher scholarship. It supplants an earlier, briefer bibliography in *A Bibliographical Guide to the Study of Western American Literature* (Lincoln: University of Nebraska Press, 1982), as well as lists compiled by George Kellogg for *American Book Collector* (September 1963) and *Western American Literature* (Spring 1970).

Editions

For the first three decades of his career, Fisher worked with several eastern publishing houses, including Houghton Mifflin in Boston and Doubleday, Harper, and Vanguard in New York. During the same period, Caxton Printers in Caldwell, Idaho, came out with regular or deluxe editions of nearly all of his books. Reception to the first seven volumes of his twelve-volume *Testament of Man* series was lukewarm, however, and Fisher struggled to find a publisher. Alan Swallow of Denver took over the series in 1956 and published the remaining five volumes, as well as *Suicide or Murder? The Strange Death of Governor Meriwether Lewis* (1962) and *Thomas Wolfe As I Knew Him, and Other Essays* (1963). Although New York firms published most of his other books, even during this period, Fisher assailed the eastern establishment, which he accused of snobbery. A brief but interesting account of Fisher's troubles with eastern publishers and critics appears in an article by Swallow, "The Mavericks" (*Critique*, Winter 1959). In addition to speculating on several possible reasons for these difficulties—including Fisher's reactionary politics, his rough style, and his rationalist approach to fiction—Swallow makes the rather bizarre accusation that people at *Time* ordered an extra copy of one of the *Testament* novels so that their researcher could "break down the scholarship of the volume." He goes on to say: "When they could not, as I infer they could not, they chose to ignore the book."

Despite these difficulties, Fisher managed to publish thirty-seven books, including two reference volumes on his home state of Idaho written for the Federal Writers' Project. Thirty years after his death, *Books in Print* lists two dozen of these books, although only *Mountain Man* (Pocket Books) is a mass market paperback. *Suicide or Murder?* (Swallow) is available in a paperback reprint edition. Libraries can order a handful of Fisher's other books, including *God or Caesar? The Writing of Fiction for Beginners* (1953), *Idaho Encyclopedia* (1938), *Idaho Lore* (Gordon Press, 1939), *The Mothers* (1943), *Pemmican* (1956), and *Tale of Valor* (Amereon, 1958). *Children of God* (Harper, 1939), Fisher's most famous book during his life, is no longer in print; however, in 1977 Opal Laurel Holmes, Fisher's widow, had it reprinted from the original plates. Others of Fisher's books in print are available from the Idaho Center for the Book and as reprints from the University of Idaho Press.

No one has published a descriptive bibliography on Fisher, but Kellogg's bibliography in *Western American Literature* (Spring 1970) includes an extensive list of the first editions published by Swallow, Houghton Mifflin, Harper, Vanguard, and other publishers, as well as the numerous deluxe editions published by Caxton and translations published in Iceland, Argentina, France, and other countries. Kellogg's earlier bibliography for *American Book Collector* (September 1963) includes two brief notes on the publishing history of *Passions Spin the Plot* (1934) and the *Testament of Man* series, along with pictures of six title pages from Fisher first editions. Scholars can find first editions, autographed copies, and other important Fisher items in the Clore and Gossett collections in the Special Collections Department at Boise State University's Albertsons Library. A list of the materials in these collections appears in *The Clore Collection of Vardis Fisher Research Materials: A Guide* (Boise: Boise State University, 1989).

Manuscripts and Letters

Collections of Fisher's papers are housed at Boise State University, the University of Idaho Library in Moscow, the Washington State University Archives in Pullman, and Yale University's Beinecke Library in New Haven, Connecticut. The most extensive is the Yale collection, which contains two file drawers of letters to or from Frederick Manfred, Alan Swallow, Harper and Brothers, and other associates and publishers, as well as typescripts for seventeen of Fisher's books. Other Fisher papers belong to Delbert Wylder.

Several letters between Fisher and Milwaukee bookseller Harry Schwartz appear in "Dear Mr. Fisher/Dear Mr. Schwartz: A Correspondence," published in the September 1974 issue of *The Bookmark*, a quarterly periodical of the University of Idaho Library. In addition to some mundane particulars related to a catalog introduction Schwartz asked Fisher to write and a limited edition of Fisher essays that Schwartz published, this correspondence contains evidence of Fisher's congeniality and humor, as well as the revelation that he "had to make a few minor concessions to the pure" to satisfy Doubleday, which was to publish *We Are*

Betrayed (1935). Even more interesting is a civil but intense debate that emerges when Schwartz, a Marxist, learns that the essays Fisher has produced for him savagely attack communists as quixotic brutes.

Biography

By far the most thorough accounts of Fisher's life are the ones he wrote himself. *In Tragic Life* (1932), the first volume of his autobiographical tetralogy, tells the story of Vardis Fisher—almost comically disguised as "Vridar Hunter"—from ancestry to adolescence. *Passions Spin the Plot* recounts the next period of Fisher's life, when he studied at the University of Utah and married Leona McMurtrey, or "Neloa Doole." Fisher continued his story in *We Are Betrayed,* an account of his graduate work at the University of Chicago and of a tragic marriage that ended in Neloa's suicide, and finally in *No Villain Need Be* (1936), an account of his second marriage and career pursuits. Still not satisfied, Fisher revised his life story in the gigantic *Orphans in Gethsemane* (1960), the twelfth and final volume of his *Testament of Man* series. Although these efforts have caused critics to compare Fisher with another confessional writer of the period, Thomas Wolfe, Fisher's autobiographical fiction stays much closer to factual reality than does Wolfe's *Look Homeward, Angel.* Indeed, Fisher's obsession with facts exasperated John Peale Bishop, who wrote of the later installments of the tetralogy: "Honesty does not consist in telling all. And that is just what Mr. Fisher does. He tells all."

More detached, if less comprehensive, accounts of Fisher's life can be found in several books and articles by scholars and acquaintances. Louie W. Attebery's essay on Fisher in *A Literary History of the American West,* ed. Thomas J. Lyon (Fort Worth: Texas Christian University Press, 1987) treats important external as well as psychological events in his subject's life, which he divides into five stages called "the early years, 1895–1915; the university period, 1915–31; the Bridwell days, 1931–34; the Federal era, 1935–39; and finally the Hagerman years, 1940–68." Of the university period Attebery writes: "First, Fisher received an education in a demanding graduate career, an education that prepared him for a life of the mind, encouraging his philosophical speculations and confirming his rejection of Mormonism. In addition, the discipline of scholarship became the servant of his maturing creativity. In the second place, his writing reached the public. The third significant element was Leona's death. For this Fisher blamed himself and subsequently identified her suicide as the great crisis of his life." Joseph M. Flora's *Vardis Fisher* (New York: Twayne Publishers, 1965) contains a brief biographical sketch that draws on Flora's acquaintance with Fisher and addresses the author's feelings about his work, family, and marriages.

The only book-length biography of Fisher is *Tiger on the Road: The Life of Vardis Fisher* (Caldwell, ID: Caxton Printers, 1989), which author Tim Woodward notes in his foreword "is not intended to be a scholarly analysis of Fisher's work" or "a definitive biography of the man." Indeed, literary scholars will find few new insights in this popular biography, which relies heavily on Fisher's own writings, as well as on previously published books and articles by Flora, Ronald W. Taber, and others. Still, even the best-read Fisher scholars will want to read *Tiger on the Road* for its scores of interesting anecdotes and impressions, which Woodward painstakingly collected through interviews with Fisher's third wife, his sister, his brother-in-law, his neighbors, and other acquaintances. In a chapter called "Old Irascible," for example, Woodward paints Fisher as a curmudgeon, prankster, carouser, and friendly neighbor—a man who could accept an invitation to a book signing and then refuse to sign books; a man who would belittle an aspiring writer and entertain a groupie for six hours; a man who was called "generous," "sentimental and compassionate," and "abrupt, aggressive, tactless." In addition to these rare glimpses of Fisher's private side, Woodward's biography contains nearly twenty photographs, excerpts from Leona Fisher's letters written just before she committed suicide, an extensive summary of Fisher's work as a newspaper columnist in Idaho, and a brief investigation of the mystery surrounding his death.

Fisher spoke at length about his life and work, as well as his ideas about writing in general, in a television interview with John R. Milton in the mid-1960s. A transcript of this interview appears in Milton's book *Three West: Conversations with Vardis Fisher, Max Evans, Michael Straight* (Vermillion, SD: Dakota Press, 1970). In addition to his novels, particularly the tetralogy and the *Testament of Man* series, Fisher discusses religion, his relationship with the harsh environment of the West, his experience as a teacher, his work on the Federal Writers' Project, realism and romance, art and scholarship, politics, the eastern literary establishment, and several fellow writers, including Wallace Stegner, Ernest Hemingway, and Thomas Wolfe. In a particularly interesting portion of the interview, Milton reads several letters to Fisher from readers who responded enthusiastically to the *Testament of Man*.

Other materials have focused on particular aspects of Fisher's life, such as his religious convictions and his relationships with other writers. Fisher's faith has been a thorny issue because of the mixed signals he sent about the subject through his actions and works. While still a teenager, Fisher renounced Mormonism, the religion of his parents. Some twenty-five years later, however, Fisher published a complex treatment of the Mormons in *Children of God,* which both angered members of the church and attracted converts to it. Later, he challenged Christianity as a whole in his *Testament of Man* series and allied himself with agnosticism and atheism. These mixed signals have left literary scholars and family members alike to speculate on what Fisher's convictions were at the time of his death in 1968. Flora opened the dialogue in 1969 with his article "Vardis Fisher and the Mormons" (*Dialogue: A Journal of Mormon Thought,* Autumn 1969), which argues that Fisher, despite his renunciation of Mormonism, showed a religious, even Mormon bent throughout his career. Citing details from *Children of God,* as well as from the essay "My Bible Heritage" and the *Testament of Man,* Flora notes that Fisher showed a deep appreciation of particular qualities of the early Hebrews and the Mormons, especially their righteousness and their similar vision of freedom.

Somewhat more strident is "The Mormon Heritage of Vardis Fisher" (*Brigham Young University Studies,* Fall 1977), in which Leonard J. Arrington and Jon Haupt argue that Fisher's break with Mormonism has been exaggerated. Early in the article, the authors make their points explicit: "(1) Fisher was not an apostate; he never renounced his religion nor did Mormonism renounce him. (2) Fisher's outlook on life and history was religious, definitely Judeo-Christian and, as he saw it, broader than the Mormonism he was acquainted with, but definitely encompassing Latter-day Saint belief and practice. And (3) Fisher was a pioneer in applying modern psychology to the Mormon experience, both past and present, and in that sense he is very much a Mormon literary prophet. He foresaw conflicts his people would have, groped with them two generations before they did, and made some progress toward a resolution of them." Marked by solid research and analysis, the article goes at least partway in making these points. The authors point out, for example, that Fisher allowed his son Grant to be baptized into the Church of Jesus Christ of Latter-day Saints. It is significant, however, that other details they cite to explain Fisher's relationship with Mormonism come from his sister Irene, a Latter-day Saint who performed temple work for Fisher after his death and presumably wanted to see her brother as a Mormon at heart.

Arrington and Haupt are on firmer ground when they analyze Fisher's early novels: *Toilers of the Hills* (1928), *Dark Bridwell* (1931), the tetralogy, and, of course, *Children of God.* Citing evidence from *In Tragic Life* (1932), for example, they make a convincing argument that Fisher's hostility toward his faith had less to do with the religion itself than with his mother's puritanical attitudes: "In fact, there is no hope in Vridar anywhere in the religion of his youth; it would be impossible for him to rid it of all the ugliness on which he was reared; agnosticism is perhaps the only way out for him." Identifying *Children of God* as "a fine indicator of

Fisher's attitudes toward Mormonism," the authors suggest that the novel shows Fisher's appreciation of the Mormons' work ethic, individuality, and social conscience. They argue that Fisher's negative portrait of Joseph Smith, whose experience with visions closely resembles Vridar's experience in *In Tragic Life,* is actually "a projection of his own unloved self." The article is valuable for other reasons. Citing research by a historian working with church archives, Arrington and Haupt provide information about Fisher's ancestry not widely available in other sources. They also cite evidence of Mormon converts who trace their interest in the Mormon church back to *Children of God* and effectively summarize the reception of the novel by both the Utah branch of the church and the Reorganized Church of Jesus Christ of Latter Day Saints.

Finally, Richard Andrews, founder of the Utah Chapter of American Atheists, has followed the lead of Fisher's widow and claimed Fisher as an atheist. More polemical than scholarly, "Vardis Fisher: An American Atheist Author" (*American Atheist,* Summer 1997) attempts no detailed investigation of Fisher's thought and is interesting mainly for its account of the battle in the 1970s and 1980s over Fisher's theology. Andrews, who corresponded with Opal Laurel Holmes, notes that the author's widow responded to scholarly claims of her husband's Mormon heritage by distributing press releases about his atheism.

Isolated by both geography and a fiery temperament, Fisher remained an outsider on the American literary scene his entire career. He did, however, develop relationships with or opinions about a few important contemporaries, and these connections have been the subjects of several articles by Flora. For example, "Vardis Fisher and Wallace Stegner: Teacher and Student" (*Western American Literature,* Summer 1970) notes the many similarities between Fisher, who taught Stegner at the University of Utah, and Paul Latour, a character in Stegner's story "The View from the Balcony." Both, for example, have sharp features, vision problems, and an affinity for hard liquor. Furthermore, both Fisher and Latour, Flora writes, use their keen, penetrating minds to analyze human behavior. Flora argues that these and other similarities not only indicate Fisher's influence on Stegner, but also point to the specific impressions Fisher left on his student. One particular characteristic that Stegner apparently noted in Fisher—and depicted in the character of Latour—is that of his penchant for detachment. Referring to Latour's brawl with a student named Charley, Flora writes: "It is an irony that Latour's animal action is really an intellectual favor to Charley and his wife. I think Fisher's own rudenesses were often attempts to prevent emotional dependencies. Fisher felt tempted to play the role of Father, but what he tried to say was: You need to be an adult. I'll tell you what I know, but don't look for me to be Big Daddy for you." Flora points out that the problem of sons' dependencies on fathers is a central theme in the *Testament of Man,* particularly in *Orphans in Gethsemane.* Turning from "The View from the Balcony," Flora traces the similarities of tone, style, setting, and characterization in Fisher's *Dark Bridwell* and Stegner's *Remembering Laughter.* He concludes that the resemblance of Stegner's Alec Stuart to Charley Bridwell, in particular, brought about Fisher's claim that Stegner's prize-winning first novel owed something to his own, commercially less successful second novel.

Between 1929 and 1931, Fisher developed a friendship with Thomas Wolfe while the two worked together as instructors at New York University. Flora's "Thomas Wolfe at NYU: His Friendship with Vardis Fisher," published in *Thomas Wolfe of North Carolina,* ed. H.G. Jones, (Chapel Hill, NC: North Caroliniana Society, Inc. and the North Carolina Collection, 1982), analyzes Fisher and Wolfe's "brief but remarkable exchange," which Fisher himself describes in an essay called "Thomas Wolfe As I Knew Him." Flora notes that Wolfe scholars have been happy to ignore Fisher's somewhat unflattering portrait of his colleague in this essay and another called "Thomas Wolfe and Maxwell Perkins," but argues that a study of their relationship reveals a great deal about both writers. First, agreeing with Fisher's own confession, Flora writes that Fisher's depiction of Wolfe as introverted, self-pitying, and contemptuous is a self-portrait. Further, Flora suggests that Wolfe, who appears as the character Robert Clark in Fisher's novel *No Villain Need Be* (1936) and later as David Hawke in Fisher's *Orphans in Gethsemane,* served as a means by which Fisher could analyze the nature and the purpose of art and artists.

Flora writes that Fisher's isolation in Idaho after 1931 largely prevented him from associating with other writers. This isolation, however, did not stop Fisher from commenting on his fellow artists' work. In "Vardis Fisher and James Branch Cabell: An Essay on Influence and Reputation" (*The Cabellian,* 1969), Flora notes Fisher's allusions to Cabell in the tetralogy and *The Neurotic Nightingale* (1935), as well as thirty-one references in *God or Caesar?* and points out that Fisher appreciated Cabell's realism and irony. Indeed, Flora argues that Cabell "taught Fisher the importance of myth" and that Vridar's increased understanding and appreciation of Cabell in the final two volumes of the tetralogy signal his control of his romanticism. Flora offers additional links between the two writers in "Vardis Fisher and James Branch Cabell: A Postscript" (*The Cabellian,* 1970), in which he argues that *Forgive Us Our Virtues* (1938) is Fisher's "attempt to do a Cabellian comedy de-mythologized."

Perhaps the most complex of Fisher's connections with fellow writers was one with a novelist who was, at times, closest to him in both geography and temperament. In "Vardis Fisher: Ernest Hemingway's Stern Idaho Critic" (*Hemingway and the Natural World,* ed. Robert Fleming, Moscow, ID: University of Idaho Press, 1999), Flora writes that Fisher "had an abiding antagonism toward Hemingway," who periodically lived in a house not far from Fisher's in Idaho. In *God or Caesar?,* Flora notes, Fisher criticizes his contemporary's reading habits and uses Hemingway as an example of a writer who sides with Caesar, pursuing fame instead of truth. In a less hostile but perhaps more perceptive section of *God or Caesar?,* Fisher calls attention to Hemingway's "essentially feminine" nature—predating, as Flora notes, Hemingway criticism by several decades. In *Orphans in Gethsemane,* Fisher writes, "Hemingway represents the child artist of the lost generation." In addition to taking cheap shots at sport hunting and bullfighting, Fisher refers to Hemingway as a boy whose rereading of his own work reveals enormous egotism. Drawing on his interview and correspondence with Fisher in the 1960s, Flora also shares some revealing anecdotes, including Fisher's expository comments on suicide and his slight of *The Old Man and the Sea.* While clearly demonstrating Fisher's antagonism, Flora's article also shows the writer's penetrating, if limited, insight into Hemingway. Indeed, he concludes that Fisher identified with Hemingway, particularly in his androgynous nature, castration complex, obsession with violence and death, anger toward his mother, and anxiety about his talent.

A handful of articles have illuminated other aspects of Fisher's life and personality. Ronald W. Taber's "Vardis Fisher and the 'Idaho Guide'" (*Pacific Northwest Quarterly,* April 1968), an interesting account of Fisher's work as director of the Idaho Federal Writers' Project, leaves one with a new appreciation of Fisher's renowned work ethic. Citing correspondence Fisher wrote to administrators in the Works Progress Administration's Federal Writers' Project, as well as other sources, Taber chronicles Fisher's success in overcoming inadequate and incompetent help, distrust in his own state, conflicting instructions, political pressures, and censorship to produce *Idaho: A Guide in Word and Picture* (1937). "Constant changes in Project personnel forced Fisher to travel thousands of miles on Idaho's poor highways and to write descriptive material about roadside views, special points of interest, and tourist accommodations," Taber writes. "In addition to these guided 'tours,' Fisher wrote all but two of the fifteen essays on Idaho history and physical attributes. He was, therefore, personally responsible for 374 of the 405 pages of text." The result, Taber shows, was the first and one of the finest of the state guides produced by the project. In "Vardis Fisher and the WLA: A Reminiscence" (*South Dakota Review,* Summer 1990), C.L. Sonnichsen recalls coordinating Fisher's address at the Western Literature Association's first convention in Salt Lake City in 1966. In tracing the controversy behind the speech, which originally had contained anti-Semitic remarks aimed at the eastern publishing powers, Sonnichsen shares passages from correspondence and interesting anecdotes, which together provide insight into Fisher's character, particularly his independence and mercurial temperament.

Finally, the Special Vardis Fisher Number of *American Book Collector* (September 1963) is a generally unscholarly, slightly queer, and wholly delightful collection of reminiscences and other "Fisherana." Among the contents are a book collector's personal responses to the tetralogy and *Testament of Man,* an essay by Opal Laurel Holmes on her husband's personality and work habits, and a reminiscence by fellow writer Ellis Foote, who describes a visit that he, George Snell, Bob Arentz, and Ray B. West, Jr., made to Fisher's home in Hagerman, Idaho. Foote's remarks are eclipsed by Fisher's own footnotes, which provide a glimpse of his sarcasm and humor. To Foote's comments on the reasons for his subject's work ethic, for example, Fisher appends this note: "Low metabolism, low pulse, and sluggish circulation. The reader should bear in mind that three of these four visitors were so sedentary that going to the bathroom was for them a long journey." The issue also contains two items by Fisher himself, "The Novelist and His Characters" and "Vardis Fisher Comments on His 'Testament of Man' Series." In the issue's sole scholarly article, "The Early Power of Vardis Fisher," Flora looks back at Fisher's first two novels, both set in the Antelope country of Idaho. Giving most of his attention to *Toilers of the Hills,* he argues that these works deserve greater recognition. In a miscellany of observations, Flora credits Fisher with introducing "a new regional literature," praises Fisher's treatment of his lonely pioneers, and contrasts his characters with the more ignorant ones of Erskine Caldwell's novels.

Criticism

Book Reviews

No one has published an extensive study of Fisher's critical reception. The best source for this information, to date, is Kich's annotated bibliography, which contains summaries of and quotations from dozens of book reviews. Kich's bibliography shows that Fisher's books attracted more than three hundred reviews, including a handful written by esteemed scholars and fellow writers. Several of these reviews, especially the ones responding to his early novels in the 1920s and 1930s, hail him as a fine, even leading American author. His first two novels, *Toilers of the Hills* and *Dark*

Bridwell, attracted favorable reviews from *The New Republic,* and the tetralogy caught the eye of Fred T. Marsh, who followed it eagerly. Writing in the December 25, 1932, edition of the *New York Times Book Review,* Marsh praises Fisher's ability to explore his own story, particularly the psychological one, without becoming sentimental. Marsh concludes his review by noting that "Mr. Fisher demands consideration as a serious and original American novelist who is blazing his own trail." Two volumes later, Marsh is still enthusiastic, writing in a review of *We Are Betrayed* that Fisher's novels have both regional and universal significance: "In their courage and rigorous honesty they are kin to the great works of confessional literature which know no national boundaries" (*New York Times Book Review,* January 20, 1935). Fisher received the consideration Marsh predicted, particularly after he published *Children of God,* which won the Harper Prize for Fiction in 1939. Praising its life and objectivity, Bernard DeVoto calls the novel "a deeply satisfying utilization of American material" and ends his review, "Millennial Millions," by saying: "It will be read for a long time, and Mr. Fisher has proved himself a mature novelist who belongs to the small company of our best" (*Saturday Review of Literature,* August 26, 1939). Alfred Kazin was more ambivalent toward the book. In "Our Last Authentic Frontier Novelist" (*New York Herald Tribune,* August 27, 1939), he notes the "superbly done scenes describing the Great Trek," but complains that "what lives in the book is, quite simply, the Mormon adventure, the Mormon suffering; but never the Mormon idea." Even the *Testament of Man* series, which some have blamed for derailing Fisher's career in the 1940s and 1950s, drew praise from high places. In a review of *Peace Like a River* (1957), in the December 8, 1957, issue of the *New York Times Book Review,* Frederick Manfred praises the series, particularly Fisher's talent for dramatizing history, and even goes so far as to say: "It is good to know we still have two more volumes coming."

The praise for Fisher's work was by no means unanimous, even during the first decade of his career. Writing in the January 6, 1934, issue of the *Saturday Review of Literature,* William Rose Benét admits that *In Tragic Life* "had its impressiveness," but that he is less impressed by *Passions Spin the Plot,* particularly its protagonist, of whom Benét writes: "God wot, I got thoroughly sick of Vridar, his hero, by the time I was through with Vridar's inhibitions and cowardly bullying and loutishness and pale-wormness." *Time* was so abusive of his later work that Fisher singled out the magazine for disdain in his book on writing fiction, *God or Caesar?* In a review that Fisher scholar John R. Milton has noted as particularly unprofessional, a *Time* writer openly ridiculed *Pemmican,* parodying what the writer saw as its gory details, ludicrous and unlikable protagonist, and "plot made of walrus blubber."

More serious and constructive critics, including fellow writers Wallace Stegner and Larry McMurtry, have recognized Fisher's achievements while also pointing out the flaws that, they believe, may have kept him from fulfilling Marsh's and DeVoto's early predictions about his great potential. In a review of *Forgive Us Our Virtues* (*Rocky Mountain Review,* Spring 1938), Stegner notes that Fisher's extreme idealism and affinity for preaching threatened his success as a novelist. Calling the tetralogy "a monumental contribution to American literature" and praising its author as "one of the two or three best candidates for the position of First American novelist," Stegner also compares his former teacher to Increase Mather and complains that his zeal for improving humanity not only is unrealistic but harms his fiction. "He deserves, whether one can agree with him the whole way or not, to be taken seriously," Stegner wrote. "The only qualification is that he should not, in my opinion, be taken as seriously as he takes himself." Decades later, Larry McMurtry also expressed ambivalence about Fisher's achievement. In "Icy Grief and a Fire of Vengeance" (*Saturday Review,* November 6, 1965), a review of *Mountain Man,* McMurtry commends Fisher's "narrative sense and his feel for the country." Glancing back at the novelist's earlier work, however, he voices a common complaint: "Fisher has a strong desire to be the scholar-artist, but his gift for narrative has not always been compatible with his yen for scholarship."

Books

Although many Fisher scholars have suggested that Fisher deserves more critical attention and appreciation, most of the book-length critical studies of his work have tended to be cursory. The exception is Joseph M. Flora's critical study *Vardis Fisher* (New York: Twayne Publishing, 1965). Combining breadth with depth, Flora covers almost all of Fisher's output while at the same time offering specific insights on individual passages and works, especially the tetralogy and *Testament of Man* series. For example, noting its similarity in form to both the novel of ideas and the Bildungsroman, Flora compares the tetralogy to the "intellectual apprenticeship" novels of James Joyce and W. Somerset Maugham. He goes on to analyze Fisher's framing device, which he notes is part of Fisher's attempt to psychoanalyze himself from a distance, and traces Fisher's application of "auto-correctivism," his psychologist brother's theory about humans' attempt to balance selfless and selfish urges in their lives. Noting Fisher's treatment of literature, puritanism, and education, Flora also argues that the "betrayal" depicted in the tetralogy "is not only Vridar's and Neloa's but the nation's as well." In a separate chapter, Flora analyzes

Orphans in Gethsemane (the final volume of the *Testament of Man,* a rewriting and expansion of the tetralogy that carries Vridar's life to the 1960s), characterizing it as another, more deliberate attempt to find larger implications in Fisher's own story, indeed "to show the present state of Western man and to account for it in terms of the race's past." Flora shows, for example, that Fisher places Vridar in a long tradition of western men who have remained children by cowering before their fathers and the Father. Because of this dependence, Flora writes, those living in the modern era of religious skepticism feel like orphans in Gethsemane.

After this analysis of the autobiographical fiction, Flora turns in later chapters to surveying Fisher's *Testament of Man* series, regional fiction, and American historical novels. Although the scope becomes wider and the criticism more evaluative, these chapters contain a number of provocative observations. In his examination of the *Testament of Man,* Flora notes the intelligence and detachment of some of Fisher's central characters, including Wuh in *Darkness and the Deep* (1943) and Harg in *The Golden Rooms* (1944), and suggests: "Generally, but not exclusively, his method is to imagine what Vridar would have done in the times Fisher considers." In "Fisher's Wessex: Antelope of Idaho," Flora examines Fisher as a regional writer, comparing him with Thomas Hardy, Erskine Caldwell, and William Faulkner. In addition to praising Fisher's vivid characterization and convincing use of dialect, Flora traces the theme of loneliness that runs through *Toilers of the Hills, Dark Bridwell, April: A Fable of Love* (1937), and the short stories in *Love and Death* (1959). "Americana," Flora's chapter on *Children of God* and the other novels of the American West, credits Fisher with moving beyond historical romance to historical realism. Particularly interesting is Flora's treatment of the generally neglected novel *Pemmican;* he suggests that Fisher's rare deviation from "the strict chronicle method" in this book grew out of the novelist's equally rare desire for public acclaim: "Anxious to revive his reputation for the sake of the *Testament,* Fisher wanted *Pemmican* to sell." Flora goes on to identify important similarities in the characters of Vridar Hunter and *Pemmican*'s David McDonald—a philosophical brother to nature. While it does not treat *Mountain Man,* which was published later, Flora's study is the seminal book on Fisher and is widely used by later critics.

Less insightful but still useful for the newcomer to Fisher's fiction is *The Uses of History in the Novels of Vardis Fisher* (New York: Revisionist Press, 1976), in which George F. Day argues that the thread uniting most of Fisher's twenty-six novels is his effort to understand himself and his fellow human beings through a study of the past. For example, Day points out in "History and the Autobiographical Novels" that Fisher's tetralogy reads like a case study showing the impact of particular episodes on an individual's life, as well as some central themes of humans in general: love, sex, and religion. In "History and the Anthropological Novels," Day writes that the novels in the *Testament of Man,* while occasionally "top-heavy with scholarship," depict humanity's debt to inherent traits such as egotism, as well as to the ideas and impulses that have emerged over the course of history. For instance, the relationship of Ghee and Kughh in *Darkness and the Deep* portrays companionship growing out of human isolation. Day also treats Fisher's ideas about the origin and evolution of war, romance, art, power, religion, and attitudes toward sex and family. He finds the same exploration of human behavior in Fisher's novels of the American West. In "History and the Americana Novels," he notes that works such as *The Mothers* and *Mountain Man,* in which characters act outside the realm of civilization, draw attention to primitive impulses, such as a mother's love for her children, and celebrate humans' potential for courage and selflessness. As a whole, *The Uses of History in the Novels of Vardis Fisher* reads more like a distillation of the ideas already prominent in Fisher's novels, rather than a fresh interpretation of the works, and is useful primarily as a guide to Fisher's plots and themes for readers new to his large oeuvre.

Other book-length critical studies on Fisher have been less satisfying, usually because the writers have done too little by attempting too much. Instead of rigorously analyzing a particular theme or genre, as they might do in studying Faulkner or Hemingway, these writers have tried to survey whole series of Fisher's novels or his entire poetic output and, consequently, have sacrificed depth for breadth. Each does little more than summarize the novels, catalog techniques, or identify general themes.

Dorys Grover has written two such broad critical studies: *A Solitary Voice: Vardis Fisher* (New York: Revisionist Press, 1973), which consists of four essays covering subjects as diverse as Fisher's poetry and elements of folklore in *Pemmican;* and *Vardis Fisher: The Novelist as Poet* (New York: Revisionist Press, 1973), in which she examines *Sonnets to an Imaginary Madonna* (1927), the Antelope People sonnets, and poems in the tetralogy. Grover notes in her preface to *A Solitary Voice* that its essays originally were written for a popular audience. Aside from a few desultory remarks, such as speculation about the influence of Edwin Arlington Robinson and other poets on Fisher, neither book ventures far beyond summary and broad interpretation.

Similarly broad is Wayne Chatterton's *Vardis Fisher: The Frontier and Regional Works* (Boise: Boise State College, 1972), which surveys Fisher's Western novels, offering a brief analysis of each. For instance, Chatterton argues that *Toilers of the Hills,* though hailed by critics as a fine addition to the country's regionalist literature, is at center "a psychological study of people bound to the land, losing track of self and time, snared in their manifold ambivalences." With the toiling Dock Hunter of this first novel, Chatterton contrasts the central character of Fisher's next published novel, *Dark Bridwell.* Charley Bridwell, Chatterton writes, is "an opposite type of frontiersman," a primitive man who "comes to the untamed land, not to tame and use it as other men do, but to become part of it." The impact of the child's experience on the man is the subject of Chatterton's analysis of *In Tragic Life;* in particular, Chatterton notes that Vridar Hunter struggles with the conflict between sex and religion and with his fear of brutal nature. Finally, Chatterton celebrates Fisher's use of historical materials in his fiction, particularly his ability to unite historical truth and dramatic art in works such as *Children of God.* As do Grover's books, Chatterton's study offers loosely connected insights on several works, but does not develop a thesis for understanding these diverse works, or focus long enough on a single novel or story to provide a detailed analysis of Fisher's achievements.

By far the strangest of the book-length studies is David Rein's *Vardis Fisher: Challenge to Evasion* (Chicago: Black Cat Press, 1937), which concerns class struggle more than Fisher's fiction. After a lengthy explanation of the means by which the establishment has dominated the lower classes throughout history through Catholicism, the illusion of democracy, and conventional moral standards, Rein complains that Fisher's diagnosis of humanity's ills in his tetralogy focuses on psychological phenomena rather than on these social forces. More Marxist propaganda than literary analysis, Rein's book is interesting primarily because it provides a glimpse of the political climate in which Fisher wrote. Indeed, the book's most striking—and odd—component is Fisher's own preface, "In Defense of the Obvious," in which Fisher disputes the book's thesis, insisting that "evasions had their beginnings, and some of their development, long before a capitalist order got on its first legs." Sketching the basic tenets of his brother's psychological theory of auto-correctivism, Fisher goes on to argue that Marxists, as well as capitalists, suffer from psychological distortions.

CHAPTERS AND COMMENTARIES IN BOOKS

Chapters on Vardis Fisher are de rigueur for encyclopedias surveying writers of the American West. In *Fifty Western Writers: A Bio-Bibliographical Sourcebook,* ed. Fred Erisman and Richard Etulain (Westport, CT: Greenwood, 1982), Joseph M. Flora assesses Fisher's place in the academy fifteen years after Fisher's death, provides a summary of his life, identifies the major themes of his work, and gives a brief analysis of the criticism on Fisher. Although Flora's chapter on Fisher in *Twentieth-Century American Western Writers,* 1st ser., ed. Richard H. Cracroft, *Dictionary of Literary Biography,* vol. 206 (Detroit: Bruccoli Clark Layman, 1999) covers some of the same ground, it more forcefully describes the vicissitudes of Fisher's career and the limitations of the artistry than does the earlier chapter. In *A Literary History of the American West,* Louie W. Attebery offers a helpful analysis of Fisher. In a particularly strong section on *Toilers of the Hills,* Attebery examines Fisher's depiction of man and nature in "equilibrium," as well as his use of folklife, which Attebery compares with the undercurrents of folk traditions in Norwegian Knut Hamsun's 1920 novel *Growth of the Soil.* While he merely glances at the tetralogy, *Children of God,* and the first eleven books of the *Testament of Man* series, Attebery is more thorough in his analysis of *Orphans in Gethsemane,* where he finds an exploration of "the web of human relationships," an understanding of fear as "the touchstone in understanding man's continuing story," criticism of eastern literary snobbery, and opinions on writing the historical novel. Attebery also briefly notes Fisher's treatment of time and the West in *Mountain Man* and concludes with an assessment of his subject's literary achievements. Borrowing Robert Frost's term "realmist," he suggests that Fisher treated universal themes in the context of his region. With perhaps some overstatement, he writes of Fisher: "As one who tried to write honestly about the West, either the West he knew or the earlier one he so carefully researched, he is close to the literary tradition of Hamlin Garland and Frank Norris, surpassing them both in range of intelligence, depth of perception, and ambition. He came to understand his region's history, its folkways, its dialect, its capacity to excite fear and terror as well as its power to inspire feelings of tenderness and rapture. Future scholars may find that in these he compares not unfavorably with William Faulkner, another realmist." *A Literary History of the American West* contains several other, briefer references to Fisher. In particular, Joseph M. Flora's essay on Wallace Stegner examines Fisher's influence on Stegner, whom Fisher taught at the University of Utah.

Other books also have focused on Fisher's role as a Western writer, sometimes using his work to support a general assessment of Western literature. In "Western Fiction and History: A Reconsideration," a chapter in *The American West* (Norman, OK: University of Oklahoma Press, 1979), for example, Richard Etulain argues that Fisher, like A.B. Guthrie, Jr., and Wallace Stegner, reveals the Western artistic pursuit of a "useful or usable past." In Etulain's analysis, Fisher was less ambitious than Guthrie, who interpreted the past, or Stegner, who explored the nature of history. Fisher's tetralogy and his *Testament of Man* series, Etulain writes, are the author's attempts to comb the past for "answers" to individual or universal questions, whereas *Mountain Man* shows him forging connections between past and present. In general, Etulain writes, Fisher's historical fiction betrays his commitment to thorough research: "Fisher seldom wrote about a subject that he had not researched as if he were writing a doctoral dissertation (he received a doctorate in English literature with high honors from the University of Chicago in 1925)." *Children of God* is among the novels Frank L. Stallings, Jr., discusses in "The West: Perpetual Mirage in Literature" (*Myths and Realities: Conflicting Values in America,* Memphis: Memphis State University, 1972). Stallings highlights the difference between settlers' visions and the severe realities of the West; he contrasts, for example, Brigham Young's illusions when he stares at the Salt Lake valley for the first time with the desiccated land and vegetation the Mormon leader finds upon closer inspection.

Barbara Meldrum examines the conflicting frontier experiences of men and women in three of Fisher's early novels in her "Vardis Fisher's Antelope People: Pursuing an Elusive Dream," a chapter in *Northwest Perspectives: Essays on the Culture of the Pacific Northwest* (Eugene: University of Oregon, 1979). Meldrum begins with the premise—developed through references to the work of Jean de Crèvecoeur, Frederick Jackson Turner, and other commentators on the pioneer experience—that the male pursuit of independence and freedom on the frontier often has stunted women's aspirations for family, civilization, and agrarian production. In her analysis of *Toilers of the Hills, Dark Bridwell,* and *April,* Meldrum succeeds in identifying these contrasting impulses of Fisher's men and women; but her argument that the women sacrifice their goals for those of their men is less satisfying. Meldrum turns to a more general subject in "Women in Western American Fiction: Images, or Real Women?" (*Women and Western Literature,* Troy, NY: Whitston, 1982), in which she analyzes two of Fisher's female characters alongside those of Willa Cather, Wallace Stegner, and other writers. Calling *Mountain Man* "one of the most eloquent tributes to woman that can be found in fiction," Meldrum notes that the novel's protagonist, Sam Minard, sincerely appreciates his wife, Lotus, respects the heroic mother Kate Bowden, and even learns from Kate's peaceful ways. On the other hand, partly by contrasting these female characters with the women on whom they were modeled, Meldrum shows that both Lotus and Kate are mere images and come across in the novel as passive and dependent. The best example of a real woman in Fisher's fiction, Meldrum writes, is Lela Bridwell, who in *Dark Bridwell* becomes "something of a protagonist herself—a thwarted artist, an individual who finally asserts herself and makes her own way in the world."

John R. Milton devotes an entire chapter of his book *The Novel of the American West* (Lincoln: University of Nebraska Press, 1980) to Fisher, particularly his efforts to combine rationalism and literature. Milton points out that Fisher's drive to dissect and understand humanity could make for unsatisfactory novels and obscure the better, more poetic parts of his work. This assessment—particularly Milton's criticism of Fisher's "excessive reliance upon the use of scholarly sources, an almost irrational passion for what he considered historical and psychological truth"—comes as no surprise to anyone familiar with the *Testament of Man*. Milton, however, shows that Fisher's rationalism shaped his other novels as well, and indeed was a guiding principle behind his literary method. Writing about *Tale of Valor,* for example, Milton points to Fisher's rationalistic tendency to examine actions from the outside: "Fisher's method is to pile it on, have three incidents do the work of one, rather than to explore the significance of the action." This observation helps explain other works as well, particularly *Children of God,* where the reader is likely to feel like Sam Minard at the end of *Mountain Man,* viewing the migrating Mormons from such a distance that they seem merely a line on the land, rather than a group of complex individuals grappling with their faith, families, and future. Milton goes on to suggest that Fisher, in writing his historical novels, chose to be "rational rather than imaginative" and so created "a feeling of distance between reader and character."

Other critics have placed Fisher in different critical camps. In his "Freudianism and the Stream-of-Consciousness," a chapter of *Lucifer at Large* (New York: Longmans, Green, and Co., 1937), C. John McCole briefly mentions Fisher, calling him one of the most "consistently Freudian" writers of the era. Focusing on the tetralogy, McCole notes Vridar Hunter's psychoanalysis of his students and his efforts to conquer his repression by giving himself over to sexual indulgences. In "The Freudians," a chapter of *Intellectual America: Ideas on the March* (New York: MacMillan, 1941), Oscar Cargill actually says little about Fisher's identity as a Freudian writer, but does voice a provocative criticism of the tetralogy: "Are there ten Vridar Hunters in the world? Nay, is there any other Vridar Hunter?...Vridar Hunter is Vridar Hunter only, and not an eye through which society may be glimpsed or evaluated" (736). George Snell places Fisher among the "Realists" in his book *The Shapers of American Fiction, 1798–1947* (New York: Cooper Square Publishers, 1961). In a section called "Erskine Caldwell and Vardis Fisher: The Nearly-Animal Kingdom," Snell provides an insightful overview of Fisher's themes and style, focusing on *In Tragic Life, Children of God,* and the first volumes of the *Testament of Man.* Calling his subject "the least read of the major American novelists," Snell also speculates productively on the reasons for popular and critical neglect of Fisher, citing his avoidance of the literary social scene, his obstinacy on matters of belief, the variety of his work, and his apparent "perverse wish to outrage" readers with his bold treatment of human weaknesses. Finally, in "Mormon Storytellers" (*Rocky Mountain Reader,* New York: E.P. Dutton, 1946), Dale L. Morgan treats Fisher as one of the numerous authors who have written novels about the Church of Jesus Christ of Latter-day Saints. Morgan calls *Children of God* the most ambitious—and, therefore, the most important—in the flood of Mormon novels published from 1939 to 1942. He offers a unique explanation for the "lifelessness" that has bothered some readers of the book, complaining that Fisher made the mistake of "peopling his pageant with a congregation of Dock Hunters" and thus omitting the "personal fulfillment and deep spirituality that were profoundly important in the inception and growth of Mormonism."

Articles in Periodicals

Although Fisher dabbled in everything from sonnets to travel guides, the bulk of his literary output can be divided fairly neatly into regional fiction, autobiographical novels, and historical novels. Likewise, most of the Fisher criticism that has appeared in periodicals has focused on one or another of these genres.

REGIONAL FICTION

Fisher's first two published novels, *Toilers of the Hills* and *Dark Bridwell,* were set in the Antelope Hills of Idaho, a region to which he returned in the autobiographical *In Tragic Life* and *April.* One of the earliest and best studies of this regional fiction is John Peale Bishop's "The Strange Case of Vardis Fisher" (*Southern Review,* Autumn 1937). Although brief, this essay provides useful insights on Fisher's pioneers—Dock Hunter, Charley Bridwell, and Joe and Prudence Hunter—whom Bishop describes as pioneers on "a very late frontier." Fisher, Bishop writes, "has explored the possibilities that open to the pioneer once he has stopped"; among those possibilities are Dock's attempts to exploit the land, Charley's atavism, and Joe and Prudence's investment in their children. Bishop is also articulate on Fisher's literary contribution, which he places below those of William Faulkner and Erskine Caldwell. Showing a particularly keen eye for Fisher's shortcomings, he writes: "His resources as an artist are limited, his taste is uncertain and his sense of form is not strong enough to allow him with impunity to discard the common conventions of the novel." Still, Bishop praises the early novels and insists that Fisher merits attention because he explores the central question for any novelist: "Granted such and such circumstances...how shall a man conduct himself so that his soul may not sicken and die?"

John R. Milton analyzes some of these same regional works in "The Primitive World of Vardis Fisher: The Idaho Novels" (*Midwest Quarterly,* 1976). Although all were written before Fisher began his *Testament of Man* series, Milton treats *Dark Bridwell, April,* and the tetralogy as if they pick up where the *Testament* left off, depicting humans' continuing struggle to rise above their animal fears and impulses. Charley and Jed Bridwell, Milton writes, "symbolize the dark origins of man, the primitive spirit, evil in its ancient sources of ignorance, base desires, and lack of intelligent control." According to Milton's analysis, even the comparatively civilized Vridar Hunter of *Passions Spin the Plot* must cope with irrational impulses, such as shyness and moral reservations. In another article, "The Western Novel: Sources and Forms" (*Chicago Review,* Summer 1963), Milton uses *Dark Bridwell* to illustrate uses of myth and treatments of nature in Western fiction.

In "Western Writers and the River: Guthrie, Fisher, Stegner" (*The Pacific Northwest Forum,* Summer 1979), Barbara Meldrum offers a brief analysis of the role of the Snake River in *Dark Bridwell* "as an indicator of change and as a reflector of personal experience." Finally, in "Vardis Fisher's 'Fierce Silent Drama' of Idaho Pioneering" (*The Redneck Review of Literature,* Spring 1990), George F. Day marks Idaho's centennial with a tribute to *Toilers of the Hills,* noting that Fisher's first published novel sketches a consummate pioneer in Dock Hunter, the complex relationship between humans and nature, and—in Dock's relationship with his wife, Opal—"a classic conflict between faith and doubt, imagination and reality, hope and fear."

AUTOBIOGRAPHICAL NOVELS

Although also set in rural Idaho, Fisher's third novel signaled a move in a slightly different direction. With *In Tragic Life,* the novelist turned to telling his own story in a series of autobiographical novels that also included *Passions Spin the Plot, We Are Betrayed, No Villain Need Be,* and *Orphans in Gethsemane.*

In "Naturalism in American Farm Fiction" (*Journal of the Central Mississippi Valley American Studies Association,* Spring 1961), Roy W. Meyer argues that the pessimism, neurotic protagonist, and dominating environment of *In Tragic Life* make it part of a tradition of naturalistic farm fiction stretching from Harold Frederic's *Seth's Brother's Wife* in 1886 to Frederick Manfred's *This Is the Year* in 1947. Speculating on the tendency of farm fiction to be naturalistic, Meyer makes two observations relevant to Fisher: he notes that most of the authors of this fiction grew up in rural settings, where they experienced nature firsthand, and that their artistic sensibilities probably did not suit them for life in such a potentially harsh environment. "Artists tend to be sensitive people," Meyer notes, "and some of those who spent their early years on the farm may have felt toward the manure pile much as Hawthorne did at Brook Farm."

In "An Early Stage of Fisher's Journey to the East: *Passions Spin the Plot*" (*South Dakota Review,* Spring 1980), Beatrice K. Morton uses Jungian ideas about the anima, an archetype representing feminine impulses in a man's psyche, to illuminate the second of Fisher's autobiographical novels. Agreeing with Joseph M. Flora's observation that protagonist Vridar Hunter suffers from a conscious internal conflict, Morton argues that Fisher's character also experiences an "unconscious projection of his anima onto Neloa."

Flora also weighs in on the autobiographical novels in his article "Concealment in Vardis Fisher's *Orphans in Gethsemane*" (*The Redneck Review of Literature,* Spring 1990). Focusing on a handful of important incidents that Fisher omitted or underplayed in an otherwise exhaustive fictional version of his own life story, Flora suggests that these incidents—as well as Fisher's "concealment" of them—reveal much about his character and work. He notes, for example, that Fisher's early dabbling with sentimental short fiction, sententious poetry, and plays set in World War I—a writing experience not chronicled in *Orphans*—reveals a writer still learning his craft: "The chief value of looking at Fisher's first published efforts in *The Pen* is to remind us how tentative he initially was about genre. His juvenilia also make clear that he had not found his subject matter—first his homeland, then himself—until after Leona McMurtrey's death." Fisher also devotes little attention to the Harper Prize for Fiction he won in 1939 for *Children of God,* and Flora speculates that the reason for this concealment is the true state of Fisher's—and Vridar's—confidence in his talents at the time. "The prize does not, in fact, lead Vridar to new confidence," Flora writes, "and this concealment is crucial to our understanding *Orphans* as an autobiographical novel." Flora suggests that by focusing on the lukewarm reception of his proposed *Testament of Man* project from an editor and publisher, Fisher emphasizes Vridar's crisis of "self-doubt" at this stage in his career rather than the surge of confidence one might expect to follow the reception of a national writing honor.

HISTORICAL NOVELS

In 1939, Fisher published his first historical novel, *Children of God,* a prize-winning epic on the origin and development of Mormonism. For the rest of his life, he wrote historical fiction almost exclusively. Many of these novels—including *The Mothers, Tale of Valor, Pemmican,* and *City of Illusion* (1941)—were similar to *Children of God* in their accounts of human survival in the American West. Others—namely, the first eleven novels of the *Testament of Man* series on the evolution of human psychology and civilization—were a dramatic departure, not only for Fisher, but for American literature in general. Whatever the discrepancies among these historical novels or the value of his other works, it is primarily as a historical novelist that Fisher is known. The large number of articles dealing with his historical novels has confirmed and perhaps even helped create this reputation.

A provocative study of Fisher's historical fiction as a whole is Ronald W. Taber's "Vardis Fisher: New Directions for the Historical Novel" (*Western American Literature,* Winter 1967). Taber notes that the work of Fisher and other novelists in the 1930s signaled a move away from historical romance and toward historical realism. He goes on to suggest that the method by which Fisher reconstructs the past resembles the ideas of British historian R.G. Collingwood, who described the role of imagination in filling the gaps between known historical guideposts. Noting Fisher's renowned research in religion, anthropology, and other fields, Taber argues that this research led Fisher to "intuitive insights" about his historical subject matter. Although Taber's analysis of this method in *Tale of Valor* is sketchy, his claim opens possibilities of research into the link between Fisher's scholarship and his historical fiction.

Fisher's best-known historical novel, however, has given at least one scholar reason to question his methods. In "*Children of God:* An Historian's Evaluation" (*Western Humanities Review,* Winter 1953), David Brion Davis cites contemporary newspapers and other sources, including correspondence and journals written by Mormon leaders Parley Pratt and William Clayton, and notes several discrepancies between Fisher's novel and the historical record. He argues, for example, that Palmyra, New York, was not a frontier settlement at the time Joseph Smith formed his church, that Smith was not a "humorless mystic," that Brigham Young knew that the Mormon settlement in the West would become part of the United States, and that the mountain man Jim Bridger actually promoted a Mormon settlement in the Great Basin next to the Great Salt Lake. More than simply a critique of Fisher's talents as a historical novelist, Davis's article helps illuminate Fisher's themes and motives. Fisher's depiction of Bridger as an outspoken critic of Young's plan, for example, supports his characterization of Young as a stubborn, persevering visionary, and his suggestion that the Mormons sought to escape the United States rather than join it, as Davis's sources imply, heightens the tragedy of the novel.

Fisher's famous Mormon novel is also the subject of the brief article "Vardis Fisher's *Children of God*: A Second Look" (*SunStone*, January–February 1979), in which Levi S. Peterson assesses Fisher's identity as a "Mormon author" and his general literary merit. While recognizing Fisher's talents, Peterson finds his subject lacking on both counts. Noting that *Children of God* emphasizes the Mormons' physical journey and largely ignores their "inner conflict," Peterson argues that Fisher lacked "the inside feel of Mormonism." Widening his scope, Peterson suggests that Fisher will not have lasting literary significance because he lacked "the fecundity of imagination and richness of intellect that makes for enduring literature" and because his fiction does not adequately treat human complexity, such as the psychological depth of Joseph Smith. Intended only as a glance at an author recently brought back into the spotlight, Peterson's article raises important questions without seeking to explore them in any depth.

Fisher's *Testament of Man* has inspired a handful of articles. In "The American West and the Archetypal Orphan" (*Western American Literature*, Fall 1970), Louie W. Attebery juxtaposes this series, Fisher's autobiographical tetralogy, and novels by James Fenimore Cooper, Mark Twain, and A. B. Guthrie. In addition to identifying the orphan, territoriality, and other archetypes in these Western novels, Attebery argues that melancholy and solitude often plague the characters involved in these archetypes, illustrating his point with passages from *Orphans in Gethsemane*. Part personal reminiscence and part literary analysis, Lester Strong's "Vardis Fisher Revisited" (*South Dakota Review*, Autumn 1986) traces the evolution of human culture and psychology, as Fisher records it in the *Testament of Man*. More interesting, though he makes it only briefly at the end of his essay, is Strong's assertion that the series "is precisely Fisher's attempt to 'embrace the totality' of twentieth century Western humanity's world, to 'mirror' that universe by showing 'its basic and essential principles' within the scope of twelve novels." The second installment of the *Testament of Man*, a novel called *The Golden Rooms*, inspired Kirby L. Duncan to make a rare case for Fisher's influence in "William Golding and Vardis Fisher: A Study in Parallels and Extensions" (*College English*, December 1965). Noting similarities in plot and characters, Duncan suggests that *The Golden Rooms* was a "possible source" for Golding's *The Inheritors*, but credits the latter writer with an innovation: "Fisher portrays a moral progress parallel to progressing evolution; but Golding's Neanderthals, in their mere innocence, represent a morality preferable to that of the Homo Sapiens who overcome them."

Mick McAllister takes up the subject of Fisher's female characters in "Survival of the Blood: Vardis Fisher's *The Mothers*" (*Vardis Fisher Newsletter*,

1990). Noting the neglect of women in historical writing and popular novels about the West, McAllister argues that Fisher routinely sketched complex female characters, including many noteworthy for their mettle. Singling out *The Mothers* for its impressive "assemblage of heroic women," McAllister notes, for example, the decisiveness and sensibility of Mary Graves, who but for the sexism of her time could have provided the leadership the Donner Party needed to survive. Quoting Fisher's comment on a woman's fierceness "when driven to the protection of her children," McAllister focuses on this motivation for heroism in the title characters of the novel.

Mountain Man, Fisher's last novel and perhaps his best known behind *Children of God,* has inspired several articles, including two by McAllister. In "Father to the Man: An Apology for Fisher's Indians" (*Vardis Fisher Newsletter,* 1990, and included in this anthology), McAllister takes on the daunting task of analyzing Fisher's treatment of his Native American characters. McAllister declares that Fisher has painted them as "the ugliest stereotype of their race that the white man has imagined." Pointing out that Fisher's view of Native Americans changed dramatically during the same period when he was composing the first seven installments of the *Testament of Man,* McAllister argues that the stereotypes in Fisher's Western novels reflect his belief in cultural evolution, the notion that cultures become more advanced over time. McAllister points out, for example, that the superstitious Native Americans in *Mountain Man* resemble the superstitious prehistoric characters of *Adam and the Serpent* (1947).

One reason for the popularity of *Mountain Man* is the 1972 film *Jeremiah Johnson,* which McAllister deftly analyzes in "You Can't Go Home: *Jeremiah Johnson* and the Wilderness" (*Western American Literature,* Spring 1978). Primarily an analysis of the movie, McAllister's article briefly treats two important transformations in his comparison of Fisher's book, Pollack's film, and the book on which both works were based, *Crow Killer: The Saga of Liver-Eating Johnson,* a biography of John Johnson [Johnston] by Raymond Thorp and Robert Bunker. First, he notes the evolution of the central character from the "uneducated, unprincipled, insensitive" and barbaric John Johnson into Fisher's Sam Minard, "a disgusted fugitive from civilization," and finally into the film's Jeremiah Johnson, "the man of good spirit and good intentions, not Everyman but the tragic hero, who carried with him into the wilderness his romantic illusions and with them the seed of the very civilization he sought to repudiate." McAllister also suggests that Native Americans, fairly portrayed in the biography and film, become in Fisher's hands mere instruments to demonstrate the author's ideas about cultural evolution.

In "The Art of the Mountain Man Novel" (*Western American Literature,* November 1985), David Stouck examines *Mountain Man* alongside A.B. Guthrie's *The Big Sky,* Frederick Manfred's *Lord Grizzly,* and other works. Stouck provides a useful summary of conventions of the mountain man novel—including the use of legend, dialect, and the journey motif—but focuses on this genre's aesthetic achievements in the areas of form, morals, psychology, and philosophy. Stouck notes, for example, how Fisher and his fellow novelists treat the question of humans' role in nature, tending to favor a primitive existence while admitting that such an existence became difficult or impossible with the exploitation and settling of the West.

Finally, Flora contrasts treatments of women in "Westering and Woman: A Thematic Study of Kesey's *One Flew over the Cuckoo's Nest* and Fisher's *Mountain Man*" (*Heritage of Kansas,* Spring 1977; reprint, *Women, Women Writers, and the West,* ed. L. L. Lee and Merrill Lewis, Troy, NY: Whitston, 1979). Seeing both books at the end of a long line of literary treatments of women's role in the American frontier by the likes of James Fenimore Cooper, Mark Twain, and William Faulkner, Flora notes that Kesey's novel, primarily through the character Big Nurse, depicts the female as the domineering figure who restricts man's freedom; the novel "vehemently cries out that Huck Finn did well to strive to escape Aunt Sally and her kind." Flora contrasts this treatment of women with the one found in *Mountain Man,* in which the characters of Lotus and Kate represent an Edenic helpmate and a motherly teacher, respectively. "Lotus does not threaten Sam's manhood," Flora writes, "but she allows him to express aspects of it hitherto subdued." He goes on to show that it is Kate who teaches Sam to forsake his quest for vengeance.

Summary Observations

At around eighty, the number of books and articles that offer substantial criticism of Fisher is still relatively small—indeed, small enough that nearly all of them could be treated here. After peaking in the 1930s—the decade of *Dark Bridwell,* the tetralogy, and *Children of God*—interest in Fisher dropped in the middle of the twentieth century, and it is now clear that contemporaries such as William Faulkner and Thomas Wolfe, with whom he has been compared, have eclipsed him in literary reputation. More than these writers, who also became identified with particular areas of the United States, Fisher seems destined to be regarded primarily as a regional writer. Especially in recent years, when a biography and several new articles have appeared, Fisher's writing continues to inspire insightful criticism, but much of this criticism has focused on his novels of the

American West or has appeared in journals such as *Western American Literature* and books such as *Women and Western Literature*. Even within this realm, Fisher's reputation as a writer worthy of scholarly attention will depend on critics' willingness to follow the lead of Flora, McAllister, and others in producing precise, thorough analyses on individual works and specific themes. Fisher's large, rich body of fiction invites such studies. Ultimately, his reputation as a leading Western writer of the twentieth century will depend on them.

Contributors

Doris Betts

Doris Betts is Alumni Distinguished Professor of English at the University of North Carolina at Chapel Hill, where she teaches creative writing. She has won numerous awards for her novels and short stories; they are the focus of Elizabeth Evans's 1998 critical study *Doris Betts*. Although much of her fiction is set in the South, Betts has set two novels in the West. *Heading West* (1981) was a Book-of-the-Month Club Selection. Her most recent novel, *The Sharp Teeth of Love* (1997), stemmed from a visit to Donner Pass, a visit that renewed her acquaintance with the work of Vardis Fisher.

Peter Blakemore

Peter Blakemore, an assistant professor of English at the University of Wisconsin, Whiteside, is a specialist in environmentalist literature. He holds a doctoral degree in English from the University of Oregon, Eugene, 1998. His dissertation on nature writing is entitled "Writing Home: Inhabitation and Imagination in American Literature."

Mark Canada

Mark Canada, assistant professor of English at the University of North Carolina at Pembroke (formerly Pembroke University), teaches courses in American literature and the English language. In addition to Vardis Fisher, his special interests include literary journalists and Southern literature, particularly that of Edgar Allan Poe. His recent publications include "The Right Brain in Poe's Creative Process" in *The Southern Quarterly* (Spring 1998).

Joseph M. Flora

Joseph M. Flora, professor of English at the University of North Carolina, has also taught at the University of Michigan and the University of New Mexico. He has been thinking and writing about Vardis Fisher since graduate school. The first president of the Western Literature Association to come from east of the Mississippi, he has made Western literature an abiding concern in his teaching and study of American literature.

Marilyn Trent Grunkemeyer

Marilyn Trent Grunkemeyer holds a Ph.D. in anthropology. Because she has a special interest in religious and moral ontogeny, she welcomed the opportunity to explore Vardis Fisher's *Testament of Man*. Her article "Belief Systems" appears in *The Encyclopedia of Cultural Anthropology*. She has also published in *Semotica* and *American Anthropologist*.

John D.W. Guice

John D.W. Guice is professor of history at the University of Southern Mississippi and a past president of the Mississippi Historical Society. He is author of *The Rocky Mountain Bench: The Territorial Supreme Courts of Colorado, Montana, and Wyoming, 1861–1890* (1973). His more recent work deals with the Southern Frontier (*Frontiers in Conflict: The Old Southwest, 1795–1830*, 1989 with Thomas D. Clark). His "A Fatal Rendezvous: The Mysterious Death of Meriwether Lewis" appeared in *The Journal of Mississippi History* (1995). The Natchez Trace is one of his professional interests.

James H. Maguire

James H. Maguire, professor of English at Boise State University, is a past president of the Western Literature Association. He has served as coeditor of the Boise State University Western Writers Series since 1972 and is the author of *Mary Hallock Foote* (1972). He has edited an anthology, *The Literature of Idaho* (1986), and is a coeditor of the anthologies *Into the Wilderness Dream* (1994) and *A Rendezvous Reader: Tall, Tangled, and True Tales of the Mountain Men, 1805–1850* (1997).

Mick McAllister

Mick McAllister, cofounder of Dancing Badger Press, has also taught Western and Native American literature. He is the author of many articles on Native American writers as well as on Vardis Fisher and Frederick Manfred.

Barbara Howard Meldrum

Barbara Howard Meldrum, professor of English emerita at the University of Idaho, is a past president of the Western Literature Association. A member of the editorial board of *Western American Literature*, she has published numerous essays on Western American writers, including Vardis Fisher. She is editor of two collections: *Under the Sun: Myth and Realism in Western American Literature* (1985) and *Old West–New West, Centennial Essays* (1993). Her monograph *Sophus Winther* (1983) was published in the Boise State University Western Writers Series.

Frederick R. Oyer

Frederick R. Oyer is an M.D. whose specialty is anesthesiology. A native Westerner, he has a passionate interest in two Idaho writers: Ernest Hemingway and Vardis Fisher. He is pursuing biographical research on Fisher.

Stephen L. Tanner

Stephen L. Tanner, Ralph A. Britsch Humanities Professor of English at Brigham Young University, is author of *Ken Kesey* (1983), *Paul Elmer More: Literary Criticism as the History of Ideas* (1987), *Lionel Trilling* (1988), and *Ernest Haycok* (1996). He is a scholar of American literature with a keen interest in the literature of the American West, his native region.

Alan Virta

Alan Virta is head of special collections at Boise State University in Idaho. Before moving west in 1988, he worked as an archivist at the Library of Congress and the University of Southern Mississippi. He holds a master's degree in library science from the University of Maryland.

Anne R. Zahlan

Anne R. Zahlan, professor of English at Eastern Illinois University, has also taught at the American University of Beruit, where she earned her undergraduate degree. An expert in twentieth-century fiction, she has taken a special interest in the literature of expatriation. The voice of the outsider helped attract her to the work of Vardis Fisher. Active in the Western Literature Association, she has presented papers there and has published essays on George Orwell, Joyce Cary, Lawrence Durrell, and Wallace Stegner.

Index